Quality:
Change Through
Teamwork

Quality: Change Through Teamwork

Rani Chaudhry-Lawton · Richard Lawton ·

Karen Murphy · Angela Terry

Best wishes
Rani Chaudhry-Lawton
July 1993

C

CENTURY
BUSINESS

This paperback edition was first published in the UK 1993
by Century Business
An imprint of Random House UK Ltd
20 Vauxhall Bridge Road, London SW1V 2SA

Random House Australia (Pty) Ltd
20 Alfred Street, Milsons Point
Sydney, NSW 2061, Australia

Random House New Zealand Ltd
18 Poland Road, Glenfield
Auckland 10, New Zealand

Random House South Africa (Pty) Ltd
PO Box 337, Bergvlei, South Africa

First published by Century Business in 1992

Typeset by ⩟ Tek Art Ltd, Croydon, Surrey
Printed and bound in Great Britain by
Mackays of Chatham PLC, Chatham, Kent

A catalogue record for this book is available from the British Library.

ISBN 0–7126–5677–4

Contents

For Three 'Home' Teams

Robert, Robyn and George

David and Morris (the cat)

John and Gwen, Nazir and Sharif

Acknowledgements

Amongst the companies who are currently using teamworking to bring about organisational change there are a number who are at the leading edge by virtue of the innovative methods they are using or because of the important lessons they have learnt about teams. We have been very fortunate in being provided with case material by a number of companies who are helping to define what it is possible to do with teamworking.

We are grateful to the following for supplying us with information and their insights in a very open fashion. Federal Express: Melvyn Tyers, Nancy McBride, Brian Hardy. BAA: Sir John Egan, Terry Morgan, Elaine Crouch, Lisa Fedden, Pam Williams. Digital: Ron Down, Alistair Wright, Ian Wallace, Chris Lever, Angie Waters. The Body Shop: Jane Corson, Gilly Forster, Fiona Thompson. Sherwood Computer Services: Bob Thomas, Richard Guy, Kevin Crane. British Aerospace (Commercial Aircraft – Hatfield): Dick Williams, Terry Taylor, Keith Davies. Wimbledon Football Club: Reg Davies. Nuclear Electric: Colin Bennett. Metropolitan Police: Ian Buchan. Galileo Associates: Peter Hartard. TMS (Team Management Systems) gave us valuable information relating to the Team Management Index and Wheel.

In addition to the corporate case material, we have benefited from discussion with a number of individuals. We are particularly grateful to Dr Meredith Belbin of Belbin Associates for his up-date on the team roles model and for the introduction to its development into Interplace. Paul Grafton, Pam Emery, Peter Farey and Melanie Hollinshead generously gave their ideas, as did the group of people who Karen Murphy affectionately refers to as her 'mafia'. George Bickerstaffe's comment, feedback and copy editing has been invaluable.

Behind the case material there is the diligent effort of Lisa Stolerman, a Mara Consultants researcher/consultant. Our special thanks go to her for conducting a large number of high quality interviews and carefully ensuring that the many clients already listed were satisfied that their comments had been accurately reproduced.

Some of the early research was carried out with the enthusiastic help of the Mara Consultants team. Helen Chew at Ashridge Management College was able to provide us with an abundance of articles and references and we are grateful to her.

Four authors, geographically scattered, working on one book creates a special problem of typing, checking and co-ordination. The problem was resolved by the skill and patience of Debbie Dudley, the Mara Consultants office manager/personal assistant and we greatly appreciate her help. Throughout the final stages she was ably assisted by Carl Hempenstall who accurately converted large volumes of rough handwritten manuscript into the finished product with great equanimity.

Throughout our first contact with Century Business we have benefited from the gentle guidance and advice of our editors Elizabeth Hennessy and Martin Liu.

The author team would not have been able to function without the help and support of 3 'home' teams. Finally, our love and thanks go to Robert, Robyn and George Terry, to David Pink, to John and Gwen Lawton, Sharon Allchild and Sharif Chaudhry-Lawton.

Rani Chaudhry-Lawton
Richard Lawton
Karen Murphy
Angela Terry

February 1992

Foreword

For the British economy and British companies, the 1990s will undoubtedly be a period of challenge and great opportunity. The opening of new markets in Eastern and Western Europe, combined with the need to recover from one of the most severe domestic recessions of modern times, make it essential that today's businesses are well equipped with the necessary skills to succeed in this period of change.

The objective of all successful businesses is relatively simple; to satisfy the customer. Achieving that simple objective can, however, be a complex managerial task. *Quality: Change through Teamwork* explores one aspect of that task – teamworking: now an essential feature of modern business.

Teamworking has been a key feature in the success of the world's premier economic powers, notably Japan and Germany. The continual search for quality in manufacturing processes, combined with that other essential ingredient, cost effectiveness, has been the bedrock for their industrial success. The key to improving quality and productivity simultaneously is the ability always to do things a better way. And here, time and time again, teamworking has been shown to be one of the most effective instruments of improvement.

The first principle of teamworking is that collectively, members of an organisation can more effectively bring about change than individuals. Teams can measure and analyse their own working methods, using their collective skills to improve quality and productivity. This process is usually best carried out by those that actually do the work on the shopfloor and so companies need to create a working culture in which people have confidence to challenge, to experiment and to seek and manage change.

Many organisations have found that this is a far from easy process and outside assistance is often required.

Quality: Change through Teamwork can provide some of that assistance. It charts the essential elements of successful teamworking, describing why and how teams are used to achieve the long term development of modern business. The book uses case studies of companies using teamworking to illustrate clearly the skills – and pitfalls – of team building and team development. Most importantly it provides some essential tips and techniques and valuable troubleshooting advice.

I have no doubt that in today's ever changing business environment the successful companies will be those that seek, and achieve, continual improvement in quality and cost effectiveness, through effective teamworking. *Quality: Change through Teamwork* is a valuable aid to all those who wish to start down the teamworking road.

Sir John Egan, Chief Executive, BAA plc

Introduction

In the 1970s there were enough good examples available of teamworking in organisations to ensure that the topic was not an oddity from the training and management development point of view. In most of the academic research (reflected also in the behaviour of management developers) there was a strong emphasis on the process adopted by teams and how internal group relationships were managed.

Ten years later an increasing number of organisations had seen the advantages of teamworking and integrated the philosophy into the culture of the firm.

Jaguar had shown the way with a remarkable turnaround. From being a loss-making company, it doubled productivity and produced a massive increase in pre-tax profits. Amongst other elements Jaguar's success is attributed to its use of multi-disciplinary teams to tackle 150 separate problems. British Airways set up Customer First Teams which involved employees at all levels. The teams were charged with the task of looking at ways of generally improving customer service.

Their successes were well publicised. Both companies were successfully floated in the mid 1980s.

Superteams was written in an attempt both to describe what was happening and to outline a model for successful teamworking that was not so heavily dependent on group processes. The model re-asserted the importance of task definition and task accomplishment. It also emphasised the key role of relationships outside a team as well as within it.

In writing *Quality: Change Through Teamwork*, we are presenting teamworking not just as a growing phenomenon or as an optional extra, but as one of the essential responses to what we regard as being the imperatives of organisational change. In doing so, we aim to go beyond reflecting the realities of the early 1990s as we see them. Our intention is to provide prescriptions for using teams to drive change forward, rather than simply responding to it.

In Section 1 we look at the reasons why teamwork provides such an excellent means of delivering on the imperatives of change outlined later in this Introduction. This includes, in Chapter 1, a model of the different ways organisations deploy teams to achieve their strategic aims. In the second chapter, we use detailed case studies to illustrate the actual experience of organisations that are using teamworking to further their corporate objectives.

If teams can deliver the powerful results described in Section 1, then it is important that they are selected and brought together in a way that maximises their chances of success. This is the main thrust of Section 2. Chapter 3 focuses on the importance of a rich and compatible mix of personality, background and working style and outlines a model for understanding the complex mix. In Chapter 4 we examine techniques for selecting a new team or revitalising an old one, and Chapter 5 describes team skills.

Teams go through development phases and these can be accelerated. It is sometimes useful to intervene in a positive way with training and development initiatives (courses, events, coaching). The two chapters comprising Section 3 explore the phases of development and their acceleration (Chapter 6), and an appraisal of techniques for enhancing the learning and growth of the team (Chapter 7). In the final section we acknowledge that even for the best selected and developed teams, there are often difficulties. Chapters 8 and 9 look at what happens when teams run into trouble and offers practical guidance to ways they can dig themselves out of it. The main concern of Chapter 8 is internal teamworking difficulties, while Chapter 9 highlights the problems teams encounter in managing external boundaries and relationships.

THE IMPERATIVES OF CHANGE

We have chosen to illustrate the Imperatives of Change using six case studies. Although the companies appear under pseudonyms, they are all real-life examples.

Case Study

1. Sitting on the Demographic Time Bomb (Save-a-Packet)

Save-a-Packet is a small food retailer with a number of outlets based in the North of England. At a recent meeting of the senior management team the Head of Personnel voiced her concern at the predicted shortfall in the supply of school and college leavers in the mid 1990s. One or two of the other managers concurred but the majority sided with the Managing Director. He pointed out that staff turnover was as low as he had ever known it, that there was no difficulty in filling such vacancies as did arise and that he really didn't think that there was much of a problem. In response the Head of Personnel pointed out that a lot of what she had been describing was probably attributable to the recession and a shortage of jobs generally, and that it only temporarily masked the underlying trend. At this point all her colleagues asked to which trend she was referring. She glanced around the room and realised that she was the only person who had any experience outside the business; she recognised that although many of her colleagues were willing to learn they relied very heavily on her to keep in touch with significant trends in their sector and in the economy as a whole.

Taking a deep breath, the Head of Personnel launched into an explanation of what she saw as the significance of falling birth rates over the last decade for the supply of labour over the next two decades. She identified it as particularly worrying for a business such as theirs, which normally had a high rate of staff turnover and was dependent on a strong intake of school and college leavers. She pointed out that the temptation for many youngsters to migrate to jobs in the South would be very strong and that some of the other European countries, facing their own similar problems, might lure away some of their workforce. There was a group amongst her colleagues who argued that if this demographic downturn ever actually materialised, they would deal with it at the time by raising wage rates. She pointed out the dangers of attempting to turn the labour market into a cattle auction, especially for a retailer which wasn't ultimately large enough to outbid the really big chains.

Perhaps the biggest shock that she managed to create during the meeting was when, sensing that she was losing ground, she pointed to the fact that Tescos had launched around 40 initiatives to combat the problem. These included measures aimed at reducing turnover (improved induction procedures, use of data from exit interviews) to expanding the labour pool by encouraging more female employees to stay or return after starting families (through flexible working patterns, or keeping in touch with those who had left).

The Head of Personnel did not win the battle in one meeting but left it with a commitment that a small Task Force, which she was to lead, would conduct some quick research and report back the following month.

Imperative No. 1 – Awareness
What the Head of Personnel brought to the meeting was an important degree of awareness of the external environment facing Save-a-Packet. She may or may not be proved right eventually but she raised an important issue for debate and one which, if the demographic experts are proved right, will distinguish between the success and failure of many businesses. At any one time, any

organisation faces a host of complex forces which may impact upon it. In the case study the key element was demographics, but there are many others. Significant improvements in transportation and communication suggest global opportunities but may also suggest global threats.

The proposed solution of a Task Force was a sane one as it shifted the focus away from one person's awareness and increased the potential pool of information. Importantly, it also increased the probability of sharing ideas about what to look for and sharing the significance of what had been found.

Case Study

2. If this Idea is so Good it has Probably Occurred to Someone Else (Granet Building Society)

By a series of mergers, the Granet Building Society has, from fairly small beginnings, managed to get itself reckoned amongst the top ten in Britain. Staying there was another problem, however, especially in the light of the steady stream of developments that had taken place within the building societies sector throughout the 1980s. It was not that the Granet was without ideas, it was just that it found itself continually limping in the race to get new ideas to the market.

The new Chief Executive, unusually for the Granet, was an outside appointment and had been brought in specifically to shake things up. At one of the early meetings of the Executive Committee, he listened to his senior management team discuss the latest suggestion for a new investment product. The General Manager of Product Development had come up with an idea for a new savings account called the Ultra-Flex, which would combine the advantages of a cheque account (with a debit card facility) at the low end of the investment range with higher rates of interest normally associated with bonds or term shares at the upper end.

Case Study

It was apparent very early on that none of the team opposed the idea and in fact most of them, with varying degrees of enthusiasm, could see its advantages. What dismayed the new Chief Executive was the elaborate process that the new savings account would have to go through before it was ready for the market. The General Manager of Branch Operations was insisting on a pilot launch in one of the regions, followed by an intensive training programme for all the managers. At the same time, the General Manager of Information Technology was expressing concern at the complex re-programming required, while the General Manager of Marketing was proposing to delay the advertising campaign until the current one was out of the way.

Having heard about as much of the discussion as he could stand, the Chief Executive vigorously challenged the amount of time that it would take to get the new account launched and pointed to the fact that Granet's competitors were not stupid and could well be working along similar lines already. He also reminded them of one of his counterparts (some years earlier) in a well known building society who, having met some internal resistance to his idea of launching a new savings account with a cheque book facility, speeded up the process by announcing it to the press. The reaction that the Granet Chief Executive received in response to his story consisted mainly of well rehearsed arguments about how long it took to do a proper job when introducing a new product.

The meeting was concluded abruptly when the Chief Executive lost patience with the discussion and made a very simple request, which was actually more of a thinly veiled command. He asked that the key players in the process should get together and, rather than addressing the question of how long it would take to launch a new product, should instead ask what needed to be done to halve the time it normally took to launch a new product. As he left the rather shocked group of managers, he added that if the answer that they first came up with still sounded too long, he might consider asking them to halve it again.

Imperative No. 2 – Speed

Although there are a number of arguments for carefully preparing the ground for a new idea it is also true that some things won't wait. In a comparatively static environment, where competitors are sleepy, market conditions are easy and it is hard to copy ideas, it might be argued that there is time to let a new idea mature. This is certainly not the situation that faces the finance sector, as the Chief Executive in the case study fully appreciated.

There are various reasons why an organisation can't move with the speed or agility it needs, but a common one is the compartmentalisation created by well defined divisions and functions. This landscape of compartments, or 'smoke-stacks' as some companies call them, may produce a strength within each compartment but its associated rigidity can make complex projects almost impossible. What the Chief Executive in the study had done, albeit in a fairly crude way, was to take the first steps towards replacing the narrow goals of functional perfectionism with the super-ordinate goal of getting a new product moving with the kind of speed demanded by market conditions.

Case Study

3. Well it Worked at the Prototype Stage (Ample Holdings)

Part of Ample Holdings is a woollen yarn spinners making carpet yarn with a high wool content (80 per cent to 100 per cent). Over the years it struggled to find a niche in a tough market dominated by a (diminishing) number of large players. Recently it looked at a new area – supplying producers of berber carpets (typically a light carpet with flecks of a darker colour). This produced some technical difficulties, as the distribution of flecks in the yarn has to be truly random or ugly running occurs when the yarn is eventually woven into a carpet. The company employed outside consultants to design some equipment to help with the randomising process. The consultants went away, did as they were instructed and reported back.

By this time they had progressed their idea a long way, even to the extent of having built a prototype, and they were understandably delighted with their progress. They asked Ample Holdings if they could do a demonstration and the company responded by offering a sample run on an old machine. The demonstration was attended by a broad cross-section of foremen and technical specialists. Although the demonstration wasn't perfect, it went well and left the consultants completely unprepared for the hostile reception that they were to receive.

First to speak was a technician who argued that the demonstration was woefully inadequate and even dangerously misleading because striping often emerged as a problem in a reasonably long production run. One of the foremen pointed out that the old machine ran at far lower speeds than the machinery currently in use. A computer aided manufacturing specialist pointed out that the control functions of the prototype would have to be made compatible with the control panels that he was installing on the machinery. The Chief Mechanic surprised everyone by announcing

Case Study

that he had tried something similar himself, made out of a garden sieve, a lawnmower box and a kitchen clock mechanism.

Sensing which way the wind was blowing, the consultants cut short the meeting and requested a private review with the Technical Director. Once they were alone with him, they apologised, acknowledged that there was a lot more expertise already within Ample Holdings than they had appreciated and offered a way forward. Their solution took as a starting point the creation of a joint project team (consisting of consultants, and technicians/foremen from Ample Holdings) whose first job would be to start with a blank sheet of paper and brainstorm alternatives.

End Case Study

Imperative No. 3 – Innovation

A phenomenon that is well understood in the training course conference room but less well on the shopfloor or in the boardroom is that given the appropriate atmosphere and encouragement most people have at least one or two ideas for improving the tasks that they have spent the majority of their working hours performing. Some people even have an abundance of ideas. If a group of people come together, ideas can be made to pinball around the table, working up fresh ideas and associations until a significant score has been achieved.

The image of the committed scientist working intensively and alone until he or she achieves a breakthrough has perhaps misled many people to focus on the inspirational element of problem solving rather than the power of a collective process in generating and sifting ideas. The consultants may have really added value to Ample Holdings by not only contributing a technical solution but also a process for resolving future problems.

Case Study

4. It may be in the Manual but is it a Good Way to do Business? (Downbridge Education Authority)

As one of the Education Authorities in a large conurbation, Downbridge does not enjoy plentiful funds, but neither is it completely starved of cash. By a combination of good luck and some careful housekeeping, it had found itself in a position to address some of its spending priorities.

Downbridge was particularly proud of its procedures for purchasing schools equipment. The movement of the inventory, both incoming and outgoing, was carefully monitored with the help of a simple computerised system. The Head of Purchasing had been appointed two years ago and was given the very clear brief of establishing an ordered and cost-effective system. Her predecessor had operated with the minimum of records and was guilty of paying over the odds for a number of purchases because he had not taken the trouble to find the best competitive price. Although she had no experience in the profit sector she quickly grasped the principle of establishing competitive tenders for big orders. She also had a safety net, in that she needed approval from the Chief Education Officer and his Deputy for any purchase over £500.

Once she had set up her systems everything ran pretty smoothly until she was asked to look into a bulk purchase of audiovisual equipment (video cassette recorders, monitors, 16mm projectors and overhead projectors) to replace some seriously outdated (and in some cases, non-existent) equipment in a number of schools. The project itself presented no major difficulties, and one of her better suppliers had contacted her with what sounded like an excellent offer. He had a job lot of heavily discounted East German equipment and was prepared to offer his own discount on top of that for a big enough sale. She had used the supplier, trusted him and the offer looked attractive. He assured her that the equipment was made by an established West German manufacturer who had recently taken over an East German producer which was discounting in order to gain market share in the UK.

The problem was that she had to make a snap decision on the equipment as the supplier had other buyers waiting. At the time the Chief Education Officer was on holiday for a fortnight, the Deputy position was vacant and there was no time to set up a competitive tender. She was not short of advice and support. There were a number of head teachers of schools under the authority's control who were quite knowledgeable about audiovisual equipment and who would have been happy to give her advice. Some of them worked closely enough with her to back her judgement, whatever she decided.

In spite of lengthy discussions with the supplier and repeated requests for more time, she decided to let the opportunity go. The supplier's deadline was firm and she feared the consequences of overturning two of her guiding principles, the competitive tender and the signing authority of her superiors. When the Chief Education Officer and Deputy returned she explained the decision that she had taken. They supported her publicly and in private grieved over the lost opportunity. Neither was prepared to suggest a re-writing of the guidelines for bulk purchasing, however.

Imperative No. 4 – Flexibility

It is a paradox of many public service functions that the very rules that are designed to protect public funds are the same ones that may ultimately waste it. The Head of Purchasing took a decision that was correct by an internal set of standards but one which made no commercial sense.

If opportunities are to be seized in the increasingly short time frames that will become feature of organisational life, then structures need to be flexible enough to allow people room for manoeuvre. This applies not only to the public sector but the profit sector also. In *Thriving on Chaos*, Tom Peters quotes the company policy manual of Nordstrom (a highly successful American retailer) as consisting simply of an exhortation to staff to use their best judgement at all times.

An ideal way of delivering flexibility is by the delegation of authority to small groups (multi-functional if possible) close to the front line of the organisation. There is an argument that says that such flexibility is dangerous in a public service but there is also a counter-argument, which says it may be vital if public money is not to be misused through missed opportunities and inefficiencies.

Case Study

5. Now I've dealt with the Meeting – I've forgotten what the Problem was (Soft Solutions)

Soft Solutions specialises in providing bespoke software computing solutions to a range of client needs. It enjoyed particular success with payroll systems.

One particular Project Leader from Soft Solutions, working on a system being installed in a major oil company, found himself in the middle of a particularly complex set of relationships. As was the custom with Soft Solutions, he would hold regular review meetings with the client. At the larger of these meetings there were often eight people present. From the client side there could be the General Manager of Information Technology plus a Technical Assistant, the General Manager of Human Resources plus the Manager of Remuneration and Benefits. From Soft Solutions, the Project Leader would often be accompanied by one of his senior consultants.

Case Study

Representatives of other computer companies were sometimes present also (a supplier of personnel information systems software and a representative from the original suppliers of the hardware).

It wasn't the number of people present at the meeting that caused the problem, but the danger of people taking entrenched positions that represented a narrow range of interests. The General Manager of Information Technology, for example, felt threatened by the number of consultants in the organisation and thought that his division should have been more involved in the early stages of the project. Unfortunately, the General Manager of Human Resources was like a straw in the wind and tended to listen to the strongest prevailing argument. He had been very vague about his requirements for a payroll system at the start of the project and everyone involved subsequently suffered from this early lack of clarity. The Manager of Remuneration and Benefits had lost interest in the fine details of implementing the payroll system and believed that his career fortunes were linked to the successful introduction of the personnel information system. This was well known to the supplier of the personnel information software, who also had designs on replacing Soft Solutions' payroll product with his own. The representative of the hardware supplies regarded the whole process with benign interest unless he was being criticised for the programme failures that were still happening. While he was prepared to accept some responsibility, he was inclined to spread the blame onto Soft Solutions' consultants or the client's Technical Assistant, whom he suspected of misguided tinkering.

The Project Leader from Soft Solutions, who was nominally responsible for co-ordinating the meetings, came to regard the whole process with a growing dissatisfaction. He was usually fairly successful at treading the narrow path between protecting Soft Solutions' interests and acting as honest broker to everyone else's conflicting needs. Somehow, though, he could not help feeling that the client's interests were getting buried under the careful manoeuvring and occasional dog fights amongst everyone around him. Although the client was to blame for some of the mess, Soft Solutions still had an obligation to do a good job for him.

The Project Leader's breakthrough came at a review meeting for which he had deliberately not prepared an agenda. When he arrived in the meeting room he made the simple request that the agenda should have only two items on it: what exactly did the client need from a personnel information system and how were all those involved going to work in partnership to produce the end result? This triggered a heated discussion with half the group arguing that they were co-operating already and the other half maintaining that they would be prepared to participate in the way the Project Leader was suggesting but they did not trust the others.

After two hours of deepening conflict it became apparent to the Project Leader that no progress was being made. He had nearly turned the meeting by offering two free consultant days of fresh diagnosis when the supplier of the personnel information systems blocked the idea because he was nervous of the potential increase in Soft Solutions' influence. In the process, the supplier had successfully paired with the Manager of Remuneration and Benefits and together they showed no signs of shifting.

Somewhat frustrated by the lack of movement in the meeting the Project Leader finally offered, quite calmly, to withdraw Soft Solutions from the process altogether. He argued that Soft Solutions liked to be able to do a quality job and that it was not going to be possible unless all those involved operated as a team. This finally galvanised the General Manager of Human Resources and the General Manager of Information Technology. They recognised that the Project Leader of Soft Solutions was trying to do a good job for

Case Study

them and that there was sense in what he was proposing. Throughout the whole discussion, the supplier of the personnel information system had begun to look increasingly partisan and in an attempt to carve out his own empire had undermined his potential for influencing events. The two General Managers made it clear that they wanted to play their part by being clearer about what they required and in return expected true co-operation between the other members of the group.

Although the struggle wasn't over, the Project Leader had managed to lay the foundations for a teamworking approach, with shared responsibilities.

End Case Study

Imperative No. 5 – Co-ordination in the Face of Complexity
As organisations become more ambitious in what they are trying to achieve and as they need to call upon more specialists, who in themselves are becoming more esoteric, so the problem of co-ordination becomes greater. The problem exists at two levels: co-ordinating the task and co-ordinating the process.

Given the position in which the Project Leader of Soft Solutions found himself, it would have been very easy to concentrate on the problem of entangling the web of interdependencies at a task level (for example, by monitoring failures in the programme and attempting to apportion responsibility for chasing and correcting faults). He knew, however, that true progress was being hampered by the lack of clarity and lack of assertiveness on the part of the General Manager of Human Resources and by the hurt feelings of the General Manager of Information Technology, both of whom hadn't been listened to in sufficient depth in the early stages. The ambitions of both the supplier of the personnel information system

15

and the Manager of Remuneration and Benefits were legitimate but were selfish enough to represent a real block, especially once the two of them started to conspire together. All the representative of the hardware suppliers wanted was not to be blamed for things that were not a hardware problem, and he was a natural supporter of a more co-operative approach.

To the uninitiated, teamworking can often feel like a messy and unco-ordinated business. It is true that teams often go through these phases, but once they start to work well together they are one of the few ways of consistently managing complex and competing elements over a long period of time.

Case Study

6. Rather Like Turkeys being asked to Vote for Christmas (Fruit Flavours Partnership)

The Fruit Flavours Partnership is a soft drinks manufacturer that had expanded from the foundation laid by a traditional family business. Once the two sons of the original founding father were approaching retirement, they expressed a keen interest in selling their shares to their fellow directors as a means of not having to sell out to the competition. There were too many shares for the other directors to absorb by themselves and after a series of long and complex negotiations, together with help from a merchant bank, it was agreed that shares would be offered to the entire workforce.

Although the re-distribution of ownership had a massive motivational effect, the firm quickly ran into technical difficulties. The retiring family directors had taken with them a lot of knowledge and experience. In desperation, the new directors turned to the workforce for a solution and together they evolved a scheme for self-managed work groups. This was a radical shift from what had formerly been a fairly traditionally structured firm. Starting with a pilot scheme in one of the factories, the initiative soon spread to the remainder of the plants.

The self-managed work groups were not without their teething troubles. Some groups did not initially have the maturity to manage budgets and costs, and awarded themselves several enhancements to their working environment before they realised the potential damage they were causing to profitability and the share scheme. In other groups the middle managers felt that the level of democracy implied by self-managed workgroups had eroded their status.

As the work groups developed and matured they enjoyed an increasing success. In fact, they were so successful that it became painfully obvious that a reduction in headcount was called for. By making the move from a traditional hierarchical structure to the flat structure of self-managed work groups a whole layer of management had become unnecessary. It was true that there were new roles to be filled but the more efficient way of working still called for a net reduction. The groups took the problem to the directors, who reminded them that self-managing meant having to take responsibility for a number of tough decisions as well as enjoying the benefits accompanying comparative autonomy.

At a series of tough meetings, each of the work groups debated the same issue: how to reduce numbers without destroying the morale of the teams. Some members felt that they should not be asked to be judge, jury and chief executioner for themselves and argued that no company should ask its employees to do such a thing. An equally strong lobby voiced the opinion that 'they' and the firm were one and the same thing and, as such, quite unlike any comparable organisations.

The solution was achieved in two ways. As a result of the fact that the tone of the meetings was very serious and that they had been going on for some time, a number of people chose to leave the company. They were mostly the group of ex-middle managers who had experienced perhaps the greatest difficulty of transition, or who had made the transition but felt that they were expendable and might have to move eventually, anyway. This did not though, release the groups from their most difficult decision, which was how to design a fair redundancy mechanism. Finally, each group came up with its own definition of fair. At one end of the scale there was a simple 'last in, first out' system. More complex systems included a definition of a core set of skills and a measure against those skills of each person's competence and flexibility in moving between a number of the team's functions. Numbers were reduced and the teams were able to move on, if not happily, at least in the knowledge that they had devised their own system to which all subscribed. This vital element of the process removed some of the resentment commonly associated with redundancy programmes.

Imperative No. 6 – Involvement

A model of an organisation in which the few command the many is fairly clear cut. It suggests a world that is reasonably straightforward, well regulated and in which the many accept the legitimacy of the directives from the few. That world is in the process of change in ways which are identified in *IGNITION! Sparking Organizational Change* as being very fast, invasive and random. Predictability is off the menu, the few may well be out of touch with the vital ingredient of the business (the customer) and the many have come to expect to play a bigger part in determining all aspects of their lives, not just the work element. The inverted triangle of the few supporting the many in their efforts to deliver their service or product to the outside world has become the new symbol of quality and customer care.

Involvement is not just a philanthropic gesture, it is now a change imperative.

The case study illustrates the benefits of involvement in what is perhaps one of the trickiest areas facing a number of organisations – making redundancies. At first glance, the notion of asking for volunteers to step over the side of the ship is somewhat bizarre. It is, however, a logical extension of the principle of self-managed teams or work groups. With involvement comes an enhanced sense of responsibility and with that comes the ability to take decisions normally reserved for the boardroom.

Section 1

The Strategic Use of Teams

1. Delivering on the Imperative of Organisational Change: How Teams are Used

INTRODUCTION

The manager or organisation who has appreciated the imperatives of change is entitled to question what the significance of teamworking is in relation to these issues and whether there are alternatives. It is this question that we address in the first section of Chapter 1. Assuming a positive answer to the question of the value and role of teamworking, a natural next step is the choice of teamworking approaches. Teamworking is an umbrella term covering a lot of different activities and teams of many different shapes and sizes. The intrepid adventurer in the teamworking area has many routes to choose from, and we provide a large-scale map of the different types of team and what informs the choice of the types. Our interest here is mainly in teams which are part of a strategy for bringing about change. Much of what we have to say in the later sections of the book about developing, bringing together and troubleshooting teams is equally applicable to established teams and not just to those spearheading change. The final question that we raise and answer in this chapter is about the circumstances under which the use of teams is *not* appropriate.

THE POWER OF THE TEAM – WHY TEAMWORKING IS IDEALLY PLACED TO DELIVER ON THE IMPERATIVES OF CHANGE

The six imperatives of change – awareness, speed, innovation, flexibility, co-ordination in the face of complexity and involvement – raise strategic issues for modern organisations because they so profoundly affect survival and growth. Faced with the imperatives, organisations can do three basic things: they can spot their significance in advance and be as proactive as possible; they can wait until the necessity for action sweeps over them; or they can ignore them and consign themselves to the scrap heap of failed businesses and inefficient public services. For organisations that are determined actually to do something about the change imperatives, there is the second decision about precisely *how* they are going to do it.

The answers to the questions raised by the change imperatives do not necessarily always involve teamworking. In our consultancy experience we have witnessed organisations enhancing their awareness by commissioning very expensive futurologists to scan some highly sophisticated crystal balls on their behalf. Some companies speed up processes by switching resources from other parts of their business or by, in effect, turning the handle faster (for example by working machines harder and asking for more overtime from the shopfloor). New ideas can be bought from the outside or worked on by the creation of bigger and better research and development divisions. Flexibility can be created by a fairly simplistic approach to human resource management; people can be moved to new jobs and locations or can be seconded to projects (how much of this is done by influence and how much by command will depend of the organisation's culture). Traditional approaches to co-ordination problems would involve greater effort put into planning and the use of increasingly sophisticated computer programmes. The concept of involvement will spur some organisations to make better use of notice-boards or invest in an internal public relations video.

All of the above can be done without teams. The only problem with the approaches mentioned is that they are rarely long-term. They do not often generate the commitment necessary to sustain progress through the next change required, and they are frequently costly. Teamworking is superbly placed to deliver on all six imperatives, often simultaneously. The next section of this chapter spells out why.

AWARENESS – COVERING THE GROUND AND KNOWING WHAT GROUND TO COVER

We noted in *IGNITION! Sparking Organisational Change* the importance of having a steady flow of rich ideas to help organisations change in an informed and valuable way (referred to as FUEL in the model). An obvious source of such ideas is constant scanning, in domestic and global markets, of political, economic, social and environmental events. Teams are well placed to do this for the three following reasons.

a) There is a lot of ground to be covered.
b) It is not possible to scan everything, and sometimes only specialists know what to look for in specialist areas.
c) The data itself is of little use unless it can be translated into action and a group of people acting together can often exert more leverage than isolated individuals.

a) In her book, *When Giants Learn To Dance*, Rosabeth Moss Kanter notes the threat posed to Kodak by competition in a number of different markets in the 1970s and 1980s. Kodak's vulnerability was caused by its relative lack of awareness of the changes going on around it at this time. As is the case with many large organisations, the opportunities presented by diversification into several markets also opened an equal number of threats.

Fuji started to produce faster, higher quality film and pioneered disposable cameras. It scored a symbolically upsetting victory over

Kodak by capturing sponsorship of the 1984 Olympics. Having managed to leapfrog Xerox in the (dry) photocopier market, Kodak lost its initiative over the next seven years, after which time the process was reversed and Xerox moved ahead. Polaroid was able to develop the highly successful Land camera (instant photographic development) after Kodak turned down Edwin Land's offer to sell it the patent.

Moss Kanter notes that the improvement in Kodak's fortunes began in the mid 1980s when it undertook major changes in its philosophy and structure. Two vital elements of the change were the creation of the flatter structure, with a shortened chain of decision making, and a strong emphasis on horizontal links and co-operation between functions and divisions.

It is not only large organisations such as Kodak that need to cover the ground. Given the huge range of developments for the majority of products and services and the variety of ways in which the developments can be monitored, there is a significant challenge presented to most organisations. In *IGNITION! Sparking Organizational Change* we identified a 'Strong Fuel' environment as one in which ideas are being generated from a number of different sources – market research, monitoring competitor activity, customer discussion groups, internal employee attitude surveys and so on. The technology might range from the sophisticated (British Airways passengers have been given access to a video recording booth in which they can comment on the service that they have received), to the simple (checking what the competition is up to).

Low-tech approaches are worth considering. One major UK retailer told us the delightful story of how it keeps an eye on its nearest rival, which is often sharing an out-of-town site. Every now and again the managers simply walk into their rival's store and have a look around.

It is not unusual for them to spread alarm through the ranks of their counterpart's staff, who, seeing a group of very obvious looking managers and assuming that they must be from their own Head Office, start apologising in advance for any mistakes that they may have made. Even the public get involved in the drama and bring their queries and complaints to the visiting managers. It would be tempting for the visiting managers to extend the role-play and inject some disinformation into the system or lure away one of the enquiring shoppers, were it not for the fact that their rivals make identical visits to their own store.

b) Being in the company of specialists can be an exciting process. Trips around factories and operations can reveal unusual insights and knowledge. For example, operatives in an electronics factory wear wristbands connected to their benches to discharge static electricity. A pile of metal turnings starts to smoke even before going into a steel furnace because the turnings are not inert and spontaneously start to combust. In a more domestic situation, a joiner, accustomed to making preliminary guesses without the help of a spirit level, can correctly judge that land destined to become a patio falls away exactly one foot from one edge to the furthest point. The average householder could not be so accurate. It is because the specialists see things that others don't that their observations can be so very stimulating.

The company of specialists can also be frustrating, if their insights remain internal and are not shared in any meaningful way. Most people working in large organisations will have experienced the frustration of a project dominated by the input of one specialist interest when it actually needed the input of rather more. Thus the Human Resources expert buys a software package to use as a database that is not properly compatible with the existing systems in the department. Alternatively, the Information Technology specialist buys a software package that will serve everyone's needs apart from Human Resources.

Awareness is not a process of randomly scanning the environment but it is better seen as an informed search with the insights being shared with all other people involved.

c) Being aware is of itself of no great value if the significance of the data being taken has been missed. British Airways knew for years that it had an appalling reputation for customer service but it took the arrival of Lord King and Sir Colin Marshall to grasp its significance and do something about it. Once they had arrived, it was notable that other events of significance, such as the development of powerful computer reservations systems by American Airlines (called Sabre), were countered quickly by British Airways with the establishment of its own system, Galileo, in partnership with other airlines.

It is common to come across organisations that have recognised the importance of gathering quality data either about markets or about employee attitudes, but have failed to guarantee the data a wide enough airing within the organisation to make it effective.

Sir John Egan, Chief Executive of BAA plc told us: 'Research surveys tell us about the quality of what we do. We know what productivity improvements we require and we have shared them with all our staff and invited them to help us improve our performance. What we do is to show the various people that we work with and alongside, the data, and demonstrate that this is unsatisfactory and try to encourage them to bring improvements.'

SPEED

In *IGNITION! Sparking Organisational Change* we highlighted the extraordinary acceleration in the rate of change and quoted examples of significantly shortened product life cycles. Two US observers of changing trends, Naisbitt and Aburdene, explore the notion of the underlying base rate of change (rather like an inflation index) and question whether it shifts over time. Whether this base rate can keep on increasing indefinitely is an interestingly speculative question, but at the moment the trend is strictly upwards.

Paradoxically, at the same time as we read about Naisbitt and Aburdene's examples of Motorola slashing the production time of electric pagers from three weeks to two hours, we know from our own work with a variety of firms that a host of employees are constantly frustrated by the slowness of their organisation's decision making processes. For example, during a recent discussion with some financial leasing specialists they revealed their annoyance with a system that enabled them to make local decisions about providing leasing finance up to a fairly low limit, but then required them to refer anything above that through two levels of hierarchy to a Special

Committee. A positive decision on the part of the committee then had to work its way back down the hierarchy. The specialists complained that the process was slow and left them at a disadvantage in relation to some of their slicker competitors. To make matters worse, the decision making processes of the Special Committee were shrouded in mystery. Most of the specialists had been told not to try to second guess the committee, which led them to putting up proposals with very little commitment and virtually no idea of their chances of success. Many of them firmly believed that the personalities on the committee at a given meeting was the best predictor of the outcome and prayed that they wouldn't get 'the hanging judge'. All of them believed the apocryphal tale of the Managing Director who, on finding that a favoured proposal of his was not approved by his colleagues on the committee, demanded a delay in the final decision. On the following day he dragged a non-executive director out of retirement to form an instant committee with himself and they agreed the proposal.

Exotic and clumsy processes such as this are not only frustrating to the business getters at the sharp end but dangerously slow from a competitive point of view. There are two enemies of speed; one is the vertical problem of hierarchy and the other is a rigidity of functional areas, which produces a problem when these areas need to integrate horizontally. Before Kodak reorganised in the mid 1980s, by decentralising and by delegating authority downwards, people reported centrally through their functional areas. Rosabeth Moss Kanter quotes one manager as saying that it needed an almost 'unanimous vote' to approve a new idea and that it was hard to advance anything that was not 'a logical extrapolation of the past'. Kodak's reorganisation attacked two problems by shortening the chain of command and by encouraging co-operation and integration horizontally across functions and divisions. The benefits included renewed organisational vigour and increased competitive edge.

A powerful way to speed up the way an organisation operates is to replace over-elaborate hierarchies with a flatter structure that also fosters a teamworking mentality. Although the British Airways privatisation success story is often told in terms of visionary top management, intensive training programmes and customer care initiatives, a vital ingredient was the removal of several layers of management so that the old RAF-style chain of command was replaced by something far shorter. In the process it helped to change the 'I'll just have to check that' culture. At the same time, every effort was made to encourage a way of thinking and a set of working practices that stressed the mutual interdependence of all parts of the airline. This has progressed to such a point that managers in Information Management now have part of their performance appraised on their ability to form partnerships with some of the other divisions that they service.

In true iconoclastic fashion, Tom Peters in *Thriving on Chaos*, recommends that organisations should limit layers of management to three or, in the case of complex operations, five at the most. In this model the majority of the workforce operates a teamworking structure either formally or informally, and the first line supervisor has a huge span of control, well beyond the norm of most current organisations. This means that the first line supervisor can't control in the traditional sense of the word but instead facilitates, coaches and speeds things up. Similarly the middle manager's job is to remove the organisational obstacles so that the supervisors can carry out their roles (in Peters' terms, an 'out-and-out expeditor').

Whether or not Peters is right about the magic formula of three management layers it is certainly true that a combination of fewer layers with a teamworking approach can help greatly to deliver on the change imperative of speed.

INNOVATION

The process of innovation is probably better understood than it is practised in many organisations. There are a number of ingredients of successful innovative processes:

1. It pays to have ideas in abundance because innovation is quite a low-yield activity in the sense that out of many new ideas only a few may emerge as useful. The few that do emerge, however, often have a potential to justify the original cost and effort.

2. New ideas come in many different shapes and forms but a very simple distinction is between those that nudge the existing

situation forward slightly and those that cause the situation to take a leap, so much so that it may almost begin to redefine the original problem. Both sorts of new idea can be invaluable and both need to be encouraged.

3.   New ideas need a certain amount of support because they tend to be puny misshapen things at birth. History is full of these ugly ducklings that eventually grew into swans.

4.   Even an idea that has had a chance to grow and stand on its own two feet needs further support as it jostles for attention amongst older, better established ideas in an organisational setting

5.   The creative process when it is working well is often experienced as unpredictable, messy and even fun.

The practice of innovation in organisations is often hampered by a number of factors. If the culture favours rules, orderliness and certainty the process of generating new ideas clashes with that culture. When fun is normally equated with irresponsible behaviour, it is hard for the guardians of established practice to believe that the laughter and energy surrounding a brainstorming session, for example, can produce useful business results. Given that fostering new ideas in their early stages requires a lot of mutual support from those involved, a highly competitive organisation culture will often not be able to change gear to provide that support. Once a new idea has emerged, backing it with time and resources can feel like a very risky enterprise to those who had grown attached to the old ideas. A risk-averse culture is not compatible with innovation.

Teamworking is an excellent vehicle for innovation, and the organisations that manage the process well understand the link. A group of people working together can, under the right circumstances, be highly creative. If there is a good mix of people (Chapter 3 looks at the things to consider in achieving the right mix) they will bring to any discussion a variety of backgrounds, experience and specialist knowledge. This is ideal for innovation, because in the vivid phrase of Tom Peters and Nancy Austin it is a process of 'irreducible sloppiness'. Excellent ideas are stumbled on by accident or borrowed from elsewhere. Peters cites the manager of the dispersed workforce who found that the newly purchased walkie-talkie, in addition to picking up the sender's communication, picked up every one else's besides. This had the beneficial spin-off of producing a very well informed workforce who were able to comment on each other's operational problems. When the next batch of walkie-talkies was purchased, rather than overcoming the 'problem' by going up-market, the manager went down-market to find equipment that would not screen out the 'interference'.

3M, the organisation that has become a byword for innovation, understands well the need for borrowing or adapting ideas from places other than the original starting point. It is run on teamworking lines in the form of a host of small autonomous product divisions and teams that push forward new product development. Part of the corporate philosophy is the requirement that each division is expected to get 35 per cent of its sales each year from products developed within the preceding five years. This leads to some highly creative pirating of ideas. In the late 1950s, 3M used its existing non-woven fibre technology to branch out from the world of packaging ribbons into that of brassière manufacture. Unfortunately the bras did not take the fashion world by storm and the suggestion of a strapless version using 3M adhesive technology did nothing to rescue the project. The basic idea finally found its place in the late 1960s when the cup shape was amended to form a surgical mask (ideal for letting air in but stopping germs from getting out). It was a short step from there to a lightweight safety mask and ultimately to a toxic-dust respirator. This 3M legend was colloquially known as 'from bust to dust'.

A teamworking mentality and the adaptation of ideas are inextricably linked. During our work with a group of aircraft maintenance supervisors we came across the phenomenon of 'robberies', people working on one particular aircraft taking parts from people working on another if they couldn't be obtained from the stores. There were two sorts of robbery, the official (properly recorded) and the unofficial, which was tolerated even though it was a source of frustration to the group being robbed. We worked hard with the supervisors to persuade them to regard themselves as a total team and to legalise robbery completely, not just in the sense of taking parts but also by borrowing the best working practices that they witnessed in other areas.

A team mix is not just about knowledge and experience, it is also about personality. In an idea generating session, the richest output comes from people making links, drawing parallels, using metaphor, humour and parody. There are two particularly important blends of personality in the process that have been identified by Professor Michael J. Kirton. The world seems to divide into the 'adaptors', who can take an existing idea and modify it at the margins, and the 'innovators', who will often go beyond the boundaries of the problem to look at something very differently. Organisations can usually only tolerate a certain amount of input from the 'innovators' and usually need the 'adaptors' to balance the equation. Both groups can generate new ideas, but the routes they choose to get there are very different.

Support is a vital element in the early stages of idea generation. People who fear risk will often express their insecurity about a new idea by criticising it. Owners of new ideas have to be very robust if they are going to run the gauntlet of negative comment. In a team setting, especially one which fosters innovation, there are usually some people who will want to give the idea a proper airing and perhaps even try it out. At the second stage when a new idea needs to start to make its way through the organisation, the support of a team can be very important.

In summary, teamworking can foster innovation by providing an effective meeting-post for ideas and creative personalities, by handling (or even creating) some of the messiness of the process and by managing the fear of risk through mutual support.

FLEXIBILITY

Responding flexibly encapsulates many elements of the preceding two categories, speed and innovation. The third ingredient has to do with ownership. Some organisations remain flexible because the people with power become wedded to unproductive or rigid ways of thinking and working. There are two basic ways to break that pattern. Either the people with power have to start operating more flexibly themselves, or they need to give some of their power to others who can do it for them. Ideally both should happen at once.

In the example of Kodak's transformation referred to under the Awareness section, Rosabeth Moss Kanter observes that not only was responsibility pushed down the organisation into smaller decentralised units, but also the three figureheads at the top of the company were working as a team.

Teams can operate flexibly by moving information around rapidly amongst themselves, by ensuring that different functions and specialisms are represented and by encouraging the movement of ideas and people across traditional boundaries. Robert Waterman quotes the US steel manufacturer, Nucor, as an example of teamwork that generates an excellent pattern of communications 'that seems uncanny to outsiders; important ideas move like quicksilver'. There is no need for constant meetings and formality and many decisions are made in corridors or over the phone. Not only do ideas move around more freely in a team setting, but people also can move across traditional boundaries when teams encourage multi-skilling.

Some organisations are fairly flexible from the word go. The story of the early days of Apple Computers with its unstructured ways of working, blurred lines of authority, large amounts of personal freedom and the ascendence of vision and values over control and discipline is by now legendary.

It was that kind of flexibility that ensured Apple's early success. But interestingly it was the comparative inflexibility of the style of management of its Chairman, Steve Jobs, that had to be overcome (effectively by Jobs' removal) before Apple could progress to its next level of maturity.

Other organisations chose flexibility late in the day to fight off a competitive threat. The development of new cars was traditionally sequential, from design to engineering to manufacturing and finally to marketing. Not only was the process naturally slow but a hitch at any stage entailed a move back to the beginning. When Ford in America brought out the Taurus it did so by means of Team Taurus, which had brought all the disciplines together at the beginning to work simultaneously as well as sequentially. Team Taurus was flexible in other ways also because it was extraordinarily responsive to new ideas and in fact began with a 'want list' of 1,401 things employees wanted to see in the design. The Taurus went onto win *Motor Trend's* Car of The Year Award.

The Coal Mine Case Study

A coal mine was about to run out of coal and three separate studies had conclusively demonstrated that the mine was uneconomical. In order to extend its life, an investment of approximately $24 million would be required.

A relatively new engineer, unaware of the rules, went underground and wandered around the coalface talking to the miners. One miner, who had worked at this mine for a long time, was perplexed by the proposed closure of the mine. He put forward a relatively inexpensive approach to keeping the mine open. The ideas sounded workable to the engineer, who put together a proposal triggered by the miner's ideas and costed it out to be approximately a $5 million project. Management finally agreed that the proposal was worth a try, if the engineer could get volunteers. The engineer asked for volunteers and within a few hours, 30 miners came forward as well as a small group of supervisors and engineers.

The project ran into problems immediately. The roof caved in as the team started to drill. The mine manager, who was sceptical about the whole project, gave the engineer a weekend to fix the problem or the whole attempt would be abandoned. That Saturday, the engineer called a meeting of the whole team, briefed them about the situation and asked for ideas. A revised scheme was quickly put together and it worked extremely well.

The project became a model of teamworking for that mine in many different ways. For example, after the original crisis meeting, the team adopted the habit of meeting every Saturday to discuss problems and progress. Part of the team's job was to repair equipment. Because of management's scepticism, the team was given the two worst machines for the job. The miners actively overhauled the old equipment during the project. The two machines became the best pieces of equipment in the mine's inventory; they were better than much newer models.

It is clearly better to prepare for flexibility in advance rather than have circumstances dictate it; teamworking gives a number of flexible options. Not every organisation will want to commit to total teamworking, however, and may want to run it in only part of the organisation or for a limited period of time, which in itself is a flexible approach. The second section of this chapter looks at the choices open to the organisation that wants to use teams flexibly.

End Case Study

Co-ordination in the Face of Complexity

The Team Taurus example above illustrates a way of gaining flexibility but also a means of achieving co-ordination. As technology and its accompanying specialisms grow and as markets become more sophisticated, the delivery of even a fairly straightforward product or service requires greater co-ordination. Often, organisations put too much emphasis on planning methods and information systems. There are times when people need to be together and to talk to each other as a team. It is important to get planners and doers together. As organisations become more progressive with their teamworking they cast the net even further to include other organisations. BAA plc has experience of the latter in its attempt to improve the total service enjoyed by passengers in British airports.

Case Study

BAA plc

BAA faces a number of significant challenges as we move towards the next century. The volume of passenger traffic through BAA's airports continues to increase. The cost of security continues to increase. The bottom line of BAA is to ensure that UK airports offer the passengers a safe, efficient and stress-free progress on and off aircraft. The aircraft business is a complex one.

Sir John Egan told us: 'Firstly, in 1990 we had a year with no growth and it looks like we're going to have a second year in 1991 with very little growth. Secondly, we have also been examined by a regulator who has decided to inflict much more severe regulations on us than before.' In July 1991, the Monopolies and Mergers Commission report on BAA stated that 'we received a considerable volume of criticism of BAA . . . . A number of airlines expressed concern about quality of service at the airports . . . . The degree of criticism is, however, to be regretted given BAA's own dependence on its user airlines for its successful development.' Some 55,000 people work at Heathrow. They do a wide variety of different jobs, for example airline staff, concessionaire operations and security. BAA employs only a small proportion of these people. It requires a cohesive policy and standard of efficiency and service right across the board; with so many different businesses and so many airport workers involved, the name of the game here is **Teamwork**.

In order to avoid organisational and commercial chaos, there is a need to identify core priorities.

Sir John also told us that: 'Under this very difficult climate, our response has been to concentrate on core business – to improve the quality and productivity of the way we run the airports.'

In the last 15 months, BAA has instituted a number of new and radical teamwork initiatives. Some elements of teamwork have always been practised within the company. The new teamworking

Case Study

approach is a more structured approach to improvement. The entire philosophy is based on the principle of 'Continuous Improvement'. Today, the company is consciously trying to take a much more proactive view in terms of dealing with problems and issues around change within the company. The other major difference is that the customer is now being involved in the monitoring of quality.

Because of the nature of the airport business, BAA is required to work alongside many other companies. This entails complicated teamworking, involving many different sectors of the airport's operations and numerous other companies.

By combining a teamworking approach and the establishment of a system for checking the quality of service (Quality Service Monitoring – QSM), BAA has been able to tackle some important customer service issues.

For example, customers were complaining about the long queues at check-in points. This involved BAA, the airlines, and the handling agents (three parties, all in close competition with each other, which made the teamworking process even more complex). When dealing with other companies where the culture, philosophy and language may differ greatly, it was important to find a common goal and acceptable ground with which to discuss achievement of this. BAA found that by using the objective, hard data made available by the QSM, it could break down defences. One manager commented, 'By helping people fix their eye on the ball (pleasing the passenger), it was possible to burn our way through difficult alleys'.

The power of a team in co-ordinating complexity can be witnessed in everyday settings. As the passenger eased down into his seat on the first leg of a two sector flight, one of the cabin crew re-packed the locker above his head to ensure that hand luggage had been stowed safely, and shortly afterwards one of her colleagues gave a faultless demonstration of the safety equipment. Although he may not have checked, the crew knew for a fact that the life jacket was underneath his seat. Throughout the flight, a stream of items appeared in front of him such as a wide selection of drinks, a pillow, blanket, newspapers, a set of headphones and even a special meal that he had requested. Had he chosen to travel first class his needs would have been attended to in even more detail, especially in the areas of food and drink. What he didn't see was all the behind-the-scenes activity, which included a briefing for all cabin crew on the allocation of working positions, route information and issues of safety. The seamless service that he witnessed was one of the many millions of daily miracles in team co-ordination.

An organisation that can't handle complexity is doomed to deliver only the most simple of products and services. More sophisticated planning methods might help but there is often no substitute for having the people involved, together, as a team.

Since the MMC report in July 1991, BAA has made considerable efforts to improve the situation. This led the CAA to comment in November 1991:

> BAA has no statutory duty, but it is apparent that it has taken the view that it should make a major effort to get closer to its users in identifying their needs and consulting them on its plans. The Authority (CAA) could not fail to be impressed by the evidence from virtually all quarters of the success of this policy. Many respondents went out of their way to comment favourably.
>
> The Authority (CAA) has been considerably impressed by the efforts now being made by BAA to involve its airline users in the decision making progress and to present a more efficient and effective service to all users of its airports.

Involvement

It has been recognised for some time now that the ideal form of motivation in the workplace is the sort that people generate for themselves because they want to strive, achieve and succeed. As long ago as the early 1960s, Frederick Herzberg recognised the limitations, for long-term results, of the kind of motivation that relies on one person (usually the manager) doing something to another (usually the subordinate). He likened this to kicking a small dog in the rear (the KITA principle) and referred to various pay and incentive schemes as a variation on the principle, attempted from the front (positive KITA). The problem with KITA, even in its positive form, is that it only has a short-term effect (Herzberg went so far as to say it only removed de-motivation by 'cleaning up' the job to make it a reasonably attractive proposition). It also requires a lot of managerial effort to keep injecting motivational stimuli.

If people once get a taste of what it means to be able to influence the nature of their work and their levels of achievement, they often come to realise the fun and challenge of pushing back what they previously saw as constraining boundaries. This can rapidly trigger an improving spiral of deeper commitment/greater achievement/ deeper commitment. Teams are often an ideal environment for fostering this virtuous spiral. Through shared responsibility and support, they can help people to take the risks necessary when taking on increased responsibility, and provide the encouragement needed once it starts to happen.

We have witnessed people in teams who have been swept up by the intensity of involvement. They are often prepared to work long hours because the boundary between what they are doing for their own satisfaction and what they are doing for the organisation has become so blurred. Their own satisfaction can be significant enough for them to describe what they are doing as fun and something that they might have chosen to do anyway, whether or not they are getting paid. Exhaustion and burnout can be a problem associated with this level of commitment but members of high-performance teams are good at looking after each other.

The transition from a traditional structure to one in which teams of highly involved individuals are shaping their own and the organisation's destiny is not without problems. Power has to transfer from individual managers to teams and the members of those teams have to find a productive way of handling it. To some people, the risk implied in this transfer sounds too great. Others have discovered that the rewards match the risk.

Case Study

One of the best US examples of the transition to involvement is that of Ralph Stayer, the CEO of Johnsonville Foods Inc. of Sheboygan, Wisconsin. He tells the story of managing a highly successful sausage manufacturing business, with the growing realisation that not only was the business under-achieving but that the employees were performing to a fraction of their potential. He came to understand that his management style removed responsibility from his staff and placed it firmly on his own shoulders, 'weighing me down and – though I didn't appreciate it at the time – crippling my subordinates and strangling the company'. In a radical move, he handed ownership of quality control completely to his line workers. Tasting sausages had formerly been the job of management, it was now the job of the people who made them.

Stayer reports his surprise at how ready his workers were to accept ownership. They formed teams to tackle quality problems and did a thorough job of surveying production practices, suppliers and even retailers. This data was then fed into improved operations and monitored for progress. It led to the startling result of a cut in rejects from 5 per cent to less than 0.5 per cent in one area. As this enthusiasm for ownership spread, the workforce started to ask for and work with data on yield, costs and human resources. In response the management at Johnsonville supplied the data and pushed responsibility further down the organisation. The teams took on the selection and training of new members and ultimately accepted responsibility for standards, schedules, budgets and capital improvements.

The acid test came when Johnsonville had to decide whether to buy a production facility from another manufacturer. This was a significant strategic decision because it was both an excellent opportunity and a possible threat if the size of the acquisition overstretched resources and compromised what had been achieved in the quality area. Strategic decisions of this sort had normally been the prerogative of Stayer and the senior managers, but after careful thought they decided that the whole of Johnsonville had to own the decision. They posed three questions to the team about what it would take to make the acquisition work, how the downside risk could be reduced and finally, whether on balance it was worth doing.

After an intense discussion and consultation period, the verdict was that the teams wanted to go ahead with the acquisition. They realised the sacrifices that they would have to make, including working a seven day week and hiring and training people to take new shifts. It was also clear that they would have to raise the already high standards of the acquired product at the same time as maintaining existing standards in the original operations. Stayer describes the decision as one of the proudest moments of his life and acknowledges that with his old traditional executive decision making he would have turned the new business down. The newly acquired production facility was a big success and quality rose on all fronts.

The power of involvement can be as liberating for the company as it can for the individual. It involves risks for both, but risks that can be managed and made to pay dividends. Even if people don't want to go as far as the Johnsonville example suggests, there is a trend in Western society towards groups and individuals wanting a bigger say in their own destiny.

MAPPING TEAMS

Using teams strategically to bring about organisational change is not completely uncharted territory, as the earlier examples have demonstrated. Some types of teamworking are still sufficiently novel, however, for it to be worth looking at some of the principles that inform the strategic choice.

1. Altering the Structure of the Organisation?

This is essentially a question about the scale and depth of the teamworking intervention. Some organisations decide to re-structure fundamentally along teamworking lines. This is usually a very far-reaching and radical move, especially if it is embraced on a permanent basis (temporary examples are rare but essentially involve tugging around a significant part of the organisation as part of a teamworking venture with another company). It may entail removing levels of management, possibly reducing the number of people, changing job, skill, selection and training requirements, altering working practices and dramatically re-distributing power.

Understandably some organisations don't see this as necessary, or they fear the risks involved. They may still see plenty of benefit in teamworking, however, and prefer instead to use teams in part of the organisation. Again there are choices. It is possible to take a whole division, say, and convert it to teamworking, or to use a few teams for specific purposes dotted round the organisation. The questions that need to be addressed revolve around whether teamworking is seen as an experiment to be used in some fairly low-risk areas, or whether there is a basic commitment to the principles, in which case areas most naturally suited to teamworking need to be identified. This begs a second major question of whether to locate a team or teams within the structure of the organisation or outside it.

2. Not altering the Structure but Inside or Outside?

A strategic intervention that alters the structure of an organisation by definition alters it on the inside. Therefore the inside/outside question only applies to structures that are in the main left unaltered by teamworking.

In the 1970s Beckhard and Harris suggested that organisations should designate special structures to do the work of managing the change while an organisation is in a state of transition. A team can take on this function, and they believe that the change efforts are best facilitated by creating a management system that is separate and different from the present management structure.

In the 1980s Stein and Moss Kanter developed Beckhard and Harris's ideas further. During an organisational transition period, they suggested that an organisation should create a parallel structure consisting of a steering committee and flexible, temporary problem-solving groups to supplement the work of the more hierarchical and bureaucratic management structure. The two organisations are intended to exist side by side and the parallel organisation is not intended in any way to replace the management hierarchy. According to Stein and Moss Kanter, parallel organisations can be both reactive (dealing with those changes made necessary by changes in the environment) and proactive (implementing change in anticipation of future developments). More recently, Moss Kanter has elaborated further on her idea by labelling the parallel structure a 'newstream'. By a mixture of autonomy, new working practices, flexible structures, new values, visions and leadership a 'newstream' cuts a channel that runs alongside the 'mainstream' organisational culture.

Parallel structures or 'newstreams' are not new and people with a passion for innovation have always found their own ways of running a creative mini-enterprise alongside their job. The Americans coined the term 'skunkworks' to capture the image of a few mad enthusiasts taking every available spare moment to go into the corner behind the machinery and, rather like skunks, snuffle through the garbage of discarded ideas and equipment until they came up with either an inspired invention or a Heath Robinson contraption. More far-sighted companies have encouraged this activity and some have even institutionalised it (3M employees can spend up to 15 per cent of their working week on any activity of their own choosing as long as it is product related). Interestingly, teams which have been set up for innovation purposes are often located in a different building away from company headquarters and the team members will often favour names, drawings, decorations and symbols that signal their separate identity. One of the early Apple Computer buildings symbolised their attitude to the rest of the established industry by displaying a skull and crossbones on the outside.

3. Permanent or Limited Life?

The duration of a teamworking initiative will depend partly on the nature of the task and partly on whether it is seen as being an experiment. Troubleshooting and problem-solving task forces will often dissolve once their work has been done. Some teams are deliberately given a limited life (or required constantly to review their membership) as a means of reaping the rewards of flexibility. Once jobs and functions become attached to people and departments on a permanent basis, the danger of staleness and complacency creeping in becomes greater. A successful teamworking philosophy will often encourage people to value their contributions to a number of projects, at different times and in different settings.

4. Putting it all Together – The Teamworking Matrix

The three choices listed above can be expressed as a matrix of six possibilities (Fig 1.1). Each is considered in detail below.

Figure 1.1: The team matrix

	Leaves the Structure of the Organization Unaltered	Alters the Structure of The Organisation
Permanent Life	A. **Inside the Structure** e.g. New venture to complement existing activities, reporting in to the Board	E. e.g. A complete restructuring along teamworking lines
	B. **Outside the Structure** e.g. Customer First Teams	
Limited Life	C. **Inside the Structure** e.g. Task Force to tackle a specific problem	F. e.g. Committing part of the organisation to a joint venture with another
	D. **Outside the Structure** e.g. New product development in the form of a mini-organisation	

A. LEAVES THE STRUCTURE OF THE ORGANISATION UNALTERED/PERMANENT LIFE/ INSIDE THE STRUCTURE

In this situation, the organisation sets up a new venture to complement its existing activities but models it along existing organisational lines and gives it only a moderate amount of autonomy. A number of companies, for example, have chosen to set up their own computer software functions or consultancy services. Over time, the relationship of these groups to the parent company may alter as they gain increasing autonomy and start to service a growing number of other organisations as well as the parent.

Case Study

Portland Holidays

Portland Holidays is a tour operator with whom the public can book directly, cutting out the travel agents and supposedly getting better value for money. Thomson Holidays, on the other hand, is a tour operator whose holidays can only be accessed through travel agents. Thomson Holidays did much in the 1970s and 1980s to develop good relationships with the travel agent network. It developed and introduced TOP, a computerised booking system. Thomson trained travel agents to use the TOP system and it also had a good reputation for quality problem solving and providing good service. Relationships with travel agents were good and also crucial to the continuing growth of Thomson Holidays.

In the late 1970s, competition started to intensify in the travel industry. The arrival of Tjaerebourg on the scene was the first real threat to Thomson Holidays. Although there had been some direct booking tour operators before, they tended to be local and small. The reason Tjaerebourg was a threat to Thomson Holidays was that it presented quality and service but was also cheaper.

Until this time, the Thomson travel portfolio consisted of Thomson Holidays, the tour operator, Lunn Poly, the travel agents and Britannia Airways, an airline. To add a direct selling tour operating company made strategic sense for the future but could in the short term jeopardise the goodwill and relationships that Thomson Holidays had with the travel agents. The TOPs systems

Case Study

and the name of Thomson Holidays in the mind of the customer suggested, however, that the threat to Thomson travel's core business, that is, Thomson Holidays, would be short-term.

The Portland Holidays Project Team

Four people were taken out to form a team, and work full time to develop the new company. They were later to become the senior managers of the new company. Secrecy was crucial. The project team was working on a special project reporting directly to the Thomson Holiday Managing Director. All members of the team were Thomson Holidays employees and each was considered to be the best in his or her own area of work.

Their task was to put together a summer programme for what was to become Portland Holidays. The range of tasks involved were:

- Choosing destinations, hotels, transfers and all the details of the travel programme.
- The staffing and technology necessary for direct operating.
- The design, marketing, PR and launch of the new company.
- Creating the image, logo and designs for the shop and the uniforms.

In fact everything that Thomson Holidays had built its reputation on needed to be included. However, politically it was seen to be important to keep a clear distinction between the two tour operators, and thereby hopefully to reduce the threat as perceived by the travel agents. Other organisations have used a similar approach. For example, Abbey National plc set up Cornerstone, the estate agency, as a separate company. The motivation here was to protect the core business, that is mortgage lending, from erosion by

Case Study

mortgages being offered through other estate agents – the 'one stop shop'.

The Thomson project team took approximately nine months to develop the concept of Portland Holidays. The original reaction from the travel agents and the travel press was as negative as had been anticipated. Interestingly, though, Portland Holidays has managed to remain separate and different from Thomson Holidays. It has established a reputation for quality and service in its own right. The original members went on to take up significant management roles and the venture has proved to be both strategically and operationally sound.

End Case Study

B. LEAVES THE STRUCTURE OF THE ORGANISATION UNALTERED/PERMANENT LIFE/ OUTSIDE THE STRUCTURE

Some teams are deliberately located outside the organisational structure in order to make it easier for them to take experimental approaches to their structure, membership and way of working. The team itself is permanent, but individual membership may change over time. Membership is generally on a voluntary basis and is not a full time commitment. Depending on the attitude of the organisation, meetings may be conducted inside or outside work time. The composition of the team and its methods will usually have no existing parallel and can therefore be said to lie outside the organisation's structure. Customer First teams (usually teams whose prime objective is to find ways of improving customer service) are often modelled along these lines.

Case Study

The World's Favourite Airline – British Airways' Customer First Teams

What is a Customer First Team?

British Airways set up 'Customer First Teams' as a component in its 'Putting the Customer First' initiative, which is already well documented. Initially the aim was to give customer contact staff the opportunity to become personally and creatively involved in improving customer service in their own areas of work.

What Do Customer First Teams Do?

The main motivation behind setting up Customer First Teams was to get employees' direct and personal involvement, which would develop ownership of the improvement process. British Airways was also trying to create positive expectations of success by tapping and developing the abilities of front-line staff.

How The Team Works

A Customer First Team was defined as a small group of volunteer staff who would meet regularly to identify, analyse and make proposals for ways of improving customer service in their areas of work. The idea was that the team would meet and try to identify areas of improvement in their own work areas. They would then develop ways of achieving this improvement and make proposals to management. The teams were also expected to get involved in implementing the change and help to monitor, evaluate and disseminate results. Each team would consist of between six and twelve customer contact staff who normally work together. It would be a natural work group. They would be led by the appropriate supervisor, supported by a local facilitator and managed by a local co-ordinator. The Customer First Teams would meet regularly, that

Case Study

is, once a week or once every two weeks, subject to their local roster arrangements. They would meet for one hour and this meeting would be held during paid work time.

In setting up the teams, training was a key element. Training was provided for facilitators, team leaders and team members. The facilitators received formal training in the philosophy behind Customer First Teams, the structure, and their own role. They were also given training in problem solving skills. The team leaders received formal training in how to set up and run the teams, team leadership, coaching skills and techniques for systematic problem-solving. The Customer First Team members were provided with coaching and instruction on how to use brainstorming, cause and effect diagrams, presentation of data and assessing benefits and costs. These techniques were to be applied immediately to look at real issues.

The benefits of Customer First Teams were seen as wide and varied. For example, the customer would benefit by having British Airways staff sensitive to and concerned for his/her needs and expectations. The staff would benefit by becoming directly involved in defining and meeting customer needs. They would also see the company making a substantial investment in its staff. The team leader would get an opportunity to extend his/her skills in developing and leading people, and overall the airline would benefit by enhancing its abilities at the grass roots level to satisfiy customers' needs. The company would also be able to move from having to persuade staff, to getting their direct involvement and hence to their ownership of the improvement process.

There were some fundamental requirements that needed to be put into place to ensure the success of Customer First Teams. They were:

- Visible senior management support.

- Sensitivity to the cultural variations within the airline.
- Managing early, visible success by implementing useful suggestions.
- Providing and maintaining an effective support system.
- Putting the emphasis on 'getting our own house in order' first.
- Voluntary membership.

These ingredients were seen as essential if this initiative was to be successful. Customer First Teams were so successful with customer contact staff that other staff also wanted to be involved, and to be part of the organisation improvement programe. Subsequently, the Customer First Team initiative was implemented throughout the airline.

Customer First Teams played an important part in the dramatic improvements in quality of service and business performance at British Airways. Examples of their achievements include improved arrangements for tracing and delivery of lost baggage, improved presentation of flight information to passengers, and better ways of dealing with unaccompanied children. Currently, British Airways is undertaking a new initiative to revitalise Customer First Teams.

In 1980, British Leyland gave the loss-making Jaguar concern a year's notice of closure unless it broke even. The turnaround of Jaguar, led by Sir John Egan, has been well publicised and was clearly a remarkable feat. Sales recovered, pre-tax profits leapt and productivity more than doubled. Jaguar was successfully floated in 1984. Jaguar's success lay in its ability to transform its product and that in turn relied on a number of key initiatives taken by Jaguar management. The changes at Jaguar were heavily dependent on teamwork and they included a restructuring of Jaguar's retail operation, a new Senior Management Team, raised standards of quality and reliability, and setting up of a parallel organisation in the form of company-wide, multi-disciplinary task forces to tackle 150 separate problems.

Various types of team and group structures can become the parallel organisation. Teams are developed to improve communication and to provide top management with feedback. Others are created to identify the critical issues which the organisation is facing and to develop projects that address them. Finally, there are teams whose purpose is to implement the change projects. Some of the teams involve all the staff, some involve natural work teams and others consist of a cross-section of the organisation.

Not only do these teams carry out and co-ordinate the change efforts, but they also perform a number of other functions. Firstly, they build commitment to the new corporate direction by providing the opportunity for large numbers of staff to become directly involved in the change process. Secondly, these teams serve as channels for information about the progress of the change effort. They provide top management with a good forum for sharing its vision. Morale is typically raised by the interaction with management at the meetings, as well as by the chance to express a wide range of feelings and reactions to the change effort. Getting feelings out in the open and sharing anxieties with other team members accelerates the process of working through the inevitable losses that all change entails. Finally, productivity improves as teams of staff engage in the task of identifying the critical issues for the organisation and of actually implementing action steps that will improve the effectiveness of the organisation.

C. LEAVES THE STRUCTURE OF THE ORGANISATION UNALTERED/LIMITED LIFE/INSIDE THE STRUCTURE

Some problems are so intractable and so fundamental to the organisation that they cannot be left to the ad hoc approach of the Customer First Team described above. In situations of this sort, an organisation may pull together a task force with the aim of solving a particular problem. Unlike Customer First Teams, membership is not usually left to chance in the form of a call for volunteers but draws on people with the necessary skills to solve the problem. Once the problem is solved, the task force disbands.

Case Study

British Aerospace

British Aerospace – (Commercial Aircraft/Hatfield) set up two different kinds of teams as part of its Quality Improvement Programme. Firstly, Quality Improvement Teams were set up to operate within each working group. The idea was that they would meet regularly to discuss, identify and solve quality problems. These meetings would be held between the supervisor and his/her direct reports.

In addition BAe Hatfield also uses Corrective Action Teams (CATs) as and when necessary. CATs are temporary, cross-functional teams spanning three or more functions. A CAT is established to identify and formulate plans to eliminate the root causes of a major defect. When problems occur across departments and where the impact goes across a number of areas, this is filtered up to the top team for authorisation to create a new cross-functional team. This allows BAe Hatfield to control the number of additional teams and acts as a balancing process within the site. A Corrective Action Team has an eight-week life span to solve the problem and to report back. Once the solution has been found, the Corrective Action Teams are formally broken up.

BAe Hatfield held a Quality Day in November 1991 to coincide with the World Quality Day. BAe estimated that £1 million worth of solutions had already been found. One executive commented '99 per cent of drives to greater efficiency have taken place in a year when it couldn't have been more difficult. We managed to push the change through'. The eight-week life span of the Corrective Action Teams helped to speed up the process considerably.

End Case Study

Case Study

BAA plc – Security Task Force

Background
Security is an issue that constantly needs attention and continuous improvement. Security is now even higher on BAA's agenda since the Gulf War and the Lockerbie air disaster. In the spring of 1991, BAA set up a special task force to look at how it could further improve security service within Terminal One at Heathrow Airport, while at the same time increasing productivity and improving the quality of service provided to passengers. The team's task was to focus its attention specifically on security operations in Terminal One, with the aim of extending any changes that were made across the other Terminals and indeed all other UK Airports.

An initial research study had already indicated that to improve security operations using the current procedures would mean employing even more staff. Thus, the task force was asked to assess current security operations, investigate ways to tighten up and improve the process and to 'trial' any newly devised security procedures that they came up with.

The Team Mix
The team was set up on the principle that it would be vital to include a number of different levels and security positions: firstly, to give the team the added value of a variety of perspectives and, secondly, so that on further communication to other staff members, there would be a team representative to communicate in the appropriate language. The team was set up by the general manager and it included four people: a Security Inspector, who was aware of the standards that needed to be maintained; a Security Guard, who knew the staff and the operational problems involved; a Security Manager; and a team leader.

Case Study

The Task

The team's overall task was to work alongside all security personnel in Terminal One to assess current security procedures, to investigate any new ideas to improve these and finally to try out the suggested new procedures. The team was specifically involved with collecting data. For example, it monitored how many bags and of what kind were passing through the Terminal, the rate of security searches and the number of passengers. Firstly the team found different ways of assessing the security procedures, including providing all security personnel with 'clickers' to record quantities of bags, passengers and so on. It then allocated tasks, monitored and collated the findings and helped to design the new security procedures. The task force was also responsible for communicating the main objective of the project and its findings to all security personnel involved.

The time allocated to this team was three months. In the initial stage, the team assessed, investigated and designed the new security procedures. However, the second stage brought in all other security personnel, thus extending the project airport wide. That part of the project is still continuing.

Sequence of the Team's Activities:

- Identify issues that needed attention.
- Decide what changes or improvements were needed.
- Decide what information had to be collected and what needed to be measured.
- Decide how this information would be recorded and when the research would be carried out.
- Communicate the objectives of the project to all security personnel.
- Allocate tasks and collect data.

Case Study

- Analyse the data.
- Brainstorm and design new ways to improve the security operation.
- Communicate these ideas to other staff.
- Put the new procedures into operation.

Daily team meetings were held to explore the findings of their research and to decide what security procedures needed modifying.

Sir John Egan told us that the teams are asked to 'get the data which describes the situation, look at your processes, and use it and try and come up with ideas for improvement, experiment with some of those ideas and any that work can then be implemented on a wider range'.

Outcomes

Initially, the reaction from other security staff was a hostile one. Data collection and trying out new work practices was considered to be a time and energy consuming process. However, as they got used to the new practices and understood the length and breadth of the project, they became involved and started taking responsibility for the changes. The task force's commitment was an essential element in their success. They were totally dedicated to the team's overall objective, aware of the importance of communication and the need to allay fears about the changes that other staff might have had.

New methods were introduced to improve the security procedures. Already vast improvements can be seen and these methods are now being implemented at all Terminals at Heathrow. They are also being put into operation at Gatwick Airport and the aim is to extend these to all other UK airports. The Terminal

Case Study

Security Manager comments: 'It is already possible to see higher productivity and significant results not seen previously'.

The task force itself was disbanded after the first three months. Each team member has returned to their normal job. The difference, however, is that they are still instrumental in pushing the new changes in security procedures through in their own place of work. They continue to play a vital role in communicating the change messages to other staff and are still 'championing the cause'. In this way, they are continuing to help secure commitment to the vision.

The Security Manager is now involved in introducing the scheme to all other airports and terminals around the country.

End Case Study

D. LEAVES THE STRUCTURE OF THE ORGANISATION UNALTERED/LIMITED LIFE/ OUTSIDE THE STRUCTURE

A task force or project team may be deliberately located outside the structure in order to break with tradition and perhaps to send signals back into the organisation about new ways of working. This would be true, for example, of an initiative located outside a Research and Development Department to develop a new product or a task force with a membership designed to represent different countries as well as representing different skills.

Many large companies have seen small businesses get ahead in the marketplace. IBM, one of the best managed companies in the world, watched Digital Equipment take the lead in minicomputers and Apple in personal computers. Clearly the tried, trusted and previously successful IBM strategies were not working in the current environment. The marketplace seemed to favour small businesses who could move fast without bureaucratic constraints.

As a result, a lot of companies like IBM, Xerox and NCR are formulating new ways of working. Their aim is to use and apply what is best about small businesses – teamworking, speed of response, flexibility, innovation – and add these to their own strengths of stability and financial security.

IBM's response to Apple was to duplicate as closely as possible the environment that generated the creativity behind Apple's success. IBM created a number of 'Independent Business Units'. These were teams designed to be outside the company's normal structure, small and flexible enough to be able to respond to the extremely volatile high-tech marketplace. 'If you are competing against people who started in a garage, you have to start in a garage', says Don Estridge, who led the IBU that came up with the PC. Estridge took a group of 12 people, on a limited budget, working in highly unattractive surroundings in Florida, people who had a lot of energy and zeal and also enjoyed freedom from the IBM headquarters in New York. This group created the IBM PC in a much shorter time-frame then anything else IBM had produced in years. IBM people think that this approach combines the best of both worlds, giving stability with speed.

In his book *The Soul of a New Machine*, author Tracy Kidder vividly describes the kind of high-energy small team innovation at Data General. The team was located separately from the Head Office in Westborough, Massachusetts. Kidder's account describes a small team's huge struggle to dominate a machine. The working of the 32 bit mini-computer Eagle was a massive task. It demanded every waking hour of a brilliant and aggressive team of young computer wizards who worked for the multi-million dollar company. They were given one year: each day the 'microkids' tested their physical, psychological and technical abilities to the limit. They finally commanded the machine's obedience and delivered Eagle. There is much to be learned from this limited-life team, which was located outside the parent organisation and given the freedom to find its own way of working.

In Japan, an 'inside-the-company-venture' was established by Hitachi. Earlier in the same year, Hitachi's president, Katsushige Mita, was approached by the Managing Director, Ozeki, and asked to create a special plant for office automation equipment, 'in order to make up for the company's serious delay in the field'. Instead of looking at whether or not such a plant would be profitable, Mita said, 'why don't you build a small shed, select a small team and start from there as our predecessors did, when they founded the company?' (This sounds very similar to what IBM's Don Estridge said when he had to find a way of competing with Apple's PC).

E.   ALTERS THE STRUCTURE OF THE ORGANISATION/PERMANENT LIFE

The benefits of teamworking are so strong that for some organisations they represent a persuasive argument for converting the whole structure to one based on teams. This is a radical move and may be driven by one or more of the change imperatives. In some cases, the whole organisation won't be ready for such a dramatic shift, but a sub-group may be. Providing that the circumstances are right, these conditions might favour an entrepreneurial group of people conducting a buy-out in order to set up a more flexible, team-based operation.

Case Study

British Aerospace (Commercial Aircraft/Hatfield)
British Aerospace (Commercial Aircraft/Hatfield) has taken a bold decision to challenge its competitive environment by setting out to restructure the entire organisation. In the late 1980s, Operations Manager Dick Williams and his colleagues were under pressure to reverse the dramatic decline in this troubled aircraft manufacturer. 'We realised that we didn't just have one business at Hatfield, we had three – supply, final assembly and customisation,' comments

Case Study

Williams. 'We needed a bold new manufacturing strategy.' The three different businesses needed to be separated physically, organisationally and financially so that they could be controlled more easily and their performances measured separately. BAe Hatfield recently announced the relocation of its final assembly operation to Woodford, Cheshire, as part of this reorganisation. The supply and customisation businesses remain at Hatfield.

For many years, BAe Hatfield had been organised into five functions – production engineering, production control, supplies, inspection and works. Williams comments: 'We began employing "cash positive restructuring" (CPR). This involves developing a strategy that allows management to take action to release cash to invest in further action which then releases more cash – in effect it offers instant pay back.'

The company used CPR to take advantage of savings generated by cutting the huge volumes of inventory on the Hatfield site. The finished goods stock was valued at £300 million, before it was cut. Early in 1989, the inventory reduction programme began. Williams formed a team of 12 people for this task. They began by mapping where inventory lay each month and displayed this on a planning sheet visible on the shop floor. The team estimated that it could drive £80 million worth of inventory from business in 1989. In fact, it eliminated £124.4 million. The team also introduced suggestion schemes on how to cut inventory. It heightened awareness throughout the factory that inventory was to be avoided at all costs.

Just telling people to cut inventory was not enough on its own. Williams says: 'We had to involve our people, gain their commitment and demolish us-and-them attitudes. Communication was the key. The general manager gave a broad presentation in December 1988. Then, over a three-month period, we presented to the entire workforce in groups of 20 to 30. We had a Lego model

Case Study

of the new site and we gave short talks on our plans for restructuring the business.

'Training and awareness have been central to what we have done. We have got everybody involved – union reps, joint staff and the executive committee'. By the end of 1989, BAe Hatfield introduced a 'pilot cell' to test its ideas. It started in October 1989. The 'door cell' was chosen because, firstly, aeroplane door manufacturing is a medium to difficult operation. Kester Vaughan, the Manufacturing Centre Manager of the pilot cell, says: 'We were concerned about having credibility with the workforce. If we chose a product they considered too simple we would lack the credibility.' The door cell was also self-contained, with raw material going in at one end and the completed product coming out at the other.

The pilot cell emphasised the BAe Hatfield management's determination to change. BAe Hatfield wanted to simplify the way it operated and optimise the use of space. It used teamworking as part of the change process, and training played a very important part in the change programme. It was aimed at building trust between mangement and the cell team. Until then there had been an us-and-them divide. To attempt to break this down, managers went through the same training at the same time as the cell team. Vaughan comments: 'In effect we were saying, "it is OK for you to participate". This was an empowerment programme, we wanted decision making from the bottom of the organisation upwards. People had never been given the chance to do that before. The training allowed members of the pilot cell to invent cell working for themselves. The team were given the principles of what we were trying to achieve. Using them and some principles they developed themselves, they invented cell working themselves.'

The Hatfield site is currently being reorganised into six manufacturing centres, each covering a particular aspect of the manufacture of an aeroplane. Within the manufacturing centres are a number of cells, which are also sub–divided. Each manufacturing centre contains a support team comprising materials management, engineering and quality teams.

Each self–contained unit is responsible for its own inventory and its own time, quality and product targets. There are approximately 10 to 12 people in each cell team. Each is an active cell member, with the role of the foreman replaced by the cell leader. There was also a move from the 'old-fashioned foreman to a new-fashioned supervision role', this being recognised as crucial to pushing the change forward.

Significant benefits have already been reported by the pilot cell teams. Cellular team working is an ongoing issue at BAe. A senior executive comments: 'Today teamwork on the site has become natural. We want to achieve world class performance, to be the most competitive and provide the best value for our customers. The process of achieving this is continuous because all our competitors are trying to do the same thing – there is no actual stopping point. Quality is a journey – not a destination.'

F.   ALTERS THE STRUCTURE OF THE ORGANISATION/LIMITED LIFE

Altering the structure of an organisation in order to capitalise on teamworking for a limited period of time does not occur very frequently, but may be justified when the project is so large that a Task Force alone is not enough. Some major joint ventures between large corporations for specific projects would be an illustration of the type of teamworking that temporarily alters at least part of the structure of both parent organisations.

On a grand scale, perhaps one of the best examples of limited life teamworking was the multi-national coalition that defeated Iraq's Saddam Hussein in the Gulf War in the earlier part of 1991. At a political level the Americans managed to hold together a loose alliance of countries composed of some very unlikely partners, such as Saudi Arabia and Israel. It was a precarious juggling act and not a solid coalition by any means but it was nevertheless strong enough to secure the vital co-operation of a number of the Arab nations.

The forces allied against Iraq agreed to accept the command of General Norman Schwarzkopf of the US. There was a general acknowledgement of the strong mutual interdependence of the forces. Thus the Americans praised the discipline of the British soldiers, the manoeuvrability of the Challenger tanks and the unrivalled ability of the British sappers to clear the Iraqi berm (sandwall) fortifications. In turn, the British acknowledged their debt to the Saudis (airfields, fuel, food), Turkey and Morocco (desert clothing) and Rumania (a 200-bed hospital). The coalition was all the more extraordinary because hitherto some countries, such as France, had sworn that their troops would never serve under anyone else's general; hence France's entry into the coalition was seen as very significant.

Forming alliances and co-operative ventures with other companies can take a number of forms from simple agreements to work more co-operatively to projects involving considerable expenditure of time and resources on joint production or service provision. These projects often alter at least part of the structure of the sponsoring organisations and often bring the groups together in one or more teams. Moss Kanter notes the fascinating phenomenon that the bonds created 'can sometimes be closer than those within their own organisations'. It is as if the co-operative venture demands high quality teamworking if it is to work at all and people unencumbered by the normal organisational roles can be free to make a team really work. Co-operation can be so close that it is sometimes difficult to distinguish between the employees of one organisation and those of another, as at Kodak, for example, where a supply room is run by the staff from a supplier.

MOVING WITHIN THE MATRIX

We have noted that organisations may want to experiment with teamworking to find out what they can do before making a more fundamental commitment. There are some good examples of the successful outcome of such experiments leading to a deeper acceptance of the concept.

Team Taurus and Johnsonville, referred to earlier, provide two illustrations. In the case of Team Taurus, its life ended with the production of the new Ford Taurus car, but the way of working had been so successful that it brought about a permanent change in the structure of Ford's new product development. At Johnsonville, the first team that set itself up under Stayer's new way of thinking concentrated mainly on quality issues. As the detailed case study in the *Involvement* section shows, teamworking spread and became such a normal way of life that ultimately strategic decisions came to be made with the help of teams company-wide.

Another way of achieving mobility within the matrix is to operate a highly fluid teamworking structure. Teams form and re-form and individuals find themselves part of a number of interlocking teams and networks. This approach is one that has been embedded in the Digital Equipment Company Ltd.

THE 'EVERYDAY' TEAM

Our main interest in this section is using teams to bring about change, but many managers will want to know what significance the strategic deployment of teams and the matrix has for the kind of teams that they have been running for years. After all, functional teams of personnel, finance, and information management specialists are not new. Similarly, some organisations, especially those involved in limited life projects (information technology, consultancy, for example) have long been accustomed to using project teams.

In terms of the matrix, both functional and project teams leave the structure of the organisation unaltered and are located inside the structure. Functional teams are usually fairly permanent, and project teams are usually limited life. More importantly, the members and leaders of these teams may find that they are already doing some of what we have described as best practice in this book. Our advice to those interested in championing teamworking, is to push the standard further by becoming even more innovative, flexible and fast and to become such a superb model of co-operative working that the rest of the organisation is stimulated to make the transition, as described in *Moving Within The Matrix*, to the permanent, total teamworking.

WHEN IS TEAMWORKING NOT APPROPRIATE?

It is tempting to be as provocative as Tom Peters and argue for 'violating common sense' by imposing a teamworking structure on 'almost anything'. Our consulting experience in the UK tells us that this may well be too much, too soon for many organisations.

There are three commonly stated reasons for not using teamworking, all of which have a reasonable basis but all of which need challenging.

1. 'We are not ready to share power'

This is rarely expressed quite so honestly as the above phrase would suggest, but this feeling often lies behind senior management's assertions about the immaturity or inexperience of the workforce when it comes to complex business matters or strategy. It is a viable strategic choice if, and only if, senior management is itself sufficiently in touch with the day-to-day realities of the customers and the minutiae of the workings of the organisation to steer a course through the difficult waters suggested by the change imperatives.

2. 'Our specialists are naturally loners'

We have heard a number of companies in the finance sector explaining or apologising for their lack of management talent or lack of cohesiveness by pointing to the elite nature of their super specialists (wholesale insurance brokers or investment directors). The argument goes that these super specialists are so good at what they do and so used to working alone that teamworking is anathema to them. It is even claimed by some that these specialists are closer to their clients than to their employing organisation.

A common fallacy amongst the super specialists is that teamworking means constantly being in meetings and reducing all group discussions to their lowest common denominator in order to accomodate the needs of the less intellectually agile. What they probably miss out on is the experience of working with a team that reduces rather than increases the number of meetings because communication and common understanding is so well developed. As *Superteams* pointed out, it is perfectly possible to manage a 'team apart' as long as the teamworking mentality exists between the scattered individuals so that they think about their responsibilities to each other even when they are separated. The lowest common denominator argument is rarely advanced by individuals who have experienced the spark and excitement of a team working in a truly innovative fashion. Without a minimum amount of teamworking the super specialists can become isolated individuals incapable of learning from or sharing their experience with the organisation that pays them, the people that provide a back-up service or from each other.

3. 'Teams are like committees and committees are disasters'

Most organisations have legendary tales (or even office cartoons) about the malfunctioning of committees. The common complaint is that they meet too often, they are over-rigid, everyone fights their corner and it is impossible to reach decisions. It is a great pity that they are sometimes associated with teams because an effective team is designed to remove all those problems.

The teams described earlier that are used to maximise speed, flexibility and innovation avoid formal procedures and rigid structures. Fighting for individual interests is accepted as long as it serves the over-arching goal of whole team, which is usually articulated so that everyone knows what it is. The need for speed creates the necessity for effective decision making procedures, which in turn mitigates against constant squabbling over narrowly defined interests. As was noted in the Nucor example (under the Flexibility section), enhanced communications in effective teams can mean fewer meetings than for the traditional committee.

It could be argued that the kinds of teams we have described as helping to change organisations draw their characteristics from the traditional mistakes of committees.

Whereas it is one thing to understand how teams can be used strategically to tackle the imperatives of change, it is another to appreciate some of the struggles and triumphs experienced by organisations in the thick of pioneering teamworking.

2. The Companies that are Doing It

INTRODUCTION

In this chapter we present four case studies to illustrate how a number of organisations have used a teamworking approach. The way they identified the need, how they assembled the teams, the type of training and development provided for the teams is also described. The case studies illustrate some of the initial results and highlight the issues that each organisation experienced as it started on the road to using teamworking. The majority are recent examples, although each organisation is at a different stage in its use of teams. However, even at this stage, important lessons can be drawn from their experiences. Each case study is from a different sector of industry and illustrates how teamwork has been used to enhance that organisation's work.

> *Case Study*

EXPERIMENTING WITH TEAMWORK AT THE BODY SHOP

Background

In 1976, Anita Roddick opened a small shop in Brighton selling the kind of simple, natural skin and hair care preparations she had seen

Case Study

women of other cultures using on her travels around the world. She decided to sell them as simply and economically as possible, with a minimum of packaging and a range of sizes so customers could buy as much or as little as they wanted. That was the first Body Shop.

The Teamwork Experiment

An experiment in teamworking without managers has been launched by The Body Shop at its latest branch in London's West End. This new experiment in a managerless shop was born out of the need to try to improve service to customers in a new and challenging way. The brief was set by the directors of The Body Shop and a team was founded to tackle the task. It was given a chance to experiment, to find a new system to strive for the best delivery of quality service to the customers. The task force consisted of eight people including the Human Resources Manager, a General Manager, an Area Manager, the Training Manager and the Field Training Officer. They used brainstorming to generate ideas and explored many different options for improving customer service. Eventually they settled on the notion of a managerless group of people, working as a team. The original idea was a spin-off from the notion of working co-operatives. The Body Shop uses co-operatives around the world for its products.

There were many questions as to how this system could work in practice in one of The Body Shop units. A new shop was to open in September 1991 in London's Oxford Street. It was decided that this would be the location for the teamworking experiment. 'The thinking behind the teamworking system was that staff should be more involved and have more incentive to want to serve the customer well,' comments Jane Corson, the Human Resources Manager of The Body Shop. The hope was that more involvement by all staff, not just management, would lead to higher levels of motivation and morale with 'more of a buzz in the atmosphere'. This, in turn, would improve customer relations and service. All those staff involved would feel some 'ownership' of the shop unit. It would create an atmosphere of excitement, high job involvement, satisfaction and fulfilment for all working there. The management group hoped that these elements would have direct repercussions on how staff interacted with customers.

Setting Up the Team
First there was identification of all the different tasks that had to be done in each shop unit. Four distinct work areas were identified: Finance, Stockroom, Personnel and Front of Shop. Twenty-four staff would be needed for the Oxford Street project. They would be split into four teams, each responsible for one of the distinct areas of work. Over time, the teams would rotate, so that each team member would have a chance to become involved in all the different aspects of running The Body Shop Unit.

Assembling the Team
The Body Shop attempted to draw parallels between retail and the theatre as it advertised for staff. The advertisement described the staff needed for this new project as 'performers'. It asked people if they would like to 'audition' for a role in this new and revolutionary project. All performers were to receive the same salary. The lack of management and the equal salaries were strong selling points in advertising the jobs and appeared to draw more applicants than usual. There were 1,000 initial inquiries, compared with a maximum of 600 on previous central London trawls. Six hundred people were auditioned, and from these, 60 applicants were deemed suitable for the assessment day. They were to be assessed in teamworking, confidence, people skills and creativity.

Case Study

A large number of exercises were put together to help observers to assess the personality, team skills and creativity of each applicant. Various exercises were designed to help illustrate how team members would interact with customers. Out of the 60 applicants, 24 people were selected to be part of the Oxford Street Unit team. The selection team was looking for particular qualities: for example, team members who could take responsibility and initiative when necessary. They did not want people who may have been strong candidates in some areas but were not happy being part of the team or who wanted to assume leadership all of the time. The selectors wanted to see people fitting together as a team, without any one person taking a dominant role.

The selection of team members 'had to be right from the start,' comments Jane Corson. 'Getting a team together means finding a balance between the team members and ensuring that you get the right mixture of people'. Selection of the team for this project also involved bringing in staff from other shops as observers for the auditions. 'They know what is necessary to make the shop work and could give insight into the skills and abilities needed in the job'. It is interesting to note that it was staff who were brought in as observers and not managers. Some managers from other shops did show a degree of suspicion and scepticism about the new project. Their worry was that if the teamworking, managerless shop was successful, it might have an effect on their own management role.

Training the Team
The whole team was trained together for four weeks. The training included operational procedures, product knowledge and training in the set tasks necessary to run the shop. The members were then asked to allocate themselves, according to their own preference, experience or particular strength, to the four working sub-teams.

Case Study

This allocation was only short-term, as the teams were expected to reshuffle and rotate later in the year.

As with the selection and assessment procedures, the training was designed so that the approach could be flexible enough to deal with whatever issues were raised by the team. Apart from the intensive team building module in the first few days of the course, team issues were looked at and dealt with using a variety of different exercises and techniques throughout the entire four-week training period.

Team members were constantly encouraged to use their own initiative and to confront any issues that concerned them. They were invited to come up with ideas on such topics as how to build trust, how to ensure clear and effective communication, and how to solve problems when they occur.

The underlying philosophy of the experiment was to allow things to happen and to evolve, when issues would emerge that needed to be clarified. The same attitude prevailed at all the different stages from selection, assessment, training and, later, to appraisal.

The training programme helped team members to emerge with a clear picture of how they wanted the team to work together, what systems they wanted to set up and how they would deal with any issues, problems or complaints as they arose. As a result of time spent on these issues during the early life of the team, so far there do not appear to have been any major clashes or problems.

Apart from operational training, specific training was also given, for example in listening skills, decision making and communication. Further training may be necessary, but first the team is being given a chance to make the teamworking system work, to identify the weak areas and find ways of fixing them.

Case Study

Teamworking in Practice

Team members decided who would do which task. This was decided on the basis of who had the most experience or desire to do a particular task. The Body Shop found that team members were willing to volunteer to do all sorts of different tasks.

As the basic idea for this project was experimental, the sentiment is to take what works and develop it further. The responsibility to try things out and change them if they don't work rests entirely with team members. The day-to-day running of the Oxford Street Unit is being left entirely to the 'performers'. They make decisions on volume of stock, training and shift patterns. Team members are accountable to each other, although the overall accountability does rest with the Area Manager. Although each team has its own area of responsibility, the operation of the unit as a whole necessitates a whole team approach. Teams are encouraged to have faith in other teams' operations or the reasons why something is done in a certain way.

If there is a problem in one working area of the shop, members are encouraged to communicate this directly to another member of that team. For example, if a personnel team member noticed a problem in the stocking of a certain item, he/she is encouraged to go directly to one of the members of the 'stock-room team' rather than to go back to his/her team and then for the two teams to have to confront each other over the issue. One-to-one communication is encouraged, in order to cut down on the 'my team/your team' situation. However, team-to-team communication meetings are now being set up to deal with inter-team issues regularly. The idea is to look at ways of supporting and helping each other, not just about shifting responsibility.

Case Study

Further Development

The idea is to let the team find its own way, to decide how members want further to develop themselves individually and the team as a whole. As far as The Body Shop Company was concerned, it hoped that this project would identify the 'movers' and the people who 'want more'. It saw this as a good way of developing management potential. This is the new breed of manager that The Body Shop is looking for, for the future: people with a participative leadership style, team builders and a teamplayers. It wants to move away from the autocratic style, which does not fit in with the company image or its values.

The Body Shop management also sees this as a way of trying out management potential and all that entails – for example, innovation, initiative, involvement and responsibility, without being called a manager. It hopes that it could be an experimental situation for future potential managers to try out the role without being under the associated pressure.

Monitoring, Reward and Recognition

The Oxford Street Unit team is meant to be self-monitoring and self-managed, although the overall responsibility rests with the Area Manager if something drastic does go wrong within the unit. Individual appraisals rest with the team. Taking the theme of the 'performance' further, each team has a 'critics' review' whereby teams review each others' performance. The critics' review is laid out as in the following example:

Case Study

THE BODY SHOP – CRITICS' REVIEW

	Thumbs Down	Thumbs Up	Rave Review
Sales satisfaction			
Appearance			
Teamwork			
Flexibility			
Communication			
Time Keeping			
Speed of work			
Initiative			
Other comments			

If a constant problem emerges, it is addressed as a team. However, Head Office does receive copies of the critics' review forms to monitor the situation, and the Area Manager would step in if necessary. The whole shop is also appraised by considering the takings, staff turnover, absenteeism and appearance of the shop. 'Mystery' customers are employed to test the team. Like the rest of The Body Shop, performers are part of a profit sharing scheme.

Emerging Problem Areas

A number of issues have emerged or are beginning to appear which need to be dealt with. Some of the most prominent ones are:

• Owing to the lack of a leader at the beginning, there were problems with decision making in the team. There appeared to be more talking and less listening to each others' views. The process of the managerless team meant that actually making decisions was difficult as no one person felt that they could take the final decision. The Body Shop adapted its training to highlight this issue and found ways of overcoming the situation. Leaders do appear to be emerging and this is seen as an additional strength by the team.

- Out of the 24 performers, six of the people selected for this project were transferred from other Body Shop Units. Performers who had been selected from outside the organisation felt that at times these six were trying to 'take over the team', as they were more familiar with The Body Shop's previous practices. The team dealt with this issue by setting up an 'honesty' session, so that constructive criticism could be given and team members were encouraged to confront this and similar sensitive issues.

- When a customer complained, who was responsible? This was a very important question. The customer was obviously not interested in dealing with a 'team', but wanted to deal with one person. This highlighted the need for effective communication between team members and the sharing of responsibility. If a particular team member was dealing with a customer problem, it was that team member's responsibility to inform all other members. All team members were encouraged to take responsibility for the whole shop, regardless of which sub-team they worked for. The experience, however, was that without a manager, people tended to 'pass the buck', thus blaming the other team for mistakes that had been made. The aim is to get the performers to take team responsibility and to let go of blaming the other teams. Further training and discussions may be needed to resolve this issue and to re-examine the communication issues.

- The attitude of some people in the company towards this new teamworking experiment has been that of suspicion and scepticism. Questions such as: 'Do we really need a manager

Case Study

when the managerless unit appears to be working without one?' are relevant questions. The Body Shop is currently discussing and debating this issue. However, now that the experiment is working people are more confident in this approach.

- Communications issues within and between the sub-teams and the shop as a whole seemed to take on great importance. The teams found that they were sometimes dealing with the teamworking issues to the detriment of manning the shop floor (i.e. they were more concerned with their own teamworking issues and as a result found that at times they neglected the customer). They found that they had to refocus on their main objective, that of improving the quality of service provided to the customer. They needed to concentrate less on 'behind the scenes' and make customers their number one priority. However, The Body Shop feels that it is important to give the team time to find its feet, to feel confident in the operation, to begin to focus less on the teamworking process and more on the customer. Jane Corson comments: 'We are well aware of this, and we are keeping tabs on it otherwise the experiment would have failed.'

Outcomes

After only three months of the teamworking system being in operation, there already appear to be clear indications of its success. As mentioned earlier, some leaders are emerging and the performers seem to be aware of this. It is seen as something positive for the team and necessary to the running of the shop. Staff are taking more initiative, being creative and making suggestions to improve service for customers. As it is up to the team to control itself, if it does not like what is happening, then the members are encouraged to confront it and put it right. If emerging leaders feel stifled, then they

Case Study

can apply for management positions coming up in other units.

According to The Body Shop's Human Resources Manager, the teamworking experiment has given the atmosphere a bit of 'spice' and in this way it has led people to start thinking about themselves and how they do their jobs. The new atmosphere has improved customer contact, enthusiasm and involvement, and performers are taking more pride in their jobs. 'In the Oxford Street project, all performers are taking great interest in all aspects of the business'.

Although the teamworking experiment had only been running for three months at the time of our research, already the Oxford Street Unit had become one of the highest earners of all the company shops. The location may have something to do with it, but The Body Shop management also attribute some of the success to the high performance of the team.

The Future

Some time down the road, this experiment may lead to particular teamworking principles being put into operation in the rest of the organisation. 'This type of teamworking approach is definitely the right way for us as a company to move', comments Jane Corson. 'It is creating a new way of thinking and maintaining momentum for change. We see the Oxford Street team as a permanent team, and if it works, we will be able to develop the new Body Shops along the same structure although there are no plans to totally reorganise the existing structures'.

The Body Shop recognises that it may be a more difficult problem when the time comes to replace team members. Logistically, it would be impossible to take all team members out of the operation to 'audition' one or two new members. The current team was selected because it worked well together. When the time comes to take on a new team member, it may alter the balance. The Body

Shop Company comments that it would need to think very carefully about recruitment. The team's progress is being monitored and reviewed constantly with the aim of finding different ways of improving the quality of service offered to customers.

The Body Shop points out that the success of the current venture is owed to two main elements. Firstly, the care, effort and time taken in selecting and training the team members, and, secondly, having the courage to allow things to evolve and find their own shape rather than setting rigid structures and panicking when things do not go right from the start. Jane Corson's closing comment to us was to 'expect mistakes; with anything new the approach must be flexible to allow for any necessary changes and improvement along the way'.

End Case Study

Case Study

THE FEDERAL EXPRESS EXPERIENCE OF DEPLOYING QUALITY ACTION TEAMS

Background
Few companies have achieved legendary status as quickly as Federal Express. It was started in 1973 by Frederick W. Smith, then aged 27. He is said to have put forward the concept of a national hub and spoke airfreight network in an undergraduate dissertation. While seeing this concept as interesting, Smith's tutor dismissed it as not feasible due to competition and regulation, and graded the paper

Case Study

with a 'C'. On his return from service in Vietnam, Smith set about trying to turn his concept into a reality.

It was a simple idea. Federal Express courier teams would be based in cities around the US, they would pick up packages and take them to a local station from where they would be flown to a central hub. Memphis was selected as the hub for Federal Express. At Memphis, packages would be unloaded, sorted out, reloaded and then flown to their various destinations where they would be delivered by a team of Federal Express couriers. Federal Express was the first company to offer overnight delivery in the US.

Federal Express lost money heavily in its earliest years, but by 1976 the company had become profitable with the help of aggressive sales and advertising policies. At this stage, Federal Express also began a major investment in information technology, creating a system called Cosmos (customer, service, master-on-line system) which was designed to provide superior customer service in the face of increasing competition.

The company grew rapidly and by the early 1980s it had become a well known national institution with slogans like 'When it absolutely, positively has to be there overnight', 'Why fool around with anybody else?' and 'It's not just a package, it's your business'.

Fred Smith is still the Chairman, Chief Executive Officer and President of The Federal Express Corporation, and his basic philosophy remains the same. He puts great emphasis on people and has stated his policy as: 'People – Service – Profits'. Federal started its service in Canada in 1979. In 1985, it started its international service and began to build up a network of routes around the world. A European hub was established in Brussels. Federal achieved its overseas expansion in part through buying existing courier firms in each national market.

By 1990, Federal Express had become one of the world's largest airlines, with a fleet of nearly 350 aircraft. They serve over 150 countries around the world. Federal Express prides itself on having one of the most sophisticated customer service systems in the world. Cosmos is a continuously updated system that can be used to trace a missing package. The notion of picking up and delivering a package and being able to offer the customer total information about its whereabouts of the package is an important one.

The Quality Initiatives

Quality has been implicit in Federal's business almost from the beginning. Its marketing and advertising certainly proclaimed its emphasis on quality, with slogans like 'Federal Express. Twice as Good as the Best in the Business' and 'Absolutely, Positively, Overnight'.

It was not until 1985, when Federal's senior managers became concerned about a possible slowdown in the business and decline in profitability, that the company first addressed quality improvement issues. The slowdown that was feared did not happen. Instead the company expanded rapidly and by 1987, the Sales and Customer Service Division was struggling with service problems that were becoming increasingly serious.

The Quality effort began with quality planning workshops for Federal's Senior Vice Presidents, their direct reports and Managing Directors from all divisions. The outcome from each workshop was a series of action plans, prioritising those problems that needed to be addressed urgently. Secondly, all managers in the sales and customer service division were trained to understand the quality process. Next, all staff in the division were trained and at this stage Quality Action Teams (QATs) were assembled. The key goal was to get teams to analyse what were often complex problems rather than coming up with instant solutions. The QATs focused on how

Case Study

quality improvement should be implemented. Training was given in a problem solving process consisting of four phases: focusing on a specific problem or opportunity; analysing information; developing solutions and action plans; and executing plans for implementing solutions. To help the QATs to perform these tasks effectively, participants were taught a range of problem solving techniques including fishbone analysis, flowcharts and cost benefit analysis.

Most problems at Federal Express were cross-functional in nature, in that one division created a certain output and passed it onto the next. The next division's problem was often directly related to what had happened earlier. By 1988 other divisions were involved in the Quality initiative (for example, Domestic Ground Operations, which employs 25,000 couriers in the US).

By examining the types of failures, the number of occurrences of each type of failure and the reasons why they occurred, Federal began to understand what needed to be done to improve the quality of service. This led Federal Express to develop the Service Quality Index or SQI (pronounced 'sky'). (The lower the index, the better the performance.)

1988 turned out to be the best year Federal had in a long time and one key reason attributed to SQI successes was that Federal had set up 12 QATs, each of which focused on a specific SQI category. Most teams were headed by a Vice President. Results were displayed each week and every three months each QAT reported to Fred Smith and his senior management team. Quarterly awards were given in four categories:

1. Greatest impact on SQI results.
2. Best use of quality tools.
3. Best understanding of root causes (identifying and working in underlying problems rather than superficial effects).

4. Best use of staff (gathering information from the people closest to the process who knew it best).

Federal Express also started efforts to facilitate a bottom-up initiative in quality improvement within the divisions. In 1988, the first Manager of Quality Improvement was appointed. At this stage, a network of quality professionals was established in each of Federal's 10 divisions. These people formed a quality advisory team and they held bi-weekly meetings to discuss successes and failures.

One Senior Quality Administrator from the ground operations felt that many of the successes that the quality programme had enjoyed were perhaps superficial successes. The real challenge was to be able to learn from these successes and reproduce them. This meant getting QATs to describe what they had actually done and how they did it, not just simply talking about the result. Federal created specially designed forms on their electronic mail systems to make it easy for QATs to record this information, while a reward system encouraged teams to share the details of their successes. In many cases Federal was able to replicate successes.

Teamworking at Federal Express – The British Experience

Federal Express has been in operation in the UK since 1986, and over 60,000 parcels go through its UK operation each day. Throughout the UK, Federal Express has 39 stations, and employs over 5,000 employees.

The Birmingham Gateway Team Brings Benefits to the Customer

A Quality award has been presented by Fred Smith and his senior team in Memphis to a recently formed Quality Action Team at the Birmingham Gateway Station for its work in forming a new customer service unit. Every day Federal Express delivers 1.9 million packages world wide; 60,000 of these will be delivered in the UK. Every package requires the correct paperwork to pass through Customs. If any information is missing – for example a VAT number, or the commercial invoice – or if the package is of dubious origin, it is placed in 'the cage', where it awaits clearance by Customs.

The problem at the Birmingham Gateway in mid 1990 was that 'the cage' was almost permanently full of packages (up to 1,000 at times), staff morale was low, people were working 70 to 80 hours a week trying to clear the cage and the number of packages coming in each day was increasing. The decision was taken to set up a QAT and give it ownership of the problem of The Birmingham Gateway. The team's charge was clear: 'to clear the cage and to improve customer care'. It was also felt that this initiative should not be seen as an 'Americanisation' of the business operation. Paul Wickes was appointed as the leader of the QAT. He recognised the importance of customers' first impressions of the company. For Federal Express, this impression will be formed when the customer first meets a member of the company and for Federal this happens thousands of times a day over the telephone. Customer Care is clearly critical to the success of Federal's business. When The Birmingham Gateway QAT met every day for two and a half weeks, it was trying to find the best way to organise the workings of the Gateway in order to improve Customer Services.

There are 250 staff at The Gateway and their work is split between three areas: handling packages; the preparation of packages for Customs clearance; and customer services. Jan Ladwa, a member of the QAT, was given responsibility for reorganising the customer service side. Ladwa comments: 'What was happening was that when a customer's package went into the cage we were not letting them know. So eventually they called our Customer Call Centre on the

0800 number (freefone) to trace their package. There they could see that the package was in the cage but didn't know why'.

This started a vicious spiral. Staff at The Gateway spent time finding out what had happened to a caged package instead of getting on with what they were supposed to be doing. 'What we decided to do was to become proactive rather than reactive in our customer relations, and for this the customer service agents needed up-to-date information on caged packages,' says Jan Ladwa.

The QAT developed a special customer service programme, which enabled the team to inform each customer regularly of the progress of the packages at any given time. Firstly, the operations team and the customer service team reached agreement on some key issues. For example, the handlers would get a list of all the packages caged overnight to Customer Services by 07:00 every morning. Customer Services would then input details of the caged package to the computer by 08:30. This meant that any Federal Express employee, anywhere in the world, could see that the package had been caged and the reason why. Finally, the Customer Service Agents undertook to call each customer by 10:30 to tell them their package was in the cage. This information was given to customers regardless of whether they specifically requested it – this being part of Federal's commitment to customer service.

Now, as the import clerks and the handlers are aware of the requirements, they can work as a team to clear the packages for the customer. The teams are responsible for an alphabetical group of customers. This means that they can build up a relationship with one person at that specific company. They know who to ask for when they call the customer and the team has also been able to keep some information about the customer; for example, if the customer has left off their VAT number, the team can fill it in for them.

This programme has not only enhanced customer loyalty but at

Case Study

the same time the infamous cage volume was drastically reduced. In July 1991, the lowest ever cage volume since 1987 was recorded, just 64 consignments. Paul Wickes comments that 'one thing that we had to do above anything else was training'. Effort is recognised to keep up the momentum for this quality initiative.

For example, recently one award was given to a member of staff, Peter Short, from the computer team. Peter Short inputs the data collected by the Customer Service Teams. This information goes to Customs, who check the details against their own summary sheet. If the information in the two files differs, the file is returned to Federal Express, the package stays in the cage and in the worst case Federal is fined for the mistake. Peter Short saw the problem and worked out how to stop it. He comments: 'What I did was to write a piece of software that would check our details with the Summary Sheet, before we sent the information to Customs. By using this software I could see if someone in the department was making regular mistakes, so that we could let them know. I was awarded the 'legendary hero's award' for producing this software'.

The scheme has been so successful that this initiative has been extended to the Gateways at Manchester, Prestwick and Heathrow and it is also being used across Europe.

In addition to this, vastly improved relations between Customs and the Federal Express Customs Clearance Team has resulted. The Gateway is working so efficiently now that Federal employs 27 fewer staff than budgeted for. Finally, Paul Wickes, the QAT's leader, comments: 'This has been the hardest 12 months' work in my life, but also the most satisfying. I think that this is because it involved working with people to improve the organisation of their teams. The results have been outstanding. Through increased business and better efficiency, we have increased our business considerably – and we haven't finished yet . . .'

End Case Study

SHERWOOD COMPUTER SERVICES AND THE TEAMWORKING 'BIG BANG'

Sherwood Computer Services plc is a specialist computer software and services company providing systems and support services to the public and financial services sectors. It has a major presence in the Lloyds and London insurance markets.

The Legend

The very name of Sherwood conjures up a legend (the link with Robin Hood is deliberate: one of its founders was previously a partner of an accounting firm called Littlejohns). In a sense, it deserves legendary status not because of its name but because it is one of the very few companies in the world that has chosen to re-model its entire structure on the basis of self-managed client teams and in a style that one of its directors describes as 'Big Bang' (i.e. all at once). From a very early stage Sherwood has had an acute sense of having to find its own way through the forest simply because there were so few examples of detailed implementation of its chosen style of teamworking. In the month of Big Bang implementation, January 1991, the Personnel Director, Kevin Crane commented: 'I know of no other company adopting such a radical approach. We do not have history waving us on and we left the academics behind four months ago.'

The top team at Sherwood is keen not to describe its progress in legendary terms, however, and is very open about acknowledging the problems and difficulties as well as the successes. Talking to the current Chairman, to the Chief Executive and some of the other members of the Business Team (a strategy team consisting of some of the former directors) is rather like discovering that Friar Tuck wasn't particularly large, that the Sheriff of Nottingham was a good father and husband, and that Robin Hood sometimes forgot to give to the poor what he had taken from the rich. The following case study is based on interviews with three key players in the change process and is an attempt not to perpetuate myths and legends but to help others who follow in Sherwood's footsteps.

Why Teamworking?

Richard Guy, the newly appointed Chief Executive, and Bob Thomas, now Chairman, then Non-Executive Director, had a clear and persistent vision of teamworking that was an important factor in the change but alone does not explain why Sherwood went in for a major re-structuring. In Thomas's words 'We had as anti-teamworking a culture as I could think of'. The tremendous independence of spirit among the specialists in the software industry created a tendency for them to want to develop their own ideas rather than share them and to focus on their own interests rather than the whole business. There was a sign of movement when the then Chairman, Terry Dicken, announced after a Board meeting that had touched on teamworking, that he had re-named the managers in one of the divisions, team captains. However, teamworking did not sweep through Sherwood in a groundswell of popular opinion.

Three main driving forces contributed to the move to teamworking; the persistent vision referred to above; the poor 1988 financial results; and a growing realisation on the part of some managers that there was a limit to what could be achieved by tinkering with hierarchical structures.

(i) The Crisis Theory

A deficit of £2 million on a turnover of £26.5 million in 1988 was a strong a spur to action; something needed to happen and quickly. The immediate response was not teamworking, however, and there

Case Study

was a fairly conventional re-structuring and a quality initiative (called QUEST) in June 1989. That year saw a return to profitability of £2 million. Although the crisis made it easier to argue for dramatic action, teamworking was by no means a foregone conclusion. Some of Sherwood's operational and financial problems actually created an obstacle to teamworking at a later stage during the crucial lull between the early summer of 1990, when the Big Bang move to teamworking had been proposed, and January 1991 when it actually happened. It was during this stage that teamworking needed to be sold heavily to the whole company, but the champions of the cause, and Richard Guy himself, found themselves distracted by fire-fighting. As Thomas sums it up: 'It was difficult to focus on the teamworking and how we were going to do it, when there were so many day-to-day operating problems'.

(ii) When the Tinkering had to Stop

Some of the opinion formers at the top of the organisation had grown weary of piecemeal reorganisations and recognised that a once and for all shape-up was probably going to be necessary. As the Personnel Director, Kevin Crane, now comments 'All we were doing (and other companies hierarchically organised, still do) was going round in circles, constantly making changes, searching for the structure then changing yet again. . . . We needed a complete change in structure, not just toying with it'.

Again, this does not by itself explain the radical nature of Sherwood's upheaval. Quite apart from anything else there were not enough opinion formers who wanted to see radical change to create a critical mass, and even those who did want change stopped short of a structure based entirely on self-managed teams.

> *Case Study*

(iii) The Persistent Vision of Two Men

Richard Guy had been appointed Chief Executive during the company's financial troubles in 1988. An accountant by training, he was convinced that the long-term solutions to a service company's problems could be provided. Quality needed improving, as did customer service generally, and there was a lot of shuffling of papers back and forth between management structures. It was a short step from the recognition of the problem to the possibility of a far flatter structure, and it was seen that the best way of achieving this was via teams of people responsible for all aspects of service to the clients. The problem was how to implement it.

Bob Thomas is a self-styled iconoclast who identifies himself as a 'strategic radicalist, long before it was popular'. He is an academic with a difference because he has used his radicalism to improve the fortunes of companies dramatically (both other people's, from a consultant's point of view, and his own business enterprises). By the late 1970s he was a convert to teamworking as one possible radical strategy, and he also had enough experience of organisational change to know that the 1988 financial crisis for Sherwood could provide the ideal lever to promote a fundamental transformation. However, from his position either as a Non-Executive Director or as an Ashridge consultant he could only influence things, not direct them.

Via different routes Thomas and Guy, unbeknown to each other, found themselves both at a workshop given in London by the master of radical change, Tom Peters, in February 1990. From that point, events happened very rapidly.

Letting the Genie Out of the Bottle

In March 1990 the Sherwood board met for a one-day workshop, with Thomas as a facilitator, and they debated the possibility of teamworking as a strategic move. It was a long and difficult meeting, as the time it took (nine hours) indicates. During the workshop, Guy was selling the idea heavily but had to contend with open opposition (including resignation threats), scepticism, pleas for caution and uncertainty. At the end of the process, however, there was agreement on a model for development starting with two design teams who would spend a month researching and working together to outline a possible system for teamworking. In what Thomas describes as an 'enormously potent move', the board offered itself as a resource to the two design teams, thereby sending out a signal about the shifting balance of power. One team took the board's offer very literally and decided to query Guy in depth on a number of issues, including the company's hopes for the future. It is widely reported that Guy more than fulfilled his role as an information-giving resource as opposed to a directives-giving Chief Executive. But even he had to swallow hard when at the end of the grilling he was firmly but politely dismissed to get on with his job, while the design team got down to the serious business of shaping the future of the company.

The design teams both carried out a detailed and diligent survey and produced recommendations. They both favoured a move to teamworking via the creation of non-hierarchical Task Teams to map out the implications and implementation plans for the various areas of the business, and the implications for rewarding and developing individuals under a teamworking structure. With the exception of the question of whether teams should have leaders (favoured by one design team but not by the other) plus one or two readily identifiable 'hobby horses', the design teams' findings were very similar.

As is often the case with organisation changes, there was something for everyone in the design teams' reports. The optimists regarded the process that the design teams had gone through as a

Case Study

testament to effective teamworking. With one or two false starts, the design teams themselves (drawn from a diagonal cross-section of people who had not previously worked together) experienced the benefits of teamworking within a very short space of time. They had stood hierarchy on its head, temporarily usurped the role of senior management in strategy formulation and had produced some very creditable results. Left more or less to their own devices they had come up with very similar findings.

At the same time, the pessimists and the sceptics had a field day. Self-styled conspiracy theorists expressed their suspicion at the similarity of the findings and pointed out that the design teams had not been left entirely to their own devices, because Ashridge tutors had done some teambuilding with them at the start of the process. The extremists claimed that it was all an Ashridge plot. Those who suspected that teamworking was an inevitability made great play of the led versus leaderless debate.

The board meeting to discuss the findings of the design teams was longer and trickier than the preceding one that had started the process. It ran from 3:00 pm on the first day to 4:00 am on the second, then again from 9:00 am to 1:00 pm. During that time one of the key directors threatened to resign. When asked to state what he was going to do next, he announced that he would set up his own company and on being asked to describe how he would run it, he amazed everyone by saying 'just in the way you've described' (i.e. using the teamworking approach). He then went on to explain that he would retain hierarchical controls as well. He was talked into withdrawing his threat and the board ultimately concluded the meeting with the acceptance of the proposal that Sherwood would re-structure itself completely by introducing self-managed, leaderless teams, without a trial experiment, in the Big Bang on January 1, 1991. The detailed implementation of the process was to be worked out by Task Teams.

Case Study

Attempting to Squeeze the Genie Back in the Bottle
Once the board had accepted the design teams' proposals, the Task Teams began their work and for the first time many of the middle managers either became involved in the Task Teams or realised the full implications of the proposals. The Task Teams had finished their work by the end of summer 1990; the Big Bang starting date was not due for another four months, during which time everyone returned to their normal jobs. It was this crucial waiting period that enabled the opponents of the change to re-group their forces, marshal their arguments and attempt to squeeze the genie back in the bottle. The range and sophistication of the opposition arguments varied greatly. It is worth capturing the flavour of some of them.

1. 'No Way'
Some people were quite simply dead set against the change. In the words of the Personnel Director, Kevin Crane, the public statements about the change to teamworking were 'a siren call for the strongest anti-reorganisationalists to come out of the woodwork with a vengeance'.

2. 'Seen it all before'
There were those who were sufficiently cynical to believe that the change was going to be just a temporary fad.

3. 'It means redundancies' and 'the best people will walk'
Middle management were very threatened by the move at the basic level of job security.

4. 'What do I tell my friends?'
A number of middle managers at the upper end of the hierarchy recognised that the flatter structure could be perceived as a massive

Case Study

loss of status and could lead to the scrapping of titles right across the board.

5. 'The clients won't like it'

This issue was expressed in a number of different ways, which included a concern that clients would need to see access to a traditional hierarchy and a worry about what to put on business cards.

6. 'It's all an academic's pipe dream'

The involvement of Thomas and Ashridge had always been problematic because the academic connections created a soft target for opponents of teamworking to shoot at. It was not helped by the fact that nobody could find another UK company using teams in exactly the same way as Sherwood was proposing, although there were some experiments in various divisions of a few organisations.

7. 'It's communism gone wild'

The idea of flat structures and teamworking offended some people's love of a natural order in which everyone knows where they stand by virtue of their title and who they report to.

8. 'Headless teams'

A group of wags christened the self-managed groups 'headless teams' to create a deliberate parallel with the expression 'headless chickens'. There were those, however, who in more reflective moods would acknowledge the advantages of teams but argue for the presence of a team leader.

9. 'Softly, softly'

There was an argument for a pilot period during which the teamworking concepts could be tested on a trial basis.

Case Study

10. 'Fine – but not for me'

From some of the calmer more mature opponents came the recognition that the intervention might well work for Sherwood but they personally were just not suited to it.

Although the four-month period of marking time towards the end of 1990 set the initiative back in many ways, there were several attempts by the teamworking champions to revitalise commitment and to communicate the benefits of the new culture. The persistent vision of Thomas and Guy was important in this phase and many have commented on a vital personality trait of Guy's, which can be seen as determination or stubbornness depending on the point of view. By this time, the ranks of those with the vision had swollen. (Crane recalls: 'Some people claimed to have had a revelation – road to Damascus stuff'.)

Another factor alongside vision and determination was the diligent efforts of the people who comprised the Task Teams. Certainly not all of them had experienced the Damascus revelation and had their own private concerns and worries. In working with some of these groups, we were impressed by their application to the enormous job of working out the final detail of implementing the broad brush vision of teamworking. Without any pathfinding examples to copy, a lot of the detail had to be worked out from scratch. Crane, in particular, was the architect of a number of detailed human resources solutions to teamworking problems. He also acted as a translator and go-between, re-interpreting academic theory, communicating it to fellow directors, relaying the message to the teams and from them back along the chain.

In spite of the lost momentum during the four months, the opposition ultimately failed to get the genie back in the bottle.

Case Study

Big Bang and the Genie Flies

On January 1 1991 Sherwood Computer Services substituted its existing matrix structure for one based on self-managed client teams. A small group of about a dozen of the most senior managers formed the Business Team, which acts as a supporting resource to the client teams and maintains a strategic overview. Central services such as finance and personnel constituted their own teams for a period and have now almost completely integrated with the client teams, giving them a greater amount of self-sufficiency.

The Sherwood example has to be regarded as a success story but not one to be mythologised. It is worth looking at some of the implementation problems and breakthroughs.

1. Costs down, productivity up

Numbers have reduced in Sherwood (from 750 in 1988 to today's figure of around 400) but with the reduced numbers, revenue per head is about £75,000 as opposed to £35,000 in 1988.

2. Happy customers

The struggle for complete customer satisfaction is never ending, but levels of satisfaction have greatly increased as the teams start to deliver on one of their main objectives, responsiveness and flexibility. With growing confidence, the client teams draw on individual members of the Business Team, Guy included, to help manage the all important interface with the client.

Customers who are concerned about how to match their understanding of business with an apparently flat structure have been given 'escalation routes' so that they are secure in the knowledge that Sherwood expertise will be supplied in a pre-determined way to sort out queries and problems. The titles on Sherwood business cards reflect an external view of the company.

3. Ownership up on balance

The negative energy accumulated by the move to teamworking has not vanished overnight and there are still pockets of resistance, both active and passive. There is still a need for more training and communications but on balance there is a growing feeling of pride and ownership among the teams for the decisions that they have made and own.

4. Learning what needs to be learned

From the philosophical standpoint, which is perhaps best captured in Guy's words ('We employ very intelligent people so we might as well let them get on with it and let them make the appropriate decisions at that level'), to the reality of asking a group of computer software specialists to draw up budgets is a big leap. Both Sherwood and the teams probably underestimated the size of the leap and the first budgeting cycle produced a lot of floundering. The lessons had been learned for the second budgeting cycle and with a combination of training and coaching, the process has greatly improved and can be regarded as a significant milestone in team development.

With hindsight, some of the Sherwood Business Team have recognised that they could have spotted in advance some of the skill and experience deficits but some were harder to see until the teams started working. More importantly, there is a greater acceptance that teams have to define training needs and the means to tackle them, for themselves.

5. Letting go of the safety net

It was the original intention that client teams should be leaderless but in the interests of allowing them reasonable autonomy, some have re-imported de facto leaders without the intervention of the Business Team to prevent them. Thomas feels that these teams have

Case Study

perhaps not yet experienced the real power of truly status-less, collaborative teamworking. Guy concludes that 'led teams are not as successful as the self-managed teams, in particular where business plans are concerned'.

6. Getting on and getting out

The fear that some talent would walk out of Sherwood as part of the reduction in headcount has, in part, been realised and put extra pressure on the teams to plug gaps in skills and experience. However, the view that a flat structure could never provide a career path and render the company unattractive to new talent has not been realised. Thanks to the efforts of Crane and others, there is now a clearly defined set of six bands of progression based on skills, qualifications and experience. Individuals who think they are eligible apply for progression through the bands, and are assessed against the criteria. There is also proof that Sherwood is attractive to outsiders who, as Crane puts it, 'want to be a part of Sherwood because we are different. We are not a normal organisation . . . we don't pretend; we know what we look like first thing in the morning'.

Perhaps the biggest getting on/getting out delimma the teams have had to face is that of having to make further reductions in the tough economic conditions prevailing in 1991. However, the teams have had the maturity to handle their own processes for selecting redundancies.

7. Autonomy at all costs

In our work with some of the client teams, we found that their drive for autonomy is very powerful. For some, it meant a full acceptance of the responsibility that went with it and they were working hard at self-sufficiency. The more mature teams had reached a level of satisfaction with their independence and could turn for support, with confidence, to the Business Team, without compromising their autonomy. Other teams behaved rather like the young adolescent who discovers the keys to the drinks cabinet and protests when the parent imposes new rules about drinking. Some things that the teams wanted to do made no sense in business terms and had to be stopped.

Learning From Sherwood

Some of the lessons to be drawn from the Sherwood experience are self evident but there are four major paradoxes that the company has had to master and is still mastering.

Paradox Number 1 – You are now in Charge of Your Own Destiny (ish)

Once a teamworking initiative is up and running it is possible to see tremendous examples of self-directing, self-motivating and self-troubleshooting people at work. In an ideal world, everyone in an organisation would be gripped by that vision and at roughly the same time so that they could all voluntarily progress to the same goal. This was not true for Sherwood, it is not true for many organisations and it is fair to assume that in many cases it never will be true. One answer is for those with the vision (often those in senior positions) to impose the solution. The big problem, however, is that this action is the very behaviour that teamworking is designed to render obsolete. Thus the teamworking initiative begins with a terrible model of how to generate commitment.

Having tried every form of persuasion known to man and having still had to use some not too subtle pressure to make teamworking happen, both Guy and Thomas are now firmly of the view that a period of imposition may be undesirable but is inevitable. Thomas sees it as leading people, preferably willingly but if not, still leading them, into an experience so good (teamworking) that they appreciate the benefits and release a self-sustaining energy. Both feel that a lot of momentum was lost in the period after the design teams had reported back. In Guy's words, 'going to the management structure was a mistake, the fire and the fervour of the initial design team investigation was watered down and broken down by the management response and in some cases teams formed out of existing departments'. He feels that 'in retrospect, we should have just imposed the new system. I think then we would be further down the line and, indeed, we have imposed the second phase of breaking up non-client central teams into true client teams'.

Sherwood still lives with the paradox of intervention. In setting up the new structure it decided that the Business Team would retain the right to intervene in situations where the business was at risk. This it chose to do very early on, to ensure the progress of a vital new product development that was seriously off target. Intervention of this sort still divides those who feel that without a secure business, the purity of the teamworking experiment is irrelevant and those who fear the destructive power of the underlying message, 'we lost patience with you and the Board of Directors had to impose old-style management to get the job done'.

Paradox Number 2 – Manage Change by Speeding up and Slowing Down

There is no doubt that the move to teamworking created a great deal of shock in the Sherwood system. A lot of communicating and persuading was done but everyone involved is unanimous that it was not enough. Crane points to the problems of large corporate briefings when individuals have a host of fears, opinions and questions that desperately need airing. Unless there is time taken to listen to people, preferably in small groups, there is the danger that as a minimum they take away very different images of what is meant to be a shared vision and in the extreme their worries grow and sow the seeds of major resistance. As Crane observes 'Subtle fears and sledgehammer solutions do not work'.

Few would dispute the importance of communication but there is a view which says that a step-by-step winning of commitment is too slow a process. Again this is acutely felt by those who saw the opportunity to seize the moment once the design teams had reported. Their views can be expressed as a recognition that large scale change is going to be messy so it is worth getting on with it.

Paradox Number 3 – Tell People What's Going to Happen to Allay Fears but Don't Get Bogged Down in Detail

As soon as it was clear that Sherwood was going to adopt teamworking there was a demand for detailed information ranging from important questions about career structure to time-honoured hobby horses such as the grade of car that specific individuals would be driving. To answer all these questions with a 'don't know' or 'we're working it out' would have massively raised anxiety levels. However, to respond at the level of detail being demanded was crippling. Guy sums it up this way 'In retrospect, I think we should have made the changes first then decided the details later. We got very bogged down trying to make everything perfect before we started.' It was also the case that in some areas the innovative nature of the Sherwood strategy meant that nobody knew exactly how things would turn out.

Paradox Number 4 – 'The Sky's the Limit – Hey What are you Doing in the Cockpit'

To help people become truly self-managing they need the confidence to be able to try things out and take their own initiatives. During the training for teamworking, a lot of energy was put into communicating the belief that everyone has huge amounts of unused potential that can be released in a team setting. Some people took this literally and did not hear, or chose to ignore, the second message about teams determining what decision making authority people had in relation to their skills and experience. This led to a number of messy episodes in which over enthusiastic novices attempted to take the controls of the aircraft in mid-flight. With varying degrees of sensitivity their colleagues or a member of the Business Team had to talk them out of the cockpit.

Of all the paradoxes, this perhaps is the one most readily solvable and Sherwood has learnt a lot about keeping levels of maturity in pace with levels of enthusiasm.

Life Beyond the Big Bang

Sherwood knows that in achieving its Big Bang implementation it has started, not ended a process. There is a clear commitment to achieving the full potential of teamworking, particularly in the areas of innovation and speed. New and creative approaches to working practices need to be found as well as processes for speeding up decision making. Close attention to the customer is a continuing imperative and one that the teams are very mindful of. Integration across the teams is a vital issue if the benefits of the cross-fertilisation of ideas are to be realised. This, of course, extends to the Business Team also.

The financial results have been impressive since 1988 and the future looks good for Sherwood not just because it has found a better way of working but because it has now introduced an extraordinarily flexible process for dealing with future challenges.

Section 2

Selecting and Bringing Teams Together

3. Models of Teams – The Importance of Mix

Introduction

This section of the book will concentrate on how to bring a team together. It will firstly review some of the models of teams that are currently being used in organisations. These models help the line manager or team leader to be aware of the intricacies of behaviour and approach that can lead to effective team performance.

Moving on from the models and case studies that illustrate their use we will look in more detail at how to select potential team members to join a particular team.

Mix and Balance

Academic literature and company research make it evident that the many models of teams generally emanate from a common belief. In bringing a team together one of the major keys to success is to ensure that there is as rich a mix as possible of personality, experience and working style. But just as this richness leads to greater creativity and capacity so it can also lead to problems of interaction and team dynamics.

To overcome these problems the team members and/or leader need to be aware of why they are happening and to have the team and process skills available to be able to deal with them. This is why it is important to blend together a balance of personality and approach in addition to a mix of background, experience and knowledge.

Balance and Imbalance in Teams

An imbalanced team has too many of its team members sharing similar work preferences. For example, an innovation team may be brought together purely on the basis of their creativity. In the short term they may work well together, because they think alike and they can relate to each other. Alternatively, they may battle because of the competitive drive to come up with the 'best' idea. Either way the team will hit additional problems of detail. Issues such as production implications, delivery mechanisms, practicality of the ideas and follow-through are some of the essential skills of teamworking that creative people often find difficult. Their creativity needs to be balanced by skills which others of a different type can bring to the team. In short, a team of people who work and think alike may well succeed but problems will eventually emerge.

Inappropriate Selection

One of the reasons why imbalance in teams exists is that often team selectors have selected people who are like themselves or people who blend with their personal style.

A medium-sized manufacturing organisation was on the edge of rapid expansion following a successful tender for a large overseas contract. The recently appointed Managing Director had some concerns about the capability of the existing team of five General Managers. They were dedicated, loyal, conscientious and excellent at managing and controlling within their functional area. He arranged for the team members to go through a battery of psychometric tests.

The base of his concern was shown to be well founded. The team members were very similar in terms of their personality type, work preferences and orientation.

The previous Managing Director had been autocratic. Dominant and directive in style, he invited managers to become General Managers who did what he said, 'ran a clean ship' and did not disagree with him. The consequence was a top team who under his tight direction were able to manage a stable organisation but who lacked the initiative, innovation, flexibility and awareness to take advantage of the challenges offered by the rapid growth potential of this new contract.

The new Managing Director restructured his team. He made two of the existing General Managers functional heads and appointed two new team members. He rightly found that they brought new skills and approaches that revitalised the whole team.

The fact that the original team members were traditional and solid was not wrong. It was the imbalance and the task that they had to address that rang warning bells.

Valuing Differences

Alistair Wright, Human Resources Director at Digital Equipment Corp., agrees that 'all styles and behaviours are valid for different tasks, times and people. Teams need to be aware of these and use them in the right operation and situation.' One of the challenges for anyone involved in selecting a team is to bring together a rich mix of people.

The Managing Director in the manufacturing company mentioned earlier used as part of the data collection on his team a model created by Dr Meredith Belbin. This gives a framework for analysing the qualities and preferences team members bring in addition to their expert knowledge and skill. Belbin researched into the nature, structure and behaviour of teams, working from the belief that 'no one person is perfect, but a team can be'. Teams give the opportunity to bring together a variety of energies and approaches to thinking, decision making, work organisation and people skills.

This model has given us a framework for understanding the constituents of a 'perfect' team and a language to describe people's behaviour and orientation in a team context.

Belbin identified eight team roles. Each team role describes patterns and behaviours that are characteristic of how team members interact with each other.

The model has been used extensively for team selection and

development. Its usefulness is derived from the way in which it enables a team to analyse itself and then make decisions about team roles that are absent, over-represented or under-represented.

Belbin's Team Roles
The eight roles that were identified are:

Company Worker: *this teamworker is practical, organised and reliable. The contribution he/she brings to the team is the capacity to turn ideas into action and see that they are carried out.*

Characteristics: practical, methodical, organised, not easily discouraged but may flounder in times of change.

Teamworker: *this person is sensitive, sociable and supporting and brings to the team the capacity to foster a team spirit by supporting team members.*
Characteristics: help communications, builds on ideas, counters friction, likeable and popular, dislikes personal confrontation and may seem 'soft'.

Chairman: *is seen as calm, controlled and self-confident, strives to get the team to work well together and produce results.*
Characteristics: clarifies, co-ordinates, is disciplined, probes, listens, brings out the best in people, not particularly creative.

Plant: *unorthodox, serious and individualistic, this team member suggests new ideas and strategies to solve problems.*
Characteristics: innovative, creative thinker, radical and imaginative, pays special attention to major issues. Can make careless mistakes on detail and may respond poorly to criticism.

Completer Finisher: *conscientious, detail conscious and delivers on time. He/she takes care that details are not overlooked and that pace is maintained.*
Characteristics: Checks details, meets deadlines, relentlessly follows through, dislikes a vague approach and can get bogged down.

Monitor Evaluator: *this team member is highly analytical and objective. Using his/her judgement, he/she evaluates the team's ideas,*

analyses problems and critiques contributions.
Characteristics: analytical 'feet on the ground', good judgement,
assimilates and assesses data. Lacks tact and fails to accept new ideas.

Resource Investigator*: enthusiastic, curious, extrovert, externally*
orientated and so creates and develops outside contacts to help the team
progress.
Characteristics: energetic, positive, masses of contacts, follows interest,
goes outside the team for information and ideas but may be poor on
follow-through. Can be elusive.

Shaper*: outgoing and dynamic, this role is about seeking to direct the*
team and its work to get results.
Characteristics: dominant and extrovert, he/she challenges and responds
to challenge. Can be seen as arrogant and abrasive. He/she gives shape
to a discussion. May be impulsive and impatient.

When groups first come together there is a tendency for
individuals to act from their functional role or specialism. For
example, an accountant is likely to become the treasurer or take care
of the figures. The most effective teams are those where members
are valued for their personal and distinct attributes as well as their
functional expertise.

Using Belbin's model, most people prefer to operate from one
or two of the team roles in preference over the others. His model is
based on the belief that no one team role is better than another – the
'best' team is one in which there is a broad spread of team roles
represented within the team.

Using Belbin's Team Profile

Using the Belbin questionnaire it is possible to build a team profile
of the team roles represented in an existing team. Equally, in
bringing together a new team, the questionnaire would be valuable
in ensuring that a spread of preferences is represented.

The team profile of the board of a manufacturing organisation
illustrates the usefulness of the model both for development and
selection.

The team was due to appoint a new member to the board and

was keen to ensure that he/she would augment the existing team base of skills and preferences. The Belbin questionnaire was used to help the team think through the type of person they needed to bring on board. It was not used to make the final selection decision and it would be unethical to use the instrument in this way.

Having completed the questionnaire the following team profile emerged:

Figure 3.1: Team profile

Chairman	Shaper

Carole (13)   PAUL (20)
Barbara (11)
	Paul (13) CAROLE (20)
	                    JAMES (25)
	                    BARBARA (18)
	                    STUART (19)

Teamworker	**Company Worker**
James (12) Barbara (10) Roy (10)	Carole (12) Barbara (10) James (13) Stuart (16) ROY (11)
Monitor Evaluator	**Plant**
ROY (11)	ROY (11)
Completer Finisher	**Resource Investigator**

Upper case = 1st preferred team role e.g. PAUL
Lower case = 2nd preferred team role e.g. Paul

Team Analysis

The Belbin team profile clearly identified some of the strengths and weaknesses of the team.

The heavy over-representation of the Shaper team role might have suggested a team made up of strong-headed individuals whose time together was spent battling for personal supremacy. Luckily this tendency was offset by their shared second preference for the role of Company Worker. This softened the Shaper abrasiveness by giving them a strong task orientation. Faced with a problem or dilemma they tuned naturally into problem solving rather than problem analysis, evaluation or idea generation mode. The pattern was to break the problem into tasks which each would then go away and deal with. This satisfied their need for framework, structure and clarity of goal (Company Worker), freedom to shape activities and resources to achieve an objective (Shaper) while maintaining the good relations in the team (Teamworker).

Paul was the Managing Director and well respected and valued by his team. His skills from the team role of Chairman enabled him to co-ordinate the activities of his competent, individualistic people.

Roy was an introvert whose fellow team members said of him 'he doesn't say much when we are together but when he does we listen'. Being respected by his colleagues, Roy was able to bring a different approach and way of thinking to their meetings. Experience had shown that his astute observations and ideas often prevented the team missing data and opportunities.

Three weaknesses within the team were highlighted through this process:

- Lack of creativity.
- Lack of follow through.
- Lack of critique and rigour.

There was a touch of the 'headless chicken' here. The team worked exceptionally hard and was always juggling an unrealistic number of tasks, projects or plans. They preferred to run harder and faster and not let anyone down (Shaper, Company Worker and Teamworker respectively) than to stop, review and evaluate activities against goals.

In defining the characteristics of the two new members to the board it was clear that they needed candidates who:

• Had an external perspective	) Resource
	) Investigator
• Were skilled networkers	)
• Had innovative flair	) Plant and
	) Resource Investigator
• Were creative	)
• Had shrewd judgement based on sound analysis	) Monitor
	) Evaluator

The Belbin model is extremely valuable as a tool to enable teams to understand their strengths and weaknesses. If a team is without a team role the realisation can help to make the team become aware that it needs to pay attention to that gap. This can lead to focused selection criteria being drawn up.

Developments of the Original Belbin Work

The original Belbin Self Perception Inventory was published some years ago. Continuing his interest and research in this area Dr Belbin has developed a computer-based assessment system called Interplace. The system is designed to handle better the many variables involved in team selection and development and to provide direct advice on the typical questions line managers raise. According to Dr Belbin the benefits of the system include:

- Assisting decisions on selection and reducing the chances of appointing misfits.
- Discovering special talents and aptitudes among employees that may have been overlooked.
- Offering leads in career progression and planning.
- Avoiding the possibility of clashes between individuals who cannot work together.
- Advising on the overall balance of a team and suggesting how roles and responsibilities might best be distributed.
- Resolving arguments between managers about prospective placements by using an acknowledged system.
- Providing individuals with feedback and counselling so that they can better understand their own strengths and weaknesses.

Interplace is a self-standing system that integrates self-reporting with observer assessments. The observers can be managers, peers, subordinates, customers or anyone involved in 'a close working relationship' with the individual concerned.

The value of this is that it overcomes some of the problems associated with self-reporting questionnaires. They are by design limited by how self-aware the individual is.

The Role of the Specialist

Following from the original research Dr Belbin had defined a ninth role – the role of the **Specialist**. This recognises those individuals who have a strong preference to become more expert and specialised in a particular area. As their careers progress they 'know more and more about less and less'. They take great pride in their work and in keeping abreast of the latest developments in their specialist area. In team settings they do not like to contribute outside their area of expertise and when contributing can sometimes give more data and detail than the listener either needs or wants. It is important not to disregard the specialist when dealing with broader issues as his/her contribution can be extremely valuable and of a depth that other team members are incapable of attaining.

Other changes to the original work have been to change the labels of two of the team roles. Both of these changes have been motivated from concerns about some misinterpretation that the original labels engendered.

The role of **Chairman** had been renamed **Co-ordinator**. This was to overcome the link between chairman and hierarchical status. **Company worker** is now referred to as **Implementer** for similar reasons. Managing Directors who showed a preference for the latter team role had some difficulty coming to terms with the label although they agreed with the team role description!

The Team Management System

Another model which can help the team selector is that devised by Charles Margerison and Dick McCann. In their reserach for the development of the Team Management System they noted that 'balanced teams encourage multiple descriptions of the same event and therefore these teams benefit from having a diversity of views to consider before making decisions.'

The model was developed following extensive worldwide research that focused on how individual work preferences match up with the necessary ingredients of a well-balanced, high-performing team. The findings led to the design and development of a questionnaire called the 'Team Management Index' (TMI).

The TMI measures four issues that occur in any work team or situation. These are:

- How people prefer to relate with others.
- How people prefer to gain or use information.
- How people prefer to make decisions.
- How people prefer to organise themselves and others.

The tool developed to show the results from the questionnaire is called the Team Management Wheel. The score from the TMI can be mapped onto the wheel to give a graphic representation of the individual's profile:

The scoring from the TMI will indicate one sector as a person's major preference and a further two as 'related' or 'back-up' roles. Thus, someone might show a preference as a Creator-Innovator with related roles as Thruster-Organiser and Concluder-Producer or as a Controller-Inspector with related roles of Concluder-Producer and Upholder-Maintainer.

Responses to the Index are analysed by a specially developed computer program to produce a 4,000-word report – a Team Management Profile. Each Profile describes an individual's work preferences in terms of their decision-making style, interpersonal skills, team building issues, leadership strengths, and so on. Below are some general characteristics of each sector on the Team Management Wheel.

Figure 3.2: Team management wheel

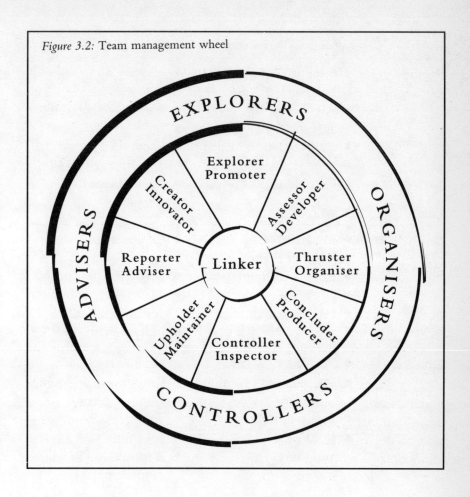

Roles	Major Characteristics	General Behaviour
Reporter – Adviser	• Supporter, helper, tolerant. • A collector of information. • Dislikes being rushed. • Knowledgeable. • Flexible.	• Usually not aggressive. • Not time conscious. • Enjoys finding out. • Issues interpreted personally. • Tends to 'put off' decisions.
Creator – Innovator	• Imaginative. • Future oriented. • Enjoys complexity. • Creative. • Likes research work.	• Often irregular work pattern. • May miss deadlines. • Continually searching for new ways. • Independent.
Explorer – Promoter	• Persuader, 'seller'. • Likes varied, exciting, stimulating work. • Easily bored. • Influential and outgoing.	• High energy level. • Knows lots of people. • Good at getting resources. • A visionary. • A good communicator.
Assessor – Developer	• Analytical and objective. • Developer of ideas. • Enjoys prototype or project work. • Experimenter.	• Moves from task to task. • Action oriented. • Dislikes routine. • Gregarious but independent. • Likes plan.

TMS material reproduced by kind permission of Prado Systems Ltd. For further information please contact Lee Kenyon on 0904 641640.

Roles	Major Characteristics	General Behaviour
Thruster – Organiser	• Organises and implements. • Quick to decide. • Results oriented. • Sets up systems. • Analytical.	• Makes things happen. • Action via deadlines. • Will exert pressure. • Impatient. • May overlook people's feelings.
Concluder – Producer	• Practical. • Production oriented. • Likes schedules and plans. • Pride in reproducing goods and services. • Values effectiveness and efficiency.	• Time conscious. • Follows through to the end. • Dislikes change. • Prefers routine. • Makes schedules work. • Emphasises outputs.
Controller – Inspector	• Strong on control. • Detail oriented. • Low need for people contact. • An inspector of standards and procedures.	• Critical of inaccuracies. • Enforcer of regulations. • Meticulous. • Quiet and reflective. • Concentrates in depth on a few issues at a time.
Upholder – Maintainer	• Conservative, loyal, supportive. • Personal values important. • Strong sense of right and wrong. • Work motivation based on purpose.	• Can help weld the team together. • Prefers advisory role. • Can negotiate well. • Usually has strong feelings. • Quiet approach. • Dedicated to what they believe in.

Using TMI and the Team Management Wheel

The questionnaire and the profile can be used to offset some of the problems that can occur in team selection and development.

It can help team members, leaders and managers to ensure that:

- Selection decisions are not based on 'in his own image'.
- Teams are balanced.
- All team members and leaders understand their own strengths, abilities and preferences.
- Roles and work are allocated in line with individual preferences and skills.
- All talents, abilities and contributions are valued and recognised.
- Team members and leaders know how to motivate and meet needs.
- Team members and leaders are aware of, and have a framework for talking about, problems.
- Activity is spread broadly across all of the preferences.

In a small team the last point often means that one person has to take on more than one role. Team members can be developed to that they can spread their skillbase to cover gaps.

Situational Leadership Model

So far in this chapter we have focused on mix and balance in the make-up of the team. In introducing the Situational Leadership model we are moving towards looking at appropriate team leadership. The model is based on the work of Hersey and Blanchard, which suggests that there is no style of leadership that is best. On the contrary, 'effective' leadership behaviour is that which is appropriate to the specific situation the leader finds him/herself in:

The model is formed around two categories of behaviour:

1. Relationship behaviour – giving encouragement, support and recognition

2. Task behaviour – giving direction, focus and structure

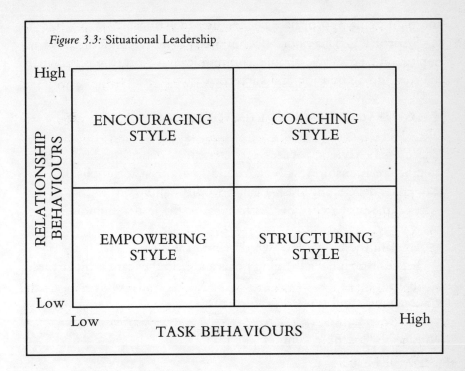

Figure 3.3: Situational Leadership

Using these as the axes of a matrix, four leadership styles can be developed. Each of the four styles can be effective when used at the right time and place. Conditions that determine whether a style is effective are:

- The willingness and ability of the team members.
- The nature of the team's goal and tasks.
- The climate of the wider organisation.

THE STRUCTURING LEADERSHIP STYLE

Here the team leader takes a major role in, first, deciding how the task can best be accomplished and when communicating this to the team members – what is expected, how to achieve it, with whom, when and where?

Close and regular monitoring is characteristic of this approach, as is showing or describing the 'how to's', then closely supervising and reinforcing appropriate behaviour and actions.

Structuring behaviours do not have to be cold, unfriendly or unpleasant. This style should communicate a sincere wish to help the team do a good job and succeed.

THE COACHING LEADERSHIP STYLE

Coaching behaviour focuses on interaction, since the leader-team member relationship revolves around two goals: accomplishing the task and developing task-related ability and commitment. To increase the probability of this happening the leader should:

- Explain the 'how' and 'why' behind the task.
- Set realistic but challenging goals and help the team achieve these goals.
- Recognise and reward performance.

Within the Coaching context, the leader:

- Elicits and listens to their ideas about the task.
- Demonstrates an interest in what they are learning.
- Gives frequent, informal feedback on how they are doing and how it fits into the larger scheme of things.
- Allows them, as they develop, to participate more and more in planning and decision making.

This style expresses the belief that 'they have potential, but hard work and learning have to occur before it is fully realised'. Coaching requires energy and commitment that is focused as much on the team's development as it is on task accomplishment.

Since this style is highly interactive and involving, meetings tend to occur frequently. It is important for leaders to have interpersonal and group process skills so that their 'boss' roles will not dampen participation and enthusiasm.

The encouraging leadership style

The main concern of the Encouraging Style is to ensure that team members are increasing their confidence and ability to perform a specific task in an understanding and independent way.

Recognising their achievements, and letting them make decisions and solve problems, is important to their development. Team members' areas of expertise are a valuable resource in the planning and decision making processes of the team. The leader can include them in meetings or consult with them. Since it is not uncommon for a leader to have more than one moderately well-developed team member, 'going to the group' can happen frequently. Therefore, an important asset to have when using this style is the mastery of group-process and participative leadership skills. The Encouraging Style calls for the skills of facilitating, listening, and two-way communiation.

The leader expresses interest in the problems and challenges the team members face to face. He/she is willing to lend an ear when needed, and able to recognise their achievements in a sincere, appreciative manner. Associated with this style is an open and supportive manner, and frequent praise for effective performance, planning and implementation.

The empowering leadership style

The dominant component of this approach is allowing the team members to proceed on their own. Occasional monitoring allows the leader to stay informed and to ensure that team members have the necessary resources. The Empowering Style requires the leader to allow team members to set their goals and be in charge of whatever planning or decision making may be involved. The primary concern of the leader is to ensure that organisational goals and policies are being met and that interferences or disruptions beyond the team members' control are dealt with.

The Empowering Style is the least interactive of the leadership styles and conveys an attitude of 'that team can get the job done without my active direction or follow-up'. There may be little day-to-day contact. Any involvement between leader and team tends to be on a factual, task-focused plane. The leader acknowledges the expertise of highly developed team members by consulting with them on relevant problems and including them, when appropriate, in organisational planning and decision making.

An Empowering relationship does not exclude warm exchanges or expressions of appreciation and support. Such behaviours are seen as tangential and not a key component, as in the Encouraging and Coaching Styles.

Concept of Maturity

In bringing a team together, team selectors need to ensure that the team leader's style is appropriate both to the task and to the team members' maturity. Maturity in this context refers not to age but to a combination of willingness and ability. A team that is bright and keen but is about to embark on an assignment outside its experience and expertise needs a team leader who can use the Structuring leadership style. This will give them task guidance and structure. As the team increases in experience and expertise so the team leader can pull back on the task-oriented style and begin to show greater concern for the members' feelings.

A team selector should be concerned to match the style of the team leader to the stage of the team's maturity. The team leader needs to have the capacity to move and change his/her style dependent upon the changes in the team's willingness and ability.

The organisational climate in which the team is operating also has an impact. The culture of Digital Equipment Corp., for example, is that of Empowerment. Teams are encouraged to determine their own goals, roles, structure and working style as they see fit.

The Digital Team Concept

Digital has provided information services and information technology in the marketplace since 1957. The heritage of Digital is in its products, but services are now earning a major and growing percentage of the total revenue. The company's area of expertise is in computing and networking, and it is the networking skills that form the basis of its teamworking approach.

The Digital Approach

Over the past few years Digital has moved away from a fragmented 'departmental' approach. There is now great emphasis on growing 'ownership' in all employees in relation to any customer issue. This means that people are encouraged to stay with a problem or issue and deal with it themselves. In the past it might have been passed around.

As far as teamwork is concerned, Ron Down, the Customer Care Manager, comments: 'We can't do business any other way.' Teamworking is a fundamental part of working life at Digital.

The teamwork approach is not new at Digital; it has been there since the start. The US founder followed the philosophy of the congregationalists whose values are to 'work together as a family'. This model is reflected in the Digital culture.

The entire paradigm, however, is seen to be shifting and changing radically. 'We are experiencing an industrial revolution in the world right now and this is being mirrored in the world of work,' says Alistair Wright, Digital's Human Resource Director.

A lot of this change is to do with interaction between people. Expectations and demands are changing. The concept of leadership is moving from an autocratic, male, hierarchical style towards more feminine principles, such as caring and coaching. This move is reflected in a shift from 'Superhuman' to 'Superteams'.

The paradigm of followers has also changed at Digital. Everyone in the company is encouraged to demonstrate what were previously held as 'leadership/management skills', such as:

- Commitment
- Energy
- Tenacity
- Innovation
- Initiative

Everyone is encouraged to grapple with current problems and issues if they want to.

The change in the roles of leader and follower has and will continue to have a dramatic affect upon the traditional role of management. Digital now recognises that there are three separate elements.

- **Leadership:** those carrying through a compelling vision for the future.
- **Coaching:** a focus on individual or team performance, development and learning.
- **Management:** a focus on productivity, the processes which yield results, and executing the vision.

Management is seen as being about the past and the present, not the future. Digital has learned from past experience that 'you cannot manage your way out of trouble, you have to *lead* your way out'. In its terms, that means having a focus on the future, the possibilities and the opportunities – 'that is what inspires people'.

New Styles of Teamworking

In Digital teams have to work synergistically, recognising the value of a common goal that they can become committed to within an honest, open and supportive culture. To achieve this there needs to be an understanding between the role of a team and the roles of individuals working together.

'Today we're trying to encourage people to break the mould, do something different, something new, something radical'. As a result there are, as we have seen, a wide variety of team types in Digital. Teams are encouraged to consider the type of team they need to be to meet organisational goals. Team types are not prescribed. The nature of the team will be based on the team, individual competencies and organisational goals. The latter focus is an essential ingredient as it is this focusing and re-focusing on the goal and contribution that has greatly enhanced teamworking in this organisation.

The Digital experience of teamworking has been founded in an organisational culture that recognises the reality of constant change, the need for continuous learning and the creative development of greater and greater flexibility.

A wide variety of teams exist.

Some of those which are currently formed are described as:

- **Virtual Teams** – pooling people from different disciplines to work in an activity-based rather than a role-based way.
- **High Performance Teams** – team members coming together around a common goal in a self-managed way.
- **Championship Teams** – teams operating within the context of a hierarchy where they are given a common goal they can commit to.
- **Joint Teams** – involving external people such as competitors or suppliers in the team activities and solutions.

The Digital culture, coupled with the level of experience and exposure employees have to teams, has led to a high maturity level in relation to teamworking. In organisations making the transition to teamworking, greater guidance and structure would be needed.

Reflection on the Imperatives of Change

Digital's teamworking approach encompasses many of the elements of the six imperatives of change.

The organisation is **aware** of its changing marketplace and the need for close anticipation of the response to these changes. Through teamworking it has grasped the need for **speed** and **flexibility**. Teams work through networks, across boundaries and are peopled by those closest to the problem. **Involvement** is the norm.

In the Introduction and Chapter 1 we addressed the six imperatives for change. The experiences described in the case studies, the work of Dr Belbin and Team Management Systems help team selectors to consider the characteristics of team members in relation to these imperatives.

Awareness

This imperative is focused on information, intelligence and intuition – the antennae that reach from the organisation to the external environment.

Bringing a team together in relation to awareness would call for team members who have the capacity both to scan for information and at the same time to know what data demands further investigation. Having an external perspective coupled with a future orientation, team members would network, question and distil data to determine possible future consequences of today's intelligence.

Awareness Skills Base

- Questioning (probe to get beyond what is being presented).
- Curious (nosey).
- Networking skills (having an external perspective).
- Sharing information (open with information).
- Information gathering (both scanning and detail).
- Future orientated (interested in 'what if' analysis and thinking).
- Intuitive (seeing beyond the data as presented).

Speed

This is the capacity to move from concept through action to results, quickly. An example of a team that is required to operate with speed is the Virtual Team as used by Digital. Here team members have access to expertise, knowledge and those who can remove barriers. Central to success is an overwhelming belief that the goal is possible and the determination to deliver.

Speed Skills Base

- Risk taker (taking 'short cuts', troubleshooting).
- Results orientated (focused on delivery).
- Creative (finding new ways to do things).
- Conviction and determination (making it happen).
- Boundary management (political skills and charm).

Innovation

The capacity to generate ideas, novel solutions, radical excursions from the tried and tested. Teamworking lends itself to rekindling innovation as teams have the capacity to support, encourage, stimulate and challenge the status quo. In the right environment team members let go of fears of incompetence, childishness and mental frigidity and are then free to innovate.

Innovation Skills Base

- Teamworker skills (support and encouragement).
- Energy and enthusiasm (capacity to let go).
- Optimistic (a belief that anything is possible).
- Spontaneous sharing (open with self and ideas).
- Creative (seeing new ways and possibilities).
- Problem solving (analysis and solution generation).

Flexibility

Being a less formal, social entity, the team represents commitment and energy directed on behalf of the team goal. Allegiance is to the team, commitment to its goal. Being so close to the point of action, team members have the capacity to adapt, reorientate and mobilise resources more readily than in more traditional structures.

Flexibility Skills Base

- Risk taker (taking short cuts, troubleshooting).
- Can deal with ambiguity (lover of change).
- Sets own goals (self starter).
- Accepts responsibility (mature).
- Adaptable (quick to respond, not sulky).
- Stamina and drive (the capacity to do it again, differently).

Co-ordination in the face of Complexity

As the number and types of teams increase so too do the complexities of co-ordination. The responsibility for co-ordination cannot rest at the centre but must be taken on board by the teams themselves. This requires a sensitivity to the information needs of others and an awareness of the drain of resource and energy that results from duplication of effect.

Co-ordination Skills Base

- Goal definition (the common purpose).
- Networking skills (external perspective).
- Communication skills (using the formal and informal communication channels).
- Respect for others (and the need to manage their anxiety through information exchange).
- Planning (what, by when and who).
- Troubleshooting (be there!).

Involvement

As complexity and speed increase the traditional team leader cannot be there to answer all the questions.

The pressure is to move towards greater involvement to maximise the value the individual can bring to the team. That means involving team members in the thinking and debate as well as the action. To do this we need to ensure that team members have the following skills.

Involvement Skills Base

- Attention to quality (pride in self, others and the task).
- Accepts responsibility (mature).
- Gives support and encouragement (a warm teamworker).
- Good communicator (involves others).
- Initiative (seeks/demands involvement).

In most teams the focus of their activity is across some or all of the change imperatives. In the next chapter we build upon the concepts of team mix, valuing differences and defining the personal characteristic of team members. The aim is to give the reader a framework for systematic team selection.

4. Bringing the Team Together Selection Methods

INTRODUCTION

There is very little generally available guidance as to how to select the 'best' team. Yet this is an area of great concern for the line manager and potential team leader. Merely bringing a group of skilled individuals together is no guarantee of team success.

CHARACTERISTICS OF 'BEST' TEAMS

Identifying the characteristics of a team that will outperform another is difficult. It is especially difficult when we consider how team members experience being a part of that team.

Successful teams bring together a strong commitment to the task coupled with commitment to each other. The gain for the individual members is personal. Each feels good in terms of task achievement, relationships with fellow team members and having real pride in the team and its performance.

Who selects and how?

The way in which teams are brought together varies tremendously. In some organisations members volunteer; in others potential members apply, are screened and some are invited to go through a highly structured selection process.

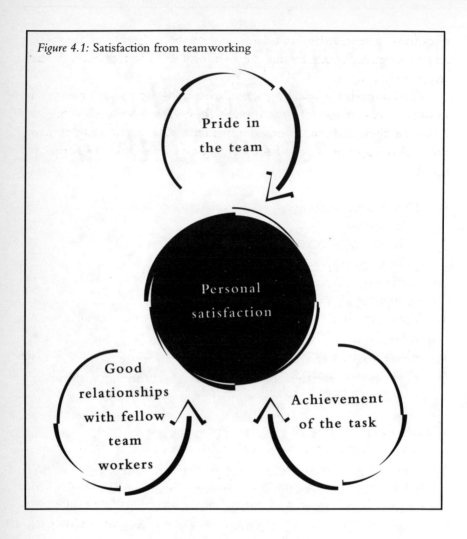

Figure 4.1: Satisfaction from teamworking

As we have seen, most commonly the team leader or perhaps the sponsor selects who will work in the team. In established teams it is usual for the team members to play a role in the selection process. This peer assessment may take place informally, perhaps over a lunch, or be part of the formal selection process. The latter is an approach used by the UK Social Services. An example is the selection of the leader for a team responsible for staffing a children's home. Following a panel interview candidates are invited to join their 'future team'. The team then asks a series of pre-prepared questions, assesses the candidates' responses and adds its feedback and recommendations to the rest of the data collected through the selection process.

The methods for selecting teams are no different from those used in other areas of recruitment though they vary from each other in terms of their structure and involvement. When choosing which method is appropriate the following questions should be borne in mind:

- Who should be involved in the selection process:
  - The sponsor?
  - The manager?
  - The team leader?
  - Other team members?
  - Customers?
- Which method of selection best matches the organisational culture?
- Which method of selection best mirrors the team's culture?
- Which method of selection gives the data the selectors need to be able to make the selection decision?

Methods of Selection

Interview – This is the most commonly used method of selection. Its validity is greatly enhanced if more than one person is involved in the interview process and candidates are all asked the same set of questions. This allows for a comparison of responses from different candidates. Obviously follow-up questions would not necessarily be pre-prepared.

Interviews are valuable in helping the selector to get a feel for the candidate in relation to how he/she interacts face-to-face with others.

Wherever possible, candidates should be asked to describe what they have done or how they have dealt with various situations. This will give a sense of how they have behaved and why they choose to behave like that.

Assessment Centre – This is a structured event that usually lasts for one day with four to eight candidates taking part.

The exercises and activities are designed to enable observers (the panel) to see the candidates in action and to gather actual examples of their work. The types of activities vary depending upon the nature of the team they are hoping to join and the team's task. Common activities are writing a report, a group discussion, a presentation, an interview and a battery of psychometric tests. The latter will probably be a mix of aptitude and personality tests.

The advantage of Assessment Centres is that they generate a range of data on each of the candidates. Although they are demanding and stressful to the candidates they are perceived as being fair in that they give individuals a variety of different situations in which to demonstrate their skills. Another advantage is that they enable the candidates to get a feel for the type of work they will be involved in and the skills they will need to use. This can sometimes help the candidate decide that this is not the team for him/her!

The disadvantages of Assessment Centres are that they require greater design, preparation and administration than the traditional interview. They are costly in terms of management time, since they require a professional co-ordinator and a panel of three to four observers.

Assessment Centres are most appropriate when the selection is for a 'key' team member, a new team where there are a number of roles to be filled or there is a large number of potentially suitable candidates.

Candidates 'have a go'

Simulations, a trial period or other processes all enable candidates to 'have a go' at the type of activity they will be required to engage in with the team. An example might be working on an oil-rig. Being a qualified engineer, experienced in the oil industry and in working in teams, does not guarantee that the candidate will be suitable for or enjoy being part of a team located on an oil-rig. By spending some time on the oil-rig both the candidate and the selector get a sense of the potential fit of the person to the team and the environment.

This method is very useful in assessing the extent to which a new team member will 'fit into' an established team. Trial periods are often three to six months but they could equally well be a week. Familiarisation days are an alternative way of letting the candidate have a look at a work setting or situation.

There are many other methods of selection available to the team selector. Some are rather 'way out', such as the much-quoted example of the Apple Corp., where potential team members were put in front of an Apple computer; if their eyes 'lit up' with joy and admiration they were in, if they were not inspired they were out!

The key to successful team selection is that it:

- Is seen to be fair.
- Gives the candidate access to the team members he or she will be joining.
- Gives the selector enough data to be able to make the selection decision.
- Gives the candidate a feel for the culture, climate and task of the team.

In and around these success criteria we would advise the team selector to be creative and to use methods in addition to the traditional interview.

What makes An Appropriate Team Mix?

An appropriate team mix in term of personalities, work styles and technical competence is essential in any team. While Chapter 3 pointed out some models that provide guidance for team mix, like most managerial practices there is a strong element of subjective judgement, 'gut feel' and hunch.

Bearing this in mind it is essential to follow a systematic process of selection, which will maximise the likelihood of:

- An appropriate mix of technical competence.
- Compatible personalities.
- Appropriate work styles.

To begin to move towards a workable checklist for selection these are some key questions to be asked:

- What is the team expected to achieve?
- What size of team is best?
- What technical expertise is needed?
- Is the team to be temporary or permanent?
- Is there to be a team leader?
- Are team members to be selected, nominated, elected or volunteered?

Let's look at each of these in turn.

What is the team expected to achieve?

One of the recurring themes in the review of successful teamworking is the recognition that setting clear goals is one of the major unifying forces. The earlier in the process that the goals are defined the better, even if later, when the team has been brought together, these goals are then refined. Having a clear sense of the expected outcome means it is then possible to break these down into the tasks that need to be accomplished and the subsequent technical skills required.

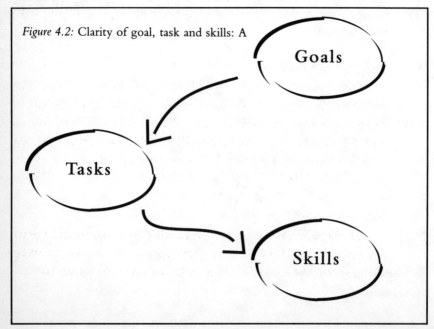

Figure 4.2: Clarity of goal, task and skills: A

Goals

Tasks

Skills

The starting point, then, for any team is to know what its overall goal is. Having stated the goal, the team can work to build up a picture of what needs to be achieved to make the goal a reality.

In the example of Portland Holidays in Chapter 1 the goal was to establish a tour operating company where the public booked their holidays direct with the tour operator rather than going through a travel agent. The advantages for the customer were lower cost and direct access to the organisation that had put the holiday together. This decreased the likelihood of errors in the booking procedure or special requirements not being actioned.

The tasks required to bring about the creation of this new company were grouped around:

– **Marketing:**
Managing the choice of design, image, logo, PR, advertising and everything involved in bringing the new company to the public's attention.

– **Operations:**
Creating the systems and procedures that would take the customer from request for a brochure to booking the holiday, to arrival and care throughout their holiday and finally their safe return.

– **Programme Design:**
This included the strategic choice of holiday type and destination, which would be the building blocks of the future market position of the company. Also involved were contact and negotiation with local hoteliers, tourist authorities and others who were central to the assurance of quality in the resorts.

– **Staffing:**
To develop a fully-fledged programme a retail outlet staffed by reservations and back-up personnel was needed, as were overseas local resort managers and holiday representatives.

- **Brochure Design and Production:**
  The selling document of any tour operator involves a mass of co-ordination of text, pictures, costs and information, all of which have to be collected, the layout designed and production managed.

There was a host of other tasks, such as securing accommodation, staffing contracts and so on.

The goal was clear, the tasks known and within the broad experience and capability of the parent organisation, Thomson Holidays. The next stage was to define the technical skills of the team that was to make Portland Holidays a reality.

It was decided that some of the tasks could be accomplished by using the existing staff from within the Thomson Holiday structure. The problem with this, however, was the importance of secrecy. Thomson Holiday's success was in part due to its good relationships with the travel agents. It was therefore crucial that the development of Portland Holidays was kept secret as long as possible and preferably to the the point of its launch. This factor alone became a major determinant of the make-up of the development team. It was decided that a small, senior team would be most appropriate to manage the political sensitivities associated with the development of the new organisation.

The technical skills and knowledge required called for a team that had experience and expertise in the areas of marketing, programme and brochure design, operations and sales. It was also decided that those who formed the 'special project team' would have sufficient capability to be the future top management team of Portland Holidays.

The team was a group of four made up of the future Managing Director who was responsible for the overall success of the project; a marketing specialist who was to become Marketing Director, the future Sales Director who had responsibility for the retailing side of the business; and the Administrator.

The above case demonstrates the need to be clear from the first about the overall goal and circumstances. From this will follow the tasks to be achieved if the overall goal is to be reached. Undoubtedly this task definition will be refined and detailed by the appointed team. At this stage an overview that gives as clear a feel as possible for the technical skills is what is necessary. (See Fig. 4.3)

SIZE OF TEAM

Optimum Team Size

Experience suggests that teams of over ten and under three perform less well. In smaller teams it is more difficult to bring together the range of skills and approaches that lead to the significant enhancement of problem solving, creativity and enthusiasm found in teams of five to seven people.

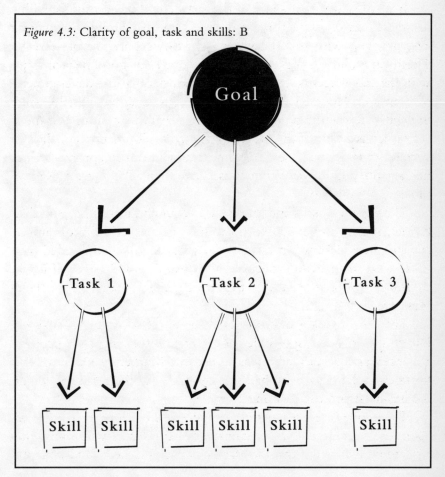

Figure 4.3: Clarity of goal, task and skills: B

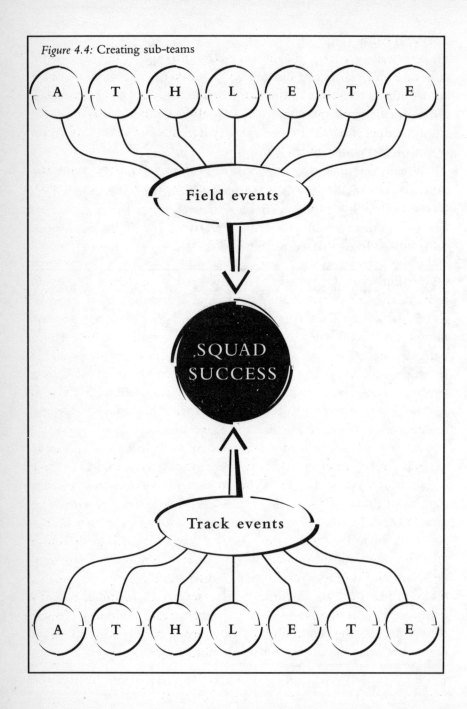

Figure 4.4: Creating sub-teams

Larger Teams

Once a team grows to beyond ten it is difficult to maintain close cohesion and teams can more readily break up into factions. This seems in part to be due to the range of activities and tasks becoming more distant from the core goal. It is always more satisfying for a team member if he/she can see directly how his/her efforts affect the overall achievement of the team.

Where the goal necessitates the creation of a large team the potential difficulties can be overcome by creating a series of sub-teams around the common goal.

Creating Sub-Teams

Take the example of an athletics team competing in an event such as the European Games. Each of the athletes is competing as an individual or in a small team of individuals sharing the same event. Their success or failure impacts directly upon their team and the nation they represent. They are therefore greatly committed to personal success and the success of their colleagues in bringing about overall team success. Each of the athletes, even in a hundred-strong squad, is clear about his/her personal contribution. The purpose is clear, the roles are clear and the performance is both measurable and capable of being traced back to the individual.

At Digital small teams are viewed as being more effective generally than larger teams. However, as they have a fairly organic organisational structure, team members tend to come and go, thus varying the size of the team at any one time. It is appreciated that some tasks necessitate the involvement of a lot of people to get the job done. Larger teams could be viewed as richer, being more creative, showing greater innovation, help and support in making decisions and problem solving. Digital has found, however, that as the number of team members increases so do difficulties with communications and issues arising between team members. This is often offset by the creation of a small core of people who call upon the expertise and contribution of peripheral members.

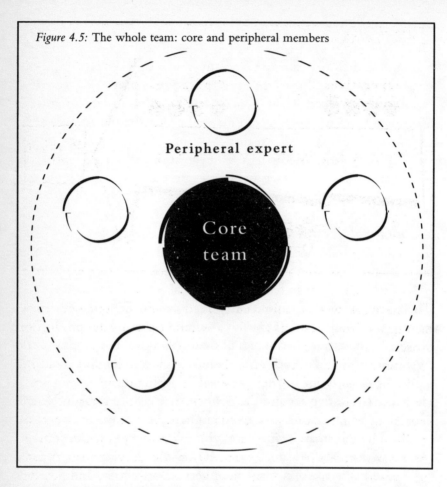

Figure 4.5: The whole team: core and peripheral members

Peripheral expert

Core
team

Here the responsibility of solving the problem or issue remains with the core team, but team members are happy to go outside to get some of the answers. This reflects how the organisation works – 'teams are there to provide support and people generally feel uninhibited about going outside the core to ask for help from another team or individual'.

An industrial example might be that of a particular form of cell manufacturing. On a recent visit to a medium sized manufacturing plant it was clear that there had been changes made to the physical arrangement of some of the work areas. The previous format had been a linear arrangement where each operative made his/her contribution to the final 'product' via a conveyor belt.

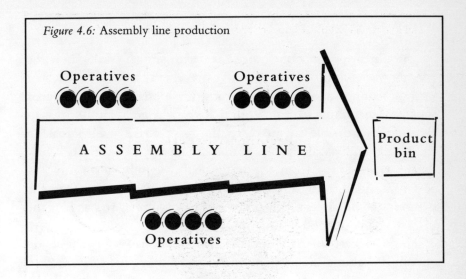

Figure 4.6: Assembly line production

The work was organised into three groups of four operatives, each group being responsible for a different part of the production process. The linear arrangement meant that there was little opportunity for communication between the three groups and the nature of the production process didn't necessitate any interaction.

The number of operatives involved in the total production process was 12. This was not too large a team, but the combination of physical separation and a lack of understanding of each operative's contribution to the final product had led to the development of three sub-groups. Each small group was very cohesive and competitive. This led to problems of flexibility when one or other of the groups were experiencing resourcing problems.

The group of 12 were brought together, initially in their three groups of four, and then as a whole group of 12 to discuss the problems. With some outside help they produced a listing of issues and possible solutions.

The issues mainly centred around not 'knowing' the operatives in the other two groups and not feeling 'at ease' with them. The reluctance to work in the other groups seemed to be directly related to how 'at home' they felt with each other, although there were some concerns about the tasks, all of which were slightly different.

It was decided that there were to be three elements to the change initiative – job rotation, multiple skill training and physical re-organisation.

The three production processes used similar skills but the ordering varied. All of the operatives received training on each of the production processes. The training was designed and delivered by each of the 'home teams'. With this knowledge of all the areas in place it was possible to move to the next phase, which was to introduce the physical changes to the organisation of the work.

The change was from the traditional assembly line format as shown in fig 4.6 to three open circles, which meant that the operatives could all see each other and that those at the end of the circles were close enough to communicate easily.

This was particularly important when the team introduced job rotation. It became the pattern for the 'new' operative to sit next to the coach from the 'new' team but at the end of the circle. He/she was therefore within easy reach of his/her 'home' team. This was important in the early days but soon fell away as the 12 became used to moving between the three groups. It was, however, important as a transition step in the process of change.

The results were marked in terms of the increased quality and quantity of production. In addition, the 12 operatives expressed a greater sense of commitment to the final product and each other. As they were now able to get to know each other better the barriers came down and the unit of 12 became more cohesive. Flexibility had been greatly increased by adopting the policies of job rotation and multiple skill training.

In re-arranging the work area to bring the larger team physically closer together there was the realisation that an open, flexible attitude to work and others became important. The previous format had not called for the operatives to be open and receptive to the wider team. The new format paid attention to the social entity of the group of 12 and the link between this and final product quality.

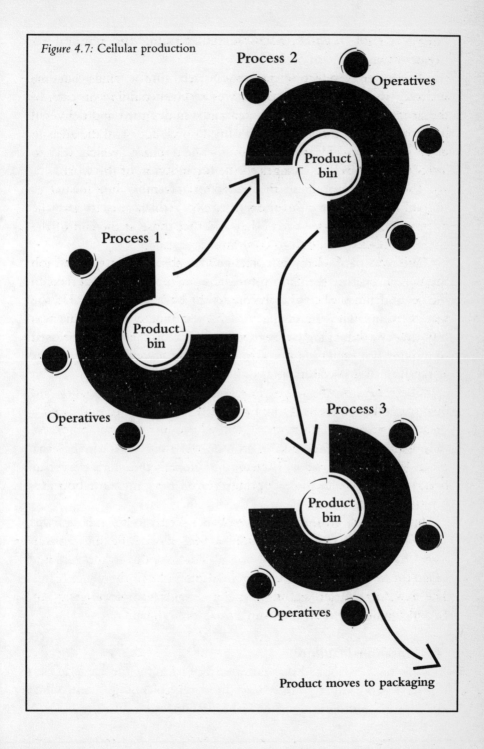

Figure 4.7: Cellular production

The Key is to Build Broader Team Commitment Irrespective of Team Size

Both the above examples reinforce the need for the team selector to be attentive to both personal commitment and skill as well as the broader team commitment. Larger teams can be, and are, successful, but they require an appreciation of:

- The personal and social needs of the individual team members.
- Potential communication breakdown in teams of more than five.
- Problems in the co-ordination of work that can arise in larger teams.

We pay attention to the voices and friendships that are closest to us. Human nature seems to pre-dispose us to building a perception of 'us and them'. In part, this is driven by a need to belong to a 'home' team. The size of this team is optiminally five to seven. In creating and managing larger teams we need to be aware of potential fragmentation and select a significant number of team members whose social skills dismantle, rather than build, walls.

SELECTING THE TEAM LEADER

We saw from the review of the models of teams in Chapter 3 that the role of the team leader is changing. Gone is the single powerful, decisive, controlling figure, to be replaced by someone who fulfils additional roles for the team as they are necessary.

The decision to appoint a team leader seems to be involved with consideration of:

- The culture of the wider organisation.
- The familiarity of the team member with teamworking.
- The complexity of the team's goal.

Organisational Culture

In Chapter 3 we looked at the move away from the mechanistic view of the team leader. Providing direction, planning, controlling, monitoring and evaluating have been transferred into the body of the teams. The leader is now more often the team member who in times of need steps in to help the team resolve problems. The skills used are likely to be those of facilitator, coach and strategic communicator. The move is from the mechanistic to the developmental.

As we found in cultures such as that within Digital, this mode of operation is known, well understood and accepted. In other organisations the move from traditional hierarchical structures to that of teamworking is proving traumatic. The situation is worsened by choosing to remove the natural focal point of control too early on in the change process. For teams in this situation the role of team leader is a necessity.

An illustration of the impact of inappropriate leadership is demonstrated in the case below. A team was bought together to solve a problem that had been around the organisation for several years. Growing irritation resulted in the team being given the challenge of 'sorting the problem out, once and for all'.

The Team
The team members were selected on the basis of their working experience, knowledge and involvement in this area of the business. A mix of levels led to the team having three Senior Managers, two Middle Managers and one Clerical member.

No Leader
The Sponsor took on a 'facilitator' role. There was no 'team leader' and all team members played a neutral role. In essence they were a 'committee' team.

Using a 'blank sheet' approach to problem solving, they set about trying to come up with a solution using a process of consensus decision making.

Absence of a Leader
In bringing the team together it was decided that there were to be no set team roles, no leader and no ground rules to guide team behaviour. As there was no one to orchestrate the team's efforts the personality of certain team members began to dictate how the team

worked, how meetings were organised and the allocation of tasks. Because of this, the same team members were 'pitching in' more than others. To have had an appointed individual or a mechanism through which ground rules were laid down and roles allocated might have helped. This would have alleviated the friction and resentment felt by some members about others and the sense that there was an uneven distribution of work.

In addition to this, the greatest difficulty experienced was over the lack of supervision and direction of the team's activities and its members. There was no one person 'championing the cause' or pulling it all together, no focal point for the team. With the lack of ground rules there was no one to monitor team activity.

Results

This team achieved its task but opportunities for the development of personal satisfaction and team pride were reduced because of the very high level of ambiguity the team members had to endure. The team members were all trained in problem solving, but they had received no formal training in group dynamics. The structure of the team called for sophisticated team skills in the areas of building relationships and managing conflict. Where these skills are not held by the team members there is a need to appoint a team leader to fulfil both a mechanistic and developmental role.

Referring back to the Situational Leadership model (presented in Chapter 3) – this team needed a coaching style of leadership, what they received was an empowerment opportunity for which they were not ready.

Models of teams are moving toward self-managed work teams where the mechanistic aspects of leadership are dealt with by the team itself. There are points of transition from a traditional structure to teamworking. The latter requires the leader to be a facilitator and coach thereby developing the teamworking skills of the members.

Looking at some of the companies we researched in putting this book together a variety of team leader criteria emerge.

The BAA Team

Leaders in BAA are seen as being those who are:

- Catalysts.
- Missionaries.
- Promoters.

Their role is to 'spark off' ideas and actions in the rest of the team. The team leader acts as a 'champion to get, and help keep, the momentum going'.

BAA is aware of who these leaders are within the company. They naturally seek out those who are receptive, gain their commitment and find out who is best to drive change.

The skills of these leaders is found in their:

- Good interpersonal skills.
- Motivational skills.
- Open minds to new ideas.

In essence, a combination of conviction, commitment, skill and attitude.

British Aerospace (Commercial Aircraft – Hatfield)

At BAe Hatfield the view of the Cell Leader is akin to that of the team captain. He/she should always be on a pitch, as a team member. The game plan needs to be explained and the other teamplayers need to be able to see what they are supposed to be doing. The aim is to harness their knowledge, break down the 'them and us' attitude and give them the opportunity to be more in control.

Assessment centres rather like the one described earlier were used to select the cell team leaders.

Part of the change at BAe Hatfield involved the move from the old foreman role to the concept of the new Cell Leader role. For some of the foremen this felt as though they had to re-apply and compete for their own jobs. In fact, the role requirements had changed and were carefully defined through the selection criteria. These are set out below.

British Aerospace – (Commercial Aircraft – Hatfield)
CELL LEADER KEY CRITERIA FOR SELECTION
Team Identity
Sees himself/herself as part of a team; prefers to work by collaborating and co-operating with others; acknowledges that success is achieved by co-operation, not competition; defines 'success' in terms of everyone's efforts; is not interested in 'one-upmanship' or in 'scoring points' off co-workers.

Management Identity
Identifies with the management role; considers himself/herself as a manager rather than as a supervisor; prepared to take the 'company line' when necessary; is committed to the aims and objectives of the company's management.

Planning and Organisation
Plans and co-ordinates people and resources; prioritises and delegates when necessary; sets up monitoring and control processes.

Flexibility
Can respond positively to change and welcome it; will alter existing plans in response to changing circumstances; can maintain quality of his/her work in difficult or ambiguous conditions; encourages others to accept and respond well to change.

Social Skill
Establishes rapport with others; is liked and accepted by them; can be warm, encouraging and supportive when necessary; is easy to get along with; displays honesty, openness and integrity; wins people's support easily.

Person Management
Can lead and encourage a team; adopts a democratic approach to team leadership; commands subordinates' respect; will attend to subordinates' training and development needs; can manage conflicts between people and make unpopular decisions when necessary; is sensitive to intra-group dynamics within his/her team.

Decisiveness

Can accept the responsibility for decision making; will make decisions at the limits of his/her jurisdiction with the minimum of hesitation and without unnecessary referral to others; will base his/her decisions on a thorough consideration of the relevant factors.

Practical Problem Solving

Is skilled in identifying problems and the causes of problems; can differentiate between relevant and irrelevant information; is mindful of the constant need for improvement and solution; can provide practical and workable solutions to problems.

Business Consciousness

Is aware of the commercial implications of his/her actions and decisions; will orient his/her actions towards maximising the profitability of the centre as a whole; will adopt a customer-oriented approach.

Commitment

Is committed to the success of the manufacturing centre; is prepared to work long and hard; is prepared to inconvenience himself/herself if necessary; will not easily give up on a problem; will show perseverance and determination; will show enthusiasm and 'staying power'.

Communication Skills

Can communicate effectively via both written and oral channels; can get ideas across easily; has a reasonable command of the language; can produce legible and easy to follow written communications; can produce explanatory diagrams and charts that are clear and easy to follow; supplements oral communications with appropriate non-verbal gestures.

People were encouraged to attend the Assessment Centre and all received skilled feedback. 'It was often very tough – heart-rending in many ways' comments one participant. Through the use of coaching and counselling, participants were able to make sense of the requirements of the new role and their development needs in relation to it.

Teamworking is still relatively new in BAe Hatfield and there is a need for the Cell Leader to maintain elements of responsibility for the mechanistic aspects such as planning control and monitoring. Proactive, positive leadership is encouraged – 'being sparky'.

Federal Express has been covered in detail earlier. However, its concept of team leadership bears repetition. He/she is usually there to:

- Focus the team rather than take the limelight.
- Facilitate quality.
- Clarify company policies and procedures.
- Remove barriers.

In summary the skills of the team leader that are recurring in the experiences of these organisations show a spectrum of skills that take the leader from a mechanistic mode to one of empowerment.

Skills of Leaders

Were:	Are becoming:
to inspire	to facilitate
to plan	to coach
to monitor	to manage boundaries
to control	to create a positive climate
to evaluate	to focus on the broader vision

The final word on team leaders goes to Ian Wallace of Digital, who describes the role of the team leader as having to 'provide an environment in which other people can be successful – to provide direction without rigidly controlling'. It is important for the team leader to ensure his/her 'vision' is understood and taken on board, to create an environment that is open, where issues or conflict can be dealt with in a tolerant and supportive way.

5. Team Skills

TEAM SKILLS

The major selection criterion for any team member is whether he/she has the technical expertise required to achieve the tasks. The only case in which this may not be true is where placement on a team is for development purposes. Here it is likely that selection would be made on the basis of future potential, though any team can only carry a small proportion of members 'in training' as they do of necessity take up the time and energy of team members.

Matching Who and What

In deciding *who* should form part of the team we need to think carefully about *what* they will be required to do. This is easier in established teams where the roles exist. Through a process of questioning and observation it is possible to draw up a list of skills that the existing job holders use. Against this one can begin to match potential team members.

Case Study

Management Consultancy

A recent assignment involved the selection of a new team member to join an established team in a management consultancy. The brief was unusual in that the team was made up of a core of full-time employees and a series of self-employed Associates. The core team numbered three and the Associates 10. The philosophy of the consultancy had always been to create a close liaison with the Associates and involve them in the development of the client base and the business. The Associates valued this and, perhaps more so, the fact that the consultancy was felt to be a 'centre of excellence' in their field. As a result of this the culture created was one of professional and personal respect. When the whole team came together there was an atmosphere charged with personal friendship and professional challenge.

The core team was made up of the two owner Directors and an Administrator. The new position was for their first full-time consultant. This was seen to be essential as the rapid growth in the business had meant that the directors were experiencing some difficulties juggling the balance between marketing, business getting and consulting.

The role was clear. They needed a bright, energetic 'mini-consultant', someone who had the intellect and potential but not necessarily the experience of the existing Associates. The aim was an individual who could relieve the directors of some of the writing and research they were currently involved in and act as a support both to themselves and the Associates. Another strand was that the individual would have credibility with the clients and be skilled in building rapport and handling relationships.

Bringing in two of the Associates, the core team drew up a list of skills and abilities they considered to be essential in a successful applicant. There criteria fell into two groupings, firstly Eligibility Criteria and Selection Criteria. Meeting the former would get an interview, the latter an invitation to join the team.

Case Study

Eligibility Criteria

Eligibility criteria are the basic requirements of the job. They include such things as:

- Age.
- Length of experience.
- Academic achievement.
- Type of industries worked in.
- Mobility.
- Languages, etc.

They are the concrete essentials the person must have to achieve success in the job.

It was decided to be fairly open in relation to this job as the consultancy needed someone who had the potential to develop further. Potential was more important then experience, although some experience was clearly needed to have the credibility required. The eligibility criteria that were identified were:

- Over 21 years old.
- Graduate calibre.
- Two years or more experience in a project or consultancy environment.
- A flair for and an enjoyment of writing.
- Living within travelling distance of Central London.
- Experience in the area of telecommunications.

Having clarified the basic requirements, any successful applicant now had to demonstrate that he/she could meet the selection criteria.

Case Study

Selection Criteria

These were put together following discussions with three of the Associates, the Directors and the Administrator. The aim was to gather as wide a view as possible of the knowledge, skills, abilities and traits the successful team member would have. Nine criteria were identified, each being of equal importance.

- **Technical/professional knowledge** – of a sufficient level to gain credibility with clients and work effectively alongside a Director/ Associate.
- **Oral communication** – effective verbal communication of ideas; speaks clearly and fluently.
- **Written communication** – expressing ideas clearly in writing, using a good style with appropriate grammar and vocabulary.
- **Impact** – creating a good first impression, commanding and maintaining attention and respect.
- **Initiative** – actively influencing events, organising action, seizing opportunities.
- **Persuasiveness** – convincing others of own point of view, gaining acceptance of plans and ideas.
- **Sensitivity** – awareness of the feelings and needs of others, able to modify own behaviour as appropriate.
- **Imagination/innovation** – producing creative solutions; capable of identifying novel or radical alternatives.
- **Teamworking** – the ability to operate in an environment where there is a lot of 'give and take', to be seen to be both supportive and confrontational.

There was an additional element that was considered important. This was an over-riding concern that centred around the importance of the person 'fitting-in'. The culture of the consultancy was not to

Case Study

be jeopardised by the appointment of a technically skilled individual who lacked some of the values that were the cornerstone of the consultancy's success. These were elements such as respect for the individual, openness, integrity and trust.

Having clarified their thinking in terms of what the new team member was to do and the knowledge, skills, abilities and traits he/she would need to be successful, the Directors invited six of the applicants to attend an Assessment Centre.

The day was designed to give each applicant the opportunity to demonstrate his/her skills. A series of activities drawn from the workplace were used. These included:

- A structured interview.
- A presentation on an area of technical expertise.
- A group discussion on a creative solution to a client complaint.
- A written proposal in response to a client request.

During the day the participants were observed or interviewed by the two Directors, two of the Associates and the Administrator. As the day progressed it became increasingly clear that only one of the applicants met the technical criteria. Another had lots of energy and enthusiasm but it was felt that he did not have the potential to develop into a consultant.

Unfortunately, the applicant who fulfilled the technical requirements fell far short of the interpersonal requirements. The heavy handed, hierarchical dealings she had had with the Administrator, together with her attitude to her fellow applicants and lack of appreciation of the role and power of the Associates, were sufficiently overwhelming as to make her politically unsuitable for this teamworking culture.

Case Study

After much energy, expense and heated discussion the 'observers' decided not to appoint!

Without the attention given to defining the criteria, the importance of this interpersonal element might have been missed. 'Fitting in' is often the key criteria for an established team.

The recruitment exercise had not been a waste as it resulted in a clearer sense of exactly what was required and, perhaps more importantly, what was not.

Three months later a letter and CV arrived at the consultancy. As a result of this and subsequent interviews and tests a bright, energetic young woman was invited to join the team.

The qualities she had? In terms of technical and academic qualifications, she was heavyweight. In relation to her commercial experience, she was lightweight. Her people skills were sensitive, proactive, and persuasive. She would 'fit'.

Six months on, the general consensus is that to have appointed the applicant from the first process would have been disastrous. Clearly she would have been difficult to assimilate into the wider team and would have disrupted the established culture and working practices of the full-time core team. The consultants were not looking for a clone, nor did they fear confrontation and change, but they knew it was imperative to maintain that core value of respect for the individual and the egalitarian culture that comes from this.

End Case Study

This case demonstrates that the process of matching the knowledge, skills, abilities and traits of the individual to the team requirements is not a scientific process. It is a combination of analysis of requirements and creating the opportunity for the applicant to demonstrate his/her skills. The team selector needs to bring these together with an element of subjective judgement as to whether the fit is close enough.

CREATING NEW TEAMS

Frequently managers are required to create new teams to undertake special projects or new types of work. This is where a systematic approach to defining the skills becomes essential. There is no one to observe. The data that exists relating to suitable team members is in the thinking and imagination of the individual commissioning the team, the sponsor, the appointed team leader or potential team members. Accessing and making sense of this data requires a combination of structure, system and hunch.

Defining a Selection Approach

To illustrate how to develop this systematic approach to the first stage of selection we will use a recent case in which we have been involved.

Case Study

Team Working in a New Factory

The company is a large, international manufacturing organisation producing specialist components for the oil industry. It has recently experienced a period of rapid growth in profit and subsequent investment in plant and machinery.

Part of the investment was in a new factory, which was highly computerised and used the latest robotic technology. In resourcing the factory the Managing Director saw the opportunity to introduce a new and, for the company, radical team approach. Until then the manufacturing process had been run on fairly traditional lines. Four years previously the organisation had introduced a Total Quality

Case Study

Programme. This was very successful and meant that most people in the company had some experience of teamworking.

With the new technology it became possible to have 24 hour manufacturing using three shifts of eight workers – the new teams. It was felt important that the structure for the new factory should be entirely flat, with the role of team leader revolving among the eight team members. For this to succeed all of the team members had to be comfortable with taking responsibility and showing initiative. At the same time it was felt to be important to maintain a degree of 'give and take'.

- **Early Success is Essential**
  As this was the first time a team philosophy had been used with a whole work group, it was felt to be important that it was seen to be successful, particularly if this way of working was to be introduced later into other parts of the organisation. The spotlight was well and truly on this, the newest part of the site.

- **Early Involvement**
  The Project Manager was the Director of Quality and Personnel. He believed it was important to recruit the team members at the earliest opportunity. He wanted them to have input into:

  - The final design of the new factory.
  - The positioning of the technology.
  - The development of working practices.
  - Selection of future team members.
  - Specification of technical and personal training needs.
  - Expansion plans for the next wave of development.

  All of these could have been developed and agreed by the senior project team, but in doing that valuable opportunities for team and personal development would have been lost.

Case Study

- **Selection Strategy**

  It was considered that success in implementing a team working philosophy and approach in the new factory would aid its introduction throughout the site. In essence the new factory was the test bed. Selection of the best possible team was crucial. The approach adopted was developed to ensure that:

  - The opportunity to apply was open to all.
  - The selection mechanism was seen to be fair and appropriate.
  - The mechanism would identify individuals' strengths and weaknesses.
  - The approach would bring together a list of people who were most suitable and ready for team working.

In dealing with each of these questions the following sources were approached:

- The developers of the technology.
- Two organisations who were already using teamworking in a related way.
- Production Director.
- Shopfloor workers who were currently working on the existing machinery which was to be replaced by the robot technology.

The aim was not to re-invent the wheel but rather to learn from best practice elsewhere and to put this together with internal views wherever possible.

SELECTION APPROACH

The selection approach in the case study had three strands to it, each being of equal importance.

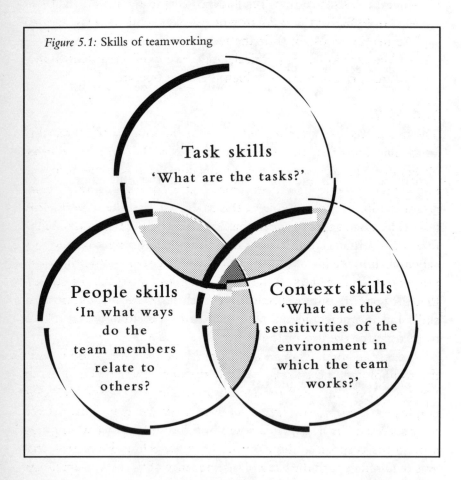

Figure 5.1: Skills of teamworking

Task skills
'What are the tasks?'

People skills
'In what ways
do the
team members
relate to
others?'

Context skills
'What are the
sensitivities of the
environment in
which the team
works?'

Case Study

In bringing a new team together the selector needs to be clear about the jobs that will need to be done, the environment the team will be working in, and the types of people who are likely to succeed in this team. These can be summarised as:

- **Task Skills:** the activities that make up the job.
- **People Skills:** the ways in which team members relate to each other and those outside the team.
- **Context Skills:** the political, social and intellectual sensitivities of the environment in which the team operates.

Task Skills

The task skills are the 'nuts and bolts' of the job. Of the three skill areas they are often the easiest to define as they are more often observable and almost tangible. Under this heading is the technical knowledge, experience and expertise that is a pre-requisite for team membership. In the example of this manufacturer, there were some task skills that made it clear that the team should include skilled fitters and electricians. It was also clear that the new technology called for knowledge and skills that existed neither within this plant nor anywhere else in the UK. It was therefore essential for success that the team members should have both the capacity to learn new skills and an interest in and aptitude for the technology as it related to this part of the production process.

To enable potential team members to get a feel for working with the technology, the company asked the developers to be available for two days, on site, to demonstrate the equipment and give employees the opportunity to see it and try using it. This proved very successful as it dispelled some of the rumours that were going around the company, about to the level of technical expertise that was required in both the use and maintenance of the new technology.

Case Study

Fear of Technology

The groups who were most hesitant were older staff and some female employees. The latter felt that they lacked the intellectual skills to be successful in using this technology. In fact although woman make up 48 per cent of the work force of the factory, eventually only three applied for the team selection process as opposed to 28 men. As a result the organisation is currently reviewing how it can get more of the very capable woman in the factory to be confident about their ability to do different jobs and tasks and move readily across teams.

In the case study of The Body Shop given earlier the task skills of the team were broken down into the four areas of Finance, Stock-room, Personnel and Front of Shop. In that case as in this, the aim was to have a team where some individuals had experience in one or other of the areas. In addition each had to have the capacity to learn the skills, knowledge and techniques used in the other areas. Using this approach the team can function from day one as the task skills are held somewhere in the team. The longer-term aim is to develop strength in depth.

It became possible in both cases, therefore, to put together a listing of task skills that had to be covered by team members from the beginning and to have a secondary listing that showed where greater depth of skill was needed for the future.

End Case Study

People Skills

People skills in teamworking are well documented. Teamworking was coined as a working methodology in the 1970s and proved very appealing to the behavioural scientists, though perhaps less attractive to the line manager. Part of the reason for this may have been the very heavy emphasis on the relationships within the team and how these were best handled. This has come to be called the process of teamworking, and in some quarters it has taken precedence over the tasks.

In reality the way in which team members interact with one another is a key to team success, but it is one of several keys. To over-emphasise its importance and thereby minimise some of the other elements is to miss the learning that the 1970s experience presented. Teams can do well together without team members 'loving' each other. The aim today is to develop warm, collaborative relationships where a respect for individual differences exists, alongside clarity of purpose and goal. This means that at times the achievement of the task takes precedence over the attention given to the relationships.

In any team, members need to be socially skilled in such a way that they can maintain warmth and respect while working under pressure. They must be able to disagree with each other and work in situations where there is a lot of change and ambiguity.

The ideal team member is one who has the capacity to be both assertive and co-operative. In our terms that means being able to push forward your own case strongly and persuasively but at other times being able to go along with the viewpoint or plans of others.

The Body Shop was clear that it wanted 'performers' who were able to take responsibility and show initiative when necessary. It did not, however, want individuals who were not happy being one of the team. In addition, applicants who wanted to be the leader all the time were not for this team.

In researching and writing *Superteams*, the authors found that team members contribute much more than their specialist knowledge and skills. They seem to bring energy, commitment and enthusiasm coupled with personal qualities that allow for quite different types of people to come together successfully around tasks and goals.

Some of the people skills that have been identified as being central to successful team working fall into three main categories:

- Building relationships with others.
- Confronting and handling conflict.
- Moving the task forward.

Building Relationships with Others

In building relationships with others a team member is concerned with drawing others out and giving them space and support. In doing this he/she seems to be using three areas of skill. Firstly, the ability to listen; secondly, the capacity to encourage and support; and, lastly, the skill of relieving tension and anxiety.

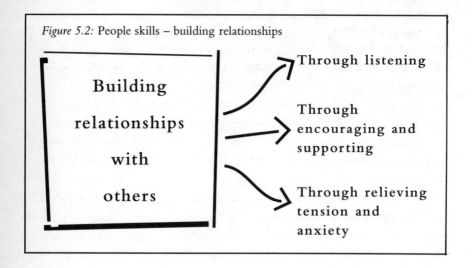

Figure 5.2: People skills – building relationships

Listening

Listening means giving the speaker full attention, and that means actively concentrating on what he/she is saying. Many teams experience problems because team members are more intent on getting their own points across than listening to what their colleagues are really saying. This is especially so when there are disagreements.

Recently, while observing a new team in action it became apparent that they were indulging in a game of verbal table-tennis. The team was a Product Innovation Team charged with coming up with a new product line for an established business. Each member had an impressive track record with the organisation and they were chosen because of this and their individuality and creativity. The result was a highly charged, combative team in which ideas flowed but were quickly criticised and discarded. The more this happened the more combative the group became. In reality each individual was so concerned with putting forward his/her idea that no one was listening to the ideas of others. Worse still, no one was building on the ideas of others. The result was that a lot of potentially good ideas never received sufficient air-time to be properly thought through and were therefore rejected. The ideas that did receive some review were those generated by the most vocal of the group.

The problem with people skills, and particularly listening, is that egos get in the way. What was happening in this team was that each of the five members was battling for supremacy based upon his/her ability to knock down the others' ideas.

The ability to listen actively to others is one that often has to be re-learned. The belief that underpins this skill is the view that others are going to say something of value. If I start off from the stance of 'my ideas are best', it is difficult to give your ideas the real attention they deserve.

So listening would have helped this Innovation Team as would building upon the ideas of others. Doing the latter actively encourages greater contribution from everyone. It creates a supportive environment in which ideas and contributions are welcomed for development and review, not instantly criticised and rejected.

Encouragement and Support

Encouragement and support are to do with 'looking out for each other'. This can include being sensitive to changes that may impact upon the team, and letting others know of the implications. A recent assignment with a medium-sized computer agency involved the merger of two Administrative Support teams. The integration of the two established teams followed an acquisition of one company by the other. The aim of the team development programme was to help to integrate the two groups through developing a teamworking culture. The challenge lay in the history of the two organisations. One had evolved a very traditional 'command and control' culture based largely on rules, checking and fear. The culture was a reflection of the autocratic style of the Owner/Managing Director, who following the acquisition was to leave the company.

The second organisation had worked hard to develop a collaborative culture where staff worked as equals demonstrating a great deal of respect for each other. One of the results of this culture was the great pride they each took in the service the support group gave to the consultants. A poorly produced proposal document was a reflection on each of them and, therefore, was rarely allowed to happen. They helped each other, they encouraged, they confronted poor standards in others and coached them to improve.

This contrasted greatly with the first group where the attitude of 'I've done my bit, that's your problem' persisted. They were not encouraged by the culture; in fact using initiative was career threatening – if you got it wrong you were dealt with publicly and severely. It is not surprising that bright young people worked quietly behind closed doors and quickly lost their creativity and enthusiasm.

It is clear from this case that encouragement and support comes through actions as well as words. People skills are as much to do with what we do as what we say.

RELIEVING TENSION AND ANXIETY

One of the realities of the commercial world of the 1990s is the continuing, rapid rate of change. Handling ambiguity, changing demands and different work assignments all add to the stress of work most of us face. Working alone can mean for some that these tensions are pushed inwards. The theory of teamworking suggests a Utopia where each is encouraged to share concerns and fears within the supportive home team. The reality for many team members is far from this.

Humour

Relief from tension and anxiety takes many forms from laughter to tears. The team member uses his/her skills through an appropriate use of humour – not at someone else's expense.

Working with many teams in a wide variety of settings shows that humour is very often used inappropriately. It becomes a veiled medium through which negative messages are communicated to fellow team members. We are all familiar with the barbed comment made at almost every meeting which still raises laughter and keeps Fred in his place!

Humour and laughter are part of the richness of teamworking and are to be valued, as is the team member who raises easy laughter when ideas are thinning or anger looming.

Moving Away

Another way of relieving tension and anxiety is knowing when to push harder and when to pull back. Moving away from a potential head-to-head and dealing with it at another time can be more successful in the longer term than battling through every disagreement as it arises.

The Marketing Team of a large pharmaceutical company was taking part in a management training exercise. The activity was based around a survival scenario and the brief was to reach an agreed team decision.

One member of the team, a Marketing Executive, was very outspoken; he was clear and committed to what he saw as the only possible decision.

As each of the items came up for discussion he assertively stated his decision and shared his reasoning with the rest of the team. As the discussion continued he systematically undermined each of his colleagues' contributions and ideas. As their resentment grew the tension and anger directed towards him increased. Unaware, he continued until one of his colleagues burst forth with a flow of anger and left the room. He was shocked and surprised that his behaviour had created such a strong reaction. He is what is called a 'stress inducer'. Just as there are people around who have the capacity to make us feel calm so there are those who can make the tension rise as they never let go or give way.

Awareness of the Impact of Behaviour

People who are skilled at relieving tension and anxiety are generally those who are aware of the impact their behaviour has on others. They are sensitive to the state of the other person and react accordingly. This reaction can vary from assertive confrontation (which is what might have helped in dealing with the Marketing

Executive in the last case) through to a comforting arm around the shoulders.

Letting Go of Emotion

Relieving tension is related to finding ways of helping others to let go of emotion. The resultant release can be laughter, anger, tears or a variety of other exclamations. To be able to let go, individuals need to feel safe and free from ridicule. The skilled teamplayer is sensitive to and aware of the needs of others and has a knack for creating an ease around him/her.

CONFRONTING AND HANDLING CONFLICT

Confrontation and the ability to manage conflict in a positive way is a state that some teams never get to. Often conflict is ignored or directed onto one person in the team – 'When Carole goes we will get on much better'.

The importance of this group of skills rests in the consequences to the team of not being able to deal with conflict as it begins to emerge. Unless dealt with openly and effectively early on, hidden conflict, and the self-orientated behaviours it creates, is very damaging to teams.

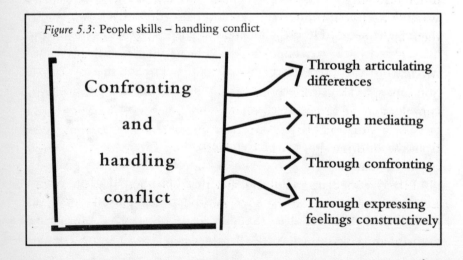

Figure 5.3: People skills – handling conflict

Articulating Differences

The key word here is 'articulating'.

Often we are aware of differences but do not say anything.

The work of Belbin and the others outlined in Chapter 3 demonstrated the need for a rich mix of approaches and styles. This is the central element of teamwork success. It is also the most difficult for some people to deal with.

Take the example again of the Marketing Executive in the survival exercise. He was certain, based upon his experience and rationale, that he was right. The stakes for him were high, his 'life' depended upon getting others to buy his series of decisions. So the discussion for him turned from reaching the best team decision to getting the team to take on his decisions, because in his view they were right. Underpinning his mind set was the belief that no one else could add value to his thinking. He was therefore closed to their contributions. One of the major values of teamworking is that it brings to any problem or situation a wide range of views, experience and capability. The increasing complexity of today's organisations requires more than any one individual can offer.

In reviewing the exercise the Marketing Team had addressed, it was shown that their team had achieved less as a team than they would have had they approached the problem individually. Teamwork requires team members to understand and respect differences in approach. When these differences are getting in the way of effective teamworking it is important to be able to deal with them appropriately by bringing the hidden situation into the open.

Mediating

Some people by nature 'pour oil on troubled waters'. Through a combination of careful questioning and listening they unravel the facts of a situation. By discovering the facts and separating them from the emotion they are able to help others move towards a more objective stance.

Effective mediators pull together the skills of Belbin's Monitor-Evaluator with those of the Chairman. They remain objective and logical while using their ability to draw others out in an unthreatening way.

It is important in any team to have team members who are concerned with finding the common ground that often exists, but which can be shaded by individual's self-orientation and hidden agendas.

Confrontation

Confrontation is an assertive response to a sense that 'all is not well'. In the example of the Marketing Executive they all knew that their colleague was behaving in a way that was driven by his personal goals rather than those of the team, but they chose not to confront him. The result of this non-confrontation was negative for him, them and the team. Result, they all lost. Team members need to have a range of people skills that enable them to be assertive as well as co-operative if the team is to perform to its potential.

Expressing One's Feelings Constructively

Often in situations of heightened emotion there is a tendency to be so concerned with 'getting back' at the other person or people that individuals are unaware of how they are feeling.

Expressing feelings helps others to understand what lies behind our words and behaviour. With this greater depth of understanding it may be possible to diffuse the conflict or to take it to a level where people begin to face up to and take responsibility for the negative feelings that exist.

Case Study

The Fabric Manufacturer's Top Team

A fabric manufacturer had set itself the target of hitting £10 million turnover within six years. Its current turnover stood at £3.5 million. The Managing Director had spent two years getting the organisation to a position where movement towards the vision was set to

Case Study

accelerate. Investment in plant, machinery and working practices had begun. A Total Quality Initiative was well underway and customers were expressing delight at the improving product quality and service standards.

We were called in to help the Managing Director assess and develop the top team of the organisation. Of the four directors, three had been with the organisation over 10 years. They had moved up as their jobs had grown with the growth of the business. Like many UK senior managers they had not invested in their development. As a result there were some questions as to whether this was the team to take the company forward.

The Managing Director was keen to give the four directors the opportunity to develop and rise to the challenges the next five years would bring.

The process of defining their individual development needs and plans started with a two-day workshop where the focus was on personal development within a teamworking context. The major aim was to establish some shared principles on how they would work together in the future to achieve the ambitious but realistic vision.

The workshop progressed well, with three of the directors being positive and open about their views, feelings towards each other and plans for the future. The fourth was holding back. It was rather like having a dormant volcano in the room: we all knew he was going to erupt, but not when, nor what would trigger the explosion.

The eruption never happened. Several of his colleagues invited him to share his obvious anger and hurt, but he was reluctant to do so. He left the workshop seething.

Three weeks after the workshop the director approached the Managing Director for a private word. Having reflected on where the organisation was going, his future role and his sense of where his strengths lay, he had decided to resign.

Case Study

The Managing Director reluctantly accepted the resignation but was confused as to why it had been offered now. The eruption happened in a combination of anger and tears. The director resented deeply the subject matter of the workshop and saw the emphasis on teamworking as a negative reflection on the way he had operated in the past. Coupled with this was the fact that he and one of his fellow directors had started at the company at the same time and he now believed that the other was favoured over him. All of this might be perceived by some as trivial and not a resignation issue. But in the area of personal self-worth, when an individual is feeling vulnerable, he/she is liable to misread the words or actions of others.

The director firmly believed that his colleagues were against him. He was unable to express his very deep sense of anger and resentment. As a result it fermented and bubbled over in a welter of blame and bitterness.

Expressing feelings can be very powerful not only in terms of managing your own emotion but also in helping others to feel better able to say how they really feel about what is going on. Without this skill feelings can become deep-seated and uncontrollable, but will break out eventually.

End Case Study

Taking the Task Forward

This grouping of skills concerns information, ideas and solutions. It is not about how to generate them but rather how a team member shares his/her ideas and information and the way in which he/she encourages this sharing in others. It is in many ways the first level of people skills, as it is totally directed towards the task and its achievement. Very often in teams, particularly in limited-life teams, these are the major skills that are required. The more complex and

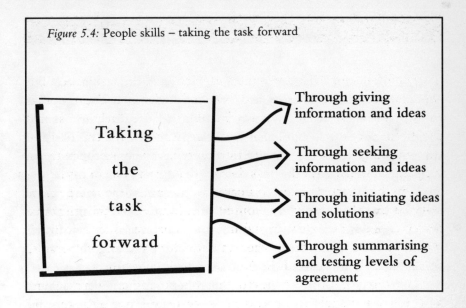

Figure 5.4: People skills – taking the task forward

uncertain the team's goals are, the more they need to use the skills of building relationships and handling conflict.

Information and Ideas

There needs to be a balance between the extent to which a team member gives information or opinions and the extent to which he/she seeks it from others. The Marketing Executive we heard of earlier was skilled at giving his views and did so very persuasively. The fact that he failed to draw others into the discussion, however, meant that the team lost the value of shared thinking and ideas. To achieve its goal successfully, a team needs to ensure that the richest possible mix of information, opinion, ideas and solutions are generated. Often this means bouncing information and opinions around – literally shaking everything out onto the table so that the team has a wide, rich raft of data on which to base its actions.

To achieve this there needs to be a mix of introverts and extraverts. Those who readily and easily open their thinking to others and those who at times need to be pressed to contribute.

Case Study

The Silent Team Member

The 1980s saw radical changes in the way in which health care is organised in the UK. We were invited into a large teaching hospital to help it put together its business strategy for the 1990s. The aim was to use the development of the strategy as a vehicle for personal and team development.

Following a series of one-to-one meetings the team came together for a one-day workshop. In the afternoon the team entered into a heated debate about matching the commercial focus of their vision of the future with the values and ethics of the caring professionals who were to be mobilised to implement the vision.

During the discussion one team member was silent. The General Manager invited him to contribute several times and each time he gave some brief comment that suggested general agreement with the direction the discussion was taking.

Later that evening the silent member was talking heatedly to one of his colleagues. The energy, passion and coherence of his thinking was impressive and would have added value to the earlier discussion. When he was asked why he had remained so quiet during the afternoon he commented: 'I had nothing to add, they were saying everthing I would have said'. In a general sense this was true; however, speaking to his colleague in the evening he had been taking the discussion further than it had moved in the afternoon.

To choose not to share thinking with fellow team members is to dilute the mix of data that the team has available to it. Team members need to share what is going on in their heads even if it is to say explicitly that they agree – this could be very supportive and helpful to a colleague.

The aim of giving and seeking information or opinions is to generate as rich a pool of data as is possible for the team to draw upon. To do this team members need to be able to state their views clearly and persuasively and to encourage others to do likewise.

Initiating Ideas and Solutions

This is about being creative. In many organisations this is an area where development is needed to revitalise the creativity that naturally exists within its employees.

Having observed a wide range of people from a host of organisations in team settings, we have found that those who have the capacity to be spontaneous and creative are disappointingly few. Teams, particularly those facing totally new and challenging problems, need to be able to free themselves from the 'tried and true' methods and products of the 1980s. To do this teams need creative players, able to share that creativity with their colleagues.

The hospital team in the last case had a creative team member who lacked confidence in her ideas. In contributing an idea or potential solution she would preface the contribution with 'I guess this won't work, but maybe we could . . .' or 'I know this will sound silly but . . .'. Not suprisingly her ideas were often lost. She didn't take them seriously so why should anyone else? Having the ideas is not enough, it is the skill of sharing them with others that is so powerful and necessary in teamworking.

Summarising and Testing Levels of Agreement

Some teams lose much of their good thinking and debate through a lack of closure. This closure is created by team members checking explicitly that everyone understands and agrees what has happened and what has been decided.

Knowing when to summarise, and how, can help a team move forward to the next stage of discussion or planning. Done skilfully it can make the difference between going round in circles indefinitely or stopping, reviewing, agreeing and moving on.

As with the technical skills, it would be unrealistic to expect to find all the necessary people skills in one person. What the selector is looking for is a balance in the team.

People Skills to be Avoided

In making selection decisions it is sometimes useful to consider which skills are not helpful to teamworking. They are in the main those skills which are directed towards meeting individual needs as opposed to the needs of the team. They are generally directed at distracting the team from the achievement of its goal whilst bolstering the needs of an individual within the team.

The behaviours are most damaging when several team members have got into the habit of using them. They can arise because individual needs are not being met in the team setting, and have often been built up over several years of bad experiences of this team, its leader or its members. The selector of a new team is well advised not to select potential team members who exhibit the following traits and behaviours.

Negative People Skills

- Aggressiveness.
- Always seeing the negatives.
- Defensiveness.
- Withdrawal.
- Distracting humour.
- Seeking sympathy.
- Playing games with the group.

In essence, a potential team member who appears to have a strong orientation towards self as opposed to a sense of the greater good of the team, may not prove to be the best team member.

CONTEXT SKILLS

These refer to the political, social and intellectual sensitivities of the environment in which the team operates. The minimum requirement for most teams under this heading is an appreciation of the broader team in which they operate. An example of this would be the advertising group of a marketing department. Team members need to be aware of the activities and priorities of other parts of the department to ensure that their efforts are not cutting across the work of others. Without this sense of the broader team, teams run the risk of becoming insular, perhaps missing opportunities for such activities as joint ventures and sharing resources, and for development. For some teams, this political sensitivity forms a part of their brief. This was certainly the case with the Portland Holidays development team. Had its goal been leaked to the media the competitive advantage offered by the broader business portfolio of the Thomson Travel Group would have been reduced. The political sensitivity surrounding this team was therefore great.

Team members need to have and use knowledge of changing situations and pressures both inside and outside the team. These may be related to social, environmental, financial or business changes that directly or indirectly affect the team's area of work.

A Financial Services organisation defined the skills under this heading as:

- Basing decisions for own team on the major influences affecting the organisation's position in the marketplace.
- Proposing ideas in the light of major external influences.
- Developing strategies to achieve the key commercial objectives of the organisation.
- Keeping up to date on latest developments in technological, economic and social fields.

People who have a flair for this area are naturally curious. They make links between the wider organisation and the team. The skills which form the basis of this selection grouping are:

- Questioning.
- Networking: building and maintaining contacts outside the team.
- Paying attention to seemingly peripheral data.
- Political 'nous'.
- Understanding the broader business context.

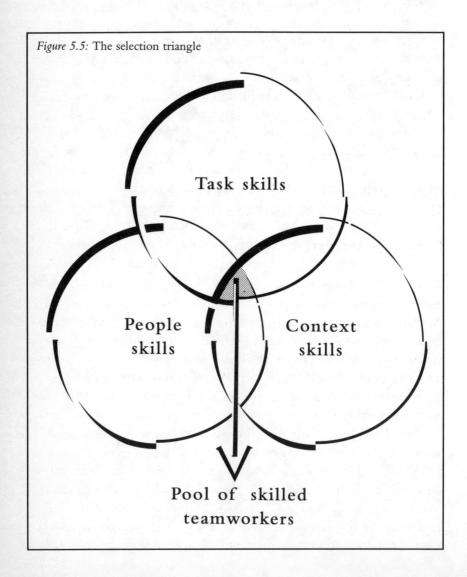

Figure 5.5: The selection triangle

In making the selection decision it is those candidates who demonstrate skills in each of the three sectors that are going to succeed, i.e. those who fall into the shaded triangle at the centre of the circles.

In summary the three areas of skills the selector needs to select against in bringing a team together are:

Task skills: defined by breaking the goal down into those activities the team members will have to achieve. From this the selector can derive a list of task skills.

People skills: split into:

- Building relationships with others.
- Confronting and handling conflict.
- Taking the task forward.

Context skills: the broader environment in which the team operates. This is where political, strategic and intuitive skills are vital.

Lifespan of the Team

As we saw in Chapter 1, teams can be temporary or permanent. A team's lifespan often depends upon the nature of its task. The Portland Holidays development team was a temporary team formed to create the basis of a future organisation. The Body Shop Oxford Street experiment put together a team to stay together, a permanent team. In both of these cases careful attention needed to be paid to the composition of the team. Technical knowledge and expertise was only the starting point; of crucial importance was the 'people mix'.

The Body Shop was determined to bring together a team of 'teamplayers' – individuals who felt comfortable accepting responsibility and taking initiative but were equally at ease following someone else's lead. To allow these attributes to emerge it was careful not to design too formal a selection procedure. This adherence to the importance of flexibility has continued into the team training and development. When bringing together a temporary team it is equally important to be aware of the process of teamworking.

Selectors sometimes make the mistake of not investing enough time in carefully choosing the team members. The assumption is that they will not be together long, so the importance of 'getting on' is less. In some ways the opposite is true. Temporary teams need to be motivated to make the effort to bring out the potential of the team just as, if not more, quickly as a team that is to stay together. A team that represents a poor mix of personality and working style is unlikely to produce the quality of solutions and outcome today's organisations require.

The selection process and the time taken to define the skills and traits of potential team members should be as comprehensive an exercise for temporary as for permanent teams.

SELECTION, NOMINATION OR VOLUNTEERING?

In most organisations the team members are chosen by the team leader or the sponsor. Because of this we have concentrated on the process by which the team leader can best identify potential team members. The benefits of spending time and energy in ensuring the best team is drawn together is well rewarded, as it minimises the likelihood of future problems because of an unsatisfactory mix of personality and work styles.

At Digital, where teamworking is part of the fabric of the organisation, individuals choose to join teams, they volunteer. Teams at Digital emerge and evolve in an almost organic way.

The norm is for teams to emerge informally. They are constantly changing, with some people closely aligned while others move in and out as their input or expertise is needed. Team membership is determined by the purpose, goal and other communications of individual members.

The teams are purpose-driven and they form because a group of people have a common purpose, interest or enthusiasm. This is mirrored at Federal Express, where teams are usually made up of a group of volunteers who may be 'equally frustrated with the same problem'. In addition to this core team, anyone can be asked to join a team to help it with its purpose. Federal Express sees the benefits of this approach as not only generating better quality solutions for the customers, but also helping to develop 'positive skills in their people to help them become better managers'.

All the members of Federal Express are seen to work as a team, even though they are split up into specialisms. 'Everyone is a team member, you go where you are needed and are freed up to participate.' Whether a person decides to join a team is an issue of judgement and priority for that individual.

Only Team Workers Can Join the Organisation

In companies where teamworking is an embedded part of the culture the teamworking selection criteria are addressed at the point of entry into the organisation. Once through the door it is assumed you have the kind of personality and approach that makes teamworking feel comfortable.

Digital introduces the concept of teamworking as part of its induction programme. Owing to the persuasive nature of teamwork at Digital, people build an understanding of what is required of them very early on. 'If they do not hold with this approach to working they would probably choose to leave the organisation.'

In organisations where teamworking is the norm, there is a larger pool of potential team members who have the skills that enable them to move from one team to another and to do so through their own choice. For those organisations that are introducing teamwork there is a need to select team members carefully and offer to augment their personal attributes with training in the skill of teamworking.

THE X FACTOR

In this chapter we have advocated a systematic approach to the definition of team skills and the mechanisms through which potential team members are identified. To leave the reader here would negate the importance of another personal attribute central to successful teamworking – 'the X factor'. This phrase was coined in a film of the 1950s. The scenario was a group of young successful executives going for the role of General Manager in a large US Corporation. As part of the rather protracted selection process, the Chief Executive Officer asked the three candidates what they thought made the difference between a mediocre and a great General Manager. One candidate hesitated in his reply and when it came it was short and mysterious. 'I don't know what it is, it's unexplainable, it's the certain something that sets them above others, makes them stand out'.

On being pressed to give more detail by the CEO the executive closed by saying 'I don't know if you have it, but if you have, you will know which of us has it'. A risky response from the ambitious young executive to the wise old CEO. Needless to say, in best Hollywood tradition he got the job.

Digital understand the importance of this ingredient in teamworking. It is described as that element in team members that enables them to 'champion' the cause, to act as 'catalysts' and push change forward. Team members are mobilised through a vision they can relate to and that they feel they can add to.

Achieving the Impossible

In one organisation, at the end of a management training programme, delegates were set the challenge of a project. One delegate decided to work on the issue of piston design and production. This process currently took 24 months and he could see there was competitive advantage to be gained by reducing this timescale. He set himself the target of creating a process through which a piston could be designed and produced in 24 weeks!

In gathering his team he approached a range of colleagues and contacts. Having outlined the nature of the task he asked each of them one question 'Do you believe it can be done'. If the response was no, or maybe, he walked away. His single selection criterion had not been met. He would only invite people to join the team who were positive about the project.

In six months the team put together a system that indeed took the development process from 24 months to 22 weeks.

The X factor in this instance was belief in the seemingly impossible and the shared drive and commitment to make it happen.

Section 3

Developing Teams

6. *Phases of Development: Accelerating the Process*

INTRODUCTION

Having accepted the challenge of a teamworking approach to change and having managed the selection process, the next issue is how to develop a group of individuals into a cohesive and effective working team. The most successful teams do not occur by magic. Interventions must be made to realise the full potential available from the team approach.

This chapter describes the various phases that teams go through in their development. Then, based on research among a variety of successful teams, it examines four key elements that have the greatest beneficial impact on team development – **CLARITY, COMMITMENT, COMMUNICATION and CELEBRATION**. These four issues are crucial to healthy team development and productivity. If they are not attended to, a team's propensity for achievement will be severely limited. It is the combination of these four elements which provides the most dynamic results. This chapter aims to emphasise which of the four elements needs to be paid most attention at each stage and to offer ideas on how best to put them into practice.

TEAM PHASES

All teams go through phases of development with varying degrees of speed, ease and success. If they do not work effectively through each phase of development then they risk either returning to an earlier phase or never fully achieving peak performance. This will inhibit their ability to bring about changes and improvements.

Clearly, in an organisational setting where both rapid and long-term productivity are of the essence it is even more critical to manage the development of the team positively.

There are a number of various models available; however we have chosen to break down and describe team development into six phases as follows:

- Getting together.
- Getting on.
- Getting going.
- Getting things done.
- Getting stuck [getting help.]
- Getting out.

Getting Together

At the outset most teams will physically come together for the first time. At this point there is probably a lack of clarity about the purpose of the team. Individuals will be concerned with 'membership' issues. Expectations will vary — expectations about leadership, of oneself, of the other members, of the task. There is likely to be some degree of anxiety and insecurity.

Success in this phase will be found in clear expression of the team's goals and purpose. The team needs direction above all else. The individual members need to be encouraged to start the process of trust and relationship building by voicing their concerns and questions.

The successful outcome from this phase is that each member of the team is clear about the team's purpose and has decided to be included in the team and its task.

There is another issue which needs to be taken into account in this phase. It matters whether the entire team is new or if only one or a few members are new. The issue is about 'grieving' for the past. Team members will need to have the opportunity to adjust to their new position. People bring 'baggage' from their past experience with them and often suffer a sense of bereavement when leaving a familiar work group.

A consultant colleague was facilitating a week-long team building event. She was helping to develop a team of varied professionals (geophysicists, accountants, engineers and so on) into a coaching team to run a corporate training event. They were each putting their professional career on hold for a period. She had a strange feeling about the way the group was 'gelling' — or not, as it seemed! Having given it a great deal of thought, in the end she confronted the group with her concerns. After lengthy debate they were able between them to identify that they had brought a sense of bereavement with them from their previous occupations. They undertook to try and surface the issues and deal with them. It took until the fourth day of the programme before all participants could say that they felt they had 'laid the ghosts of their past'.

Getting On

After the initial 'set-up' phase a team will begin to sort out how it will work together. The politeness and caution typical during the 'Getting Together' phase develop into a more purposeful approach to establishing the ground rules for working together. Having accepted inclusion in the team everyone will feel they have a right to contribute to agreeing working procedures, standards of performance and communication lines. The fragile process of trust building needs to be assisted by clearly defined fall back positions, 'just in case'.

Relationships, roles and responsibilities will begin to clarify. People will begin to get a sense of their position in, and value to, the team.

Getting Going

At some point fairly early on in the development of the team they need to really roll their sleeves up and thrash things out together. Although it appeared that everyone agreed and contributed to the setting up of task and team 'rules and regulations' they will now be railed against. If there is a leader, he/she can expect to be challenged on his/her role as can each member of the team.

It is in this phase that the last vestiges of politeness and caution associated with the two start-up phases must be shed. This will be a period of challenge and conflict. Who can do what? Who will do what? How? How well? Who says so? What happens if they don't?

Alliances will be set up and fall down again. Individuals may well flout the previously agreed procedures. Uncomfortable though this phase may be, it is imperative for the future success of the team that members can see and believe that it is possible to live through this experience. It is like the domestic strife that families know to be part of the fabric that bonds them together.

After this phase people will settle down and realise that it is OK to flex their muscles and that they do not have to be on their best behaviour all the time; that it really is acceptable to contribute openly and honestly without risk to their position in the team.

If this phase is not gone through it is likely that the team will become stilted; one where people dare not jeopardise their feelings and 'reputation'. This leaves little hope of them working effectively together in the next phase.

Getting Things Done

Phase Four is where all the niggles have been worked out between the team. They are clear on their purpose, task(s), roles, responsibilities and relationships. They have methods for dealing with problems. Members will work alone, in splinter groups or all together. They trust one another and value each other's contribution. Achievement leads to good feelings, which generates more motivation – the commitment/achievement/commitment spiral mentioned in Chapter 1. The team can go from strength to strength and will be recognised for its accomplishments.

Getting Stuck

At any time there is the risk of the team development being arrested. It can come about for a variety of reasons. (See Section 4 on Troubleshooting.) It may be that the team has moved quickly through the phases but not thoroughly enough. In this case old issues may arise. Internal relationship conflict may be the problem or it may be that external influences and pressures (either personal or organisational) are affecting the smooth working. Perhaps the task is the sticking point and because the team feels unable to move on team development and relationships suffer.

What if there has been a major task accomplishment? The team needs to review and reassess its purpose and membership.

Getting Help

The group might be able to resolve its own sticking points. Often, though, an intervention from an external source will be the most profitable route. Chief among the reasons for this being a better option is the likelihood that an 'outsider' will view the overall situation with a more objective and less biased eye. He or she will be able to put all the issues into perspective more easily without being as emotionally attached as team members are likely to be.

Getting Out

At some point the team's natural life will come to an end. Clearly, a team set up as a limited-life team is likely to be more aware of this and will be better placed to anticipate and deal with the situation when it arises. Other teams may reach this phase for reasons other than that their planned life is at an end. Either the task is complete; the world has moved on and the team's purpose no longer exists; maybe the energy for the task has diminished within the team; maybe the leader and/or some members are moving on. It is vital that teams recognise when their usefulness is at an end, otherwise they may wallow fruitlessly and detract from any previous good results.

The team needs to work out its next step. Remain together? Regroup? Reform? Refocus? Retire? Abandon?

Another element to consider is how best to integrate new members – this needs careful management whatever phase the team is at, as The Body Shop clearly recognises in its leaderless team experiment.

Ideas on how to facilitate development through each of these stages will be given in the remainder of this chapter.

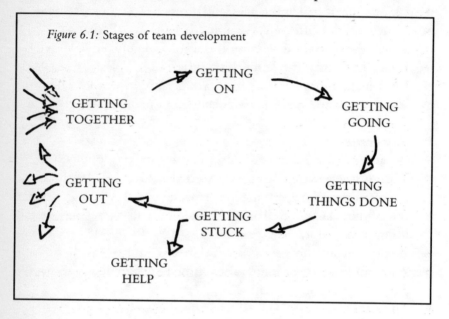

Figure 6.1: Stages of team development

WHAT SUCCESSFUL TEAMS SAY

The following quotes are drawn from research where team members were asked about their experiences of being in good teams that achieved results. Specifically they were asked 'What was it that contributed to making the team successful?'. As well as various organisational work teams, the teams included football teams, skirmish teams, amateur dramatics teams, army teams, police teams and tutor teams.

- Clear about what I had to do.
- Knew how important the job was and why.
- Understood my part/responsibility and that of the others.
- It was enjoyable.

- It was something we wanted to do.
- I felt I counted and was valued.
- There was a sense of equality.
- We were treated like humans.
- Everyone was fully involved.
- I knew what was going on.
- I knew what was expected of me.
- I knew what I could expect of the others.
- I knew how to do it – or how to get it done.
- I was confident of my ability to deliver and confident in others.
- I just got a buzz from belonging.
- There was a real feeling of camaraderie and of having 'our own place'.
- The excitement was being a part of it.
- We worked hard and played hard.
- There was an element of rebellion and/or competition; overcoming the odds.
- It was 'our way' – we thumbed our noses at the establishment, we could bend the rules.
- We got on well together – and socialised together.
- The leader was very clear about what he wanted but was never 'bossy'.
- The size was important – it was a manageable number.
- We could and did try new things.
- There was always a challenge – we can do it better.
- We positively enjoyed what we were doing.
- It was a special occasion.
- We were prepared to *try*.
- We were unconstrained by existing rules or culture.
- The rewards were OK.
- There was character – and characters.
- Tenacity and determination.
- We had agreements – like contracts.
- Loyalty.
- Shared values and beliefs.
- Celebrating our successes together.

The themes threaded through these quotes are clear: roles and expectations; understanding; wanting to be involved in doing the job; positive and equal involvement; challenge; excitement; loyalty; belonging and ownership; camaraderie; good leadership; freedom; and enjoyment. We have distilled these into the four key elements, CLARITY, COMMITMENT, COMMUNICATION and CELEBRATION.

Commitment and Clarity in Balance

It is in the very first phases of team development that Clarity and Commitment play their greatest part. It is only by achieving a positive balance between Commitment and Clarity that the team can be set up with any possibility of real achievement. Once each individual is absolutely clear about his/her role and responsibilities and is alight with commitment, the potential for the results of their synergy can be astonishing.

Figure 6.2: Commitment and clarity

VERY COMMITTED

Helpful blundering	The sky's the limit
(*Only Fools & Horses*)	(*Top Gun*)

HAVEN'T THE FOGGIEST ———————————— **CRYSTAL CLEAR**

Lost/no chance	You go your way, I'll go mine.
(*The Dirty Dozen*)	(*A Fistful of Dollars*)

NOT COMMITTED

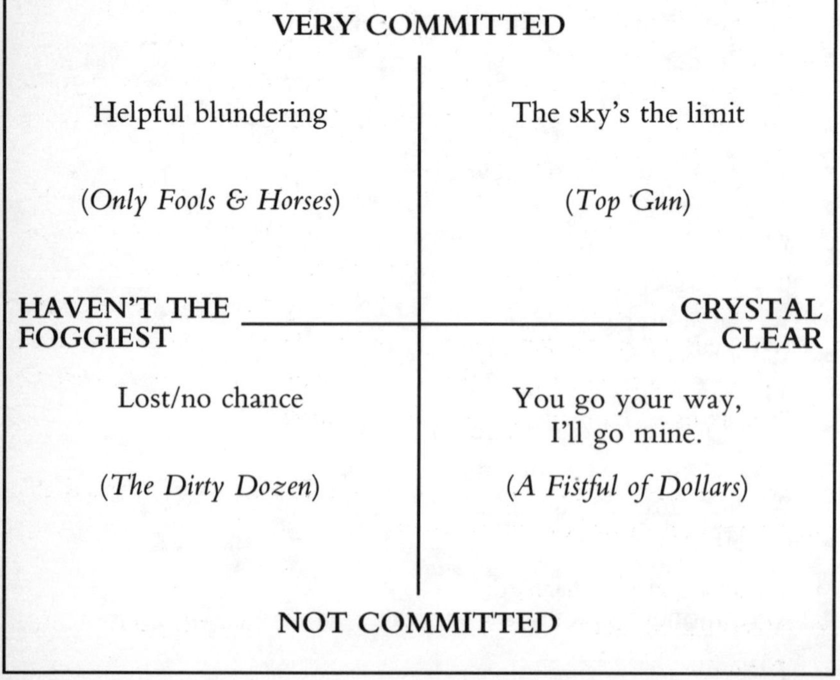

On the other hand if there is total Commitment but the goals/roles are unclear, there is risk of chaos as each individual devotes his/her energies to whatever he/she sees as the most important task or activity but with no common goal or co-ordination of effort. Equally if there is Clarity of task/roles/responsibility and so on but people do not want to be involved then, there is little hope of the team working effectively, especially not together!

Figure 6.2 illustrates the essential relationship of Commitment and Clarity required to take real advantage of the opportunities that teamworking provides to drive change and quality improvement. The titles of contemporary films in brackets aim to demonstrate the 'character' of each quadrant.

> *Wimbledon Football Club made the historic rise from non-league football to the First Division in the space of nine years and won the FA Cup two years later in 1988. It is a story fraught with difficulty and set-backs but has many points that illustrate the importance of Clarity and Commitment.*
>
> *The club underwent a 'commercialisation' programme starting in 1977, got elected to League Division Four and was promoted in its first two league seasons. However, it dropped back down very quickly. There was a financial crisis and a new owner took over. He stated his vision – **'We will be in the First Division in seven years' time'.** They achieved this goal in 1986.*
>
> *Now the vision was* **'We will win the F A Cup in three years'.** *They won it in 1988. (There were those who laughed at this vision and who had a 'sub-vision' simply to stay in the First Division.)*
>
> *They are currently working on* **'Winning the European Cup in five years!'.** *As the first two visions have been so accurately realised, although this is an even tougher one, there are fewer sceptics. Belief in their abilities has grown with each new success.*

So what are the keys to this success? What can be learned that can be applied in organisational teams?

- Clearly stated vision/goal.
- Vision/goal stated with a high degree of enthusiasm, even passion.

- Vision/goal stretching but just about within the bounds of reason!
- Vision/goal relevant to the team.
- Vision/goal exciting and motivating.
- Vision/goal worth going for.
- Purpose is crystal clear.
- Everyone can be involved.
- Vision/goal made public.

Each of the above learning points shows the importance of absolute Clarity and how the starting point for success depends on being able to gain the Commitment of all team members.

Additionally, what is not explicit above but which is apparent on further investigation and demonstrates the absolute commitment from the owner is that:

- He means what he says! It is not just lip-service. He is prepared to 'put his money where his mouth is' – literally – and 'walk his talk' to coin two currently popular phrases!
- The vision is supported with detailed plans, goals, structures, resources.
- Those needing to implement the vision have the necessary skills, knowledge and qualities to make it happen.
- Individuals are in a position to take decisions and action.

CLARITY

'Everyone is talking about quality and they've split us up into all these teams and seem to expect us to do something about it; but nothing has changed and people are getting really fed up because no one really understands what is going on,' says Dominic. He works for an engineering company that recently embarked on a Total Quality Management programme.

Put yourself in Dominic's position. He has been in his organisation for three and a half years. The company has been doing reasonably well but is competing under the same difficult conditions as any other. It is faced with the challenge to increase productivity and profit while managing with reducing resources. The board has decided to take on a Quality focus. The message has gone out: 'Things are going to change round here. We have a vision of our future and how things need to be. We will work in a more collaborative way. We require greater and more active participation from every employee. The new challenges will be exciting and stimulating. We will all benefit from the potential rewards.'

Dominic's anguished comment may be alarming but unfortunately not unusual. It is heard in many organisations that are ostensibly doing all they can to improve the quality of their output. If they have thought about their workforce at all it is likely that they feel they have communicated their intentions to the workforce and encouraged them to be involved. Dominic's quote makes it apparent that there is a major ingredient missing. Clarity.

In the list of quotes from members of 'good' teams earlier in this chapter it is noticeable how many references there are to Clarity as a key part of the success of the team, such as 'Clear about what I had to do'; 'Knew how important the job was and why'; 'Understood my part/responsibility and that of the others'; and so on.

Where companies are undergoing major changes it is especially important that teams have a focus so that they can find a way forward despite organisational insecurity and instability. It will be helpful to know of those things that will not change as well as those that will. This more immediate understanding will enable them to see where they fit in and how their contribution counts.

There are also the important issues of people's ability to live with ambiguity, their emotional responses and the debilitating effects of stress, that make it worth the while of any manager to ensure that his/her people have as much Clarity in their work as is feasible.

Clarity has an implication of simplicity. What is frequently the case in organisational change is that the complexity of the transition itself is communicated in complex language that a fair proportion of the workforce finds difficult to understand and accept. Strategic 'business speak' often needs a translation into 'what this means for you is . . .' in simple language that is relevant to the recipient.

Clarity is difficult. Getting simplicity is difficult. Clarity and simplicity are often mistaken for stupidity and banality. There is a fear that because things may appear easier if written clearly and simply, they risk being seen as lacking in business 'weight' and 'depth'. There is a tendency to beef things up with jargon and business-ese, which unfortunately can cloud the real messages.

In our experience the messages can change daily. This is no reason not to have a clear message each day.

Clarity involves the skill of taking information from a variety of sources and making it appropriate, relevant and usable to the team. It is not just passing on messages.

BAA intended that information given to the top 10 executives in weekly meetings should be cascaded down through all levels. It was found that only three levels down people were recounting the exact wording of the message without modifying it to reflect different work environments. BAA realised that any change message has to be communicated in a style applicable to the person being communicated to and to their specific responsibility and aspirations. Otherwise staff 'hear' the message but are given no direction as to how to achieve it. What is then missing are the tools for the team!

Clarity has such a major effect in so many areas that it is broken down here into three categories. If team leaders and/or members are lacking clarity in any of these areas, organisations run the risk of not maximising the opportunities available from successful change through teamworking. The three categories are Context, Task and People. In Chapter 4 they are explained as sensitivity to operative environment, the job and relating to other people respectively.

First then a brief explanation of what we mean by **Context, Task and People** in relation to Clarity.

Context: We have heard people talk cynically about corporate 'buzz words' such as 'the big picture' and 'global overview'. This, in our experience, is most likely due to over- and mis-use of such phrases; for example when they are used in such a way as to baffle or overawe as in 'I can see that this may seem incomprehensible to you now, that is because you do not have the global overview'. What we are suggesting is that explanations of why changes, improvements, restructurings etc. are necessary and must cover global, political, social, industry-wide, organisational and strategic reasons and angles. The long-term and large-scale risks and benefits must be made clear.

Task: This is perhaps the easiest of the three. What is the 'job' that needs doing? Task is setting the performance parameters and standards. This is definition of the more tangible and measureable outputs. It is not a blow by blow account of how the job will be done

People: The people part is about members knowing their role and responsibility in the team, knowing what to expect of others and what is expected of them. It is the relationship/emotional part of the equation. Looking at the comments from successful teams it is interesting to note how many of them contain 'feeling' words. Historically this is the factor that has received least attention in organisational teamworking. It is our belief, therefore, that this is the area where there are the greatest opportunities to be gained.

The next section of this chapter is given over to exploring these categories further, establishing the critical nature of each and explaining ways of achieving them.

CONTEXT

For the individual to be able to put his/her role and contribution in perspective he/she needs to know the broader context. This includes a bold declaration and clear explanation of the corporate vision/mission/goals and strategic philosophy. Thinking back to Dominic, he is likely to be wondering: 'What is happening? Why is it happening and what has it got to do with me?'

In a number of organisations it would be true to say that there is no clearly defined philosophy or goals. In this case the team will need to take responsibility for establishing as much Clarity as it can for itself. Not being directed from above is not an excuse for having no Clarity within the team of the context within which it is working. The team as a whole and/or its leader has a responsibility to fight continually for Clarity from the sponsor. If this does not happen then the likelihood is that results will not match expectations. As a last resort, if the team wishes for any sense of accomplishment even on its own terms, it will need to clarify for itself, as far as it can without organisational guidance, what is the context within which it must function.

Example 1: In the 1980s British Airways had very clearly defined its mission and goals and run a company wide Customer First Campaign, which set out to re-educate all its staff to adopt a customer-oriented approach to their work, no matter in which area they worked. Following this BA set up 'Customer First Teams' in various departments. Their brief was to identify ways in which Customer Service could be improved in their area. Specific improvements were recommended and implemented which did make a significant difference. For example, wheelchair facilities and arrangements in the terminals were improved; assistance to special needs passengers was improved in the form of 'care cards' which outlined specific help offered in a variety of foreign languages.

Example 2: Recently a departmental manager from another organisation said that he felt there was merit in the idea of a teamworking approach to quality improvement and had decided to put it into practice. He got together a group of employees and told them that they had a blank sheet of paper to come up with any quality improvements they could think of and that he would consider implementing any that he felt worthwhile. They went to their task with great gusto. In his own words the results of their efforts were 'like a trade union negotiation shopping list'. All of their ideas were to do with employee benefits and welfare. None had specific or direct impact on corporate quality improvement. He was in a very difficult position because he now had to return to his Quality Improvement Team and tell them that none of their ideas were acceptable. This was likely to increase their levels of dissatisfaction.

Clarity of context is vital because it helps allay people's natural concerns about change. If they can see better where they fit in to the strategic and operational whole it is easier for them to understand and accept the change challenge more easily. It helps teams see other viewpoints and share a sense of common purpose and belonging to the change. Once a team is aligned behind the corporate goal, creative energy can be focused on achievement.

Context information which will help:

- Industry wide and competitor information.
- Statement of corporate strategy and goals.
- Explanation of how the organisation arrived at its strategy and goals.
- What changes can be expected.
- What will remain the same.
- Where the team fits in relation to the new structure.
- Continuous repetition and updating.

Change of Organisational Structure

The move to a teamworking model from a traditional corporate structure can create enormous uncertainty and discomfort. This change will have a far more significant impact on the daily life of each employee as it asks for a fundamental change in the way people go about their work. It completely alters the company that they were employed by and as such may cause the sensation of now being a square peg in a round hole where once they fitted reasonably comfortably. It requires a more active role to be played by everyone. If people clearly understand what is behind the change it is much more likely that they will be able to make the transition smoothly and more quickly make a positive and useful contribution in the new structure. In this situation if people are really not clear about what is happening and why, the risk is that at best that they move too slowly for the good of the organisation's intentions and at worst (and highly likely) they will find ways to actively sabotage the change and the teamworking processes.

Special Task Force or Project Team

Where the change is less drastic but a special limited life team has been put together the need for clarity of context is still pivotal for results. Without a clear understanding of the corporate or departmental requirements of the team it stands less chance of producing positive outcomes. One of the main risks is that team members will work away at the task but without being able accurately to truly reflect the wider needs of the organisation. They will be unknowing of the impact and implications of their actions until perhaps it is too late.

Functional Team

Even if the type of team is simply the departmental team, how can it, with the best will in the world, be aligned with the organisation if it has no background information or frame of reference to explain the need for, and meaning of, the change?

> Recently we were consulting with a manager in an organisation moving rapidly to a more customer-focused approach (internally and externally) who spoke contemptuously of the staff in a technical support area who 'had no concept of the significance of the changes going on in the rest of the organisation. They are getting on with things the way they always have done. Even those who have understood the need for change have no idea how to go about implementation.' On further discussion it was clear that no one had advised the support staff of the background to change or explained the relevance of it to them in their area. On speaking to them it became apparent that they were quite prepared to accept the challenge of the changes, despite not totally understanding the need for them. They were deeply concerned that they might get left behind, because they suspected that they were ill-equipped to work in the new ways. They were very keen to get re-skilled and to become more customer orientated, although rather nervous about what it might mean to them in practice

TASK

Once people are aware of the context of change within the organisation they have a better chance of understanding the purpose of the team and more readily identify and accept tasks that need to be achieved.

There are three ways in which a task can be defined.

A) Badly.
B) Absolutely clearly with no room for manoeuvre.
C) Clearly but with freedom for interpretation and initiative.

Example A. A team in a medium-sized UK organisation was given this briefing from the board via their boss: 'We want you to find a way to communicate our new corporate strategy to the rest of the organisation.' They went away and researched, planned and put together arrangements for a superb 'lights, laser and dry ice' show in a glitzy auditorium for all the staff, in two sittings, with a professional compère. It involved the members of the board being on stage and taking part in two-way communication with staff members. It would be challenging, exciting – and high risk. The team reported back to their boss who reported back to the board. They loved the idea of a big glitzy show. One problem was that the plan was well in excess of budget. The second was that very few of the board members were prepared to put themselves in such an exposed position. The plan was vetoed and a 'talking-heads' video produced – by a different team.

Example B. The briefing could have been: 'We want to communicate our new corporate strategy to the rest of the workforce. We want to make a 20-minute professionally produced video where the Chairman and each member of the board has the opportunity to contribute. We would like help with scripting it. The budget will be £25,000.'

This describes absolutely what needs doing. It provides the team only with a research task. The decision has been taken. The team simply has to make it happen.

Example C. Alternatively: 'We want to communicate our new strategy to the entire workforce. We would like you as a team to investigate the various options and come up with at least four for us to choose from. Please cost each option and give pros and cons for each and make recommendations.' While still clear, this variation provides greater opportunity for challenge, initiative and creativity.

Clarity of task does not mean then that every single detail of the job to be done has been described and that the team simply has to carry out the instructions. This clearly does not make best use of the synergistic potential of the team and the same results could be achieved by a group of capable individuals.

Clarity of task means letting people know the parameters of the job at hand. It provides them with a picture of what the end result would look like. The clearer this picture, the less work needs to be done later on putting things back on track or chasing to re-establish clarity. This is because energies can all be directed at the correct focal point from the outset.

Clarity in the first place helps deliver on the second imperative of change – speed. It is also in support of the quality maxim: right on time, first time, every time.

The information the team requires includes:

- What needs to be achieved.
- By when.
- To what standard.
- Who is the sponsor/customer.
- The limits of responsibility.
- Budget available.
- Other resources available.
- How will success be measured.

The method chosen to clarify the task will depend on the maturity of the team. At the 'Getting Together' phase clarity of context and task are the two most essential components. Without them the new team is doomed to a very difficult time and little likelihood of travelling successfully through the other phases of development. Do they need telling, having both the what and the how explained, and then galvanising into action? Do they need to be involved in the clarification process? Do they just need a nudge to be set off and running? Are they clued up enough to be able to get on with it by themselves? The Situational Leadership model referred to in Chapter 3 is particularly relevant to the leader in developing his/her team.

PEOPLE

For members to be enough at ease to be able to focus on the task they need to have certain ground rules established. This is the stage of development where the team moves on from Getting Together to Getting On. The team can make a fair attempt at the task without the 'people' issues being dealt with but evidence suggests that they are likely to be significantly less effective. The 'people' issues that are fundamental to teamworking success are:

- Why was I chosen for this team?
- What particular part do I play?
- Am I capable of this?
- What are the rules governing behaviour?
- What do people expect of me?
- What can I expect from other members?
- Is there an official leader?
- What are the values of this team? ie, what do we believe in?
- Where can I go for help/support?

The aim in achieving clarity here is to establish the roles, responsibilities, talents, relationships and so on, so that there is a balanced focus on both the task and the way in which it is achieved by the individuals that make up the team. If members do not feel valued, if they have low self-esteem or low opinions of colleagues or lack of trust it makes the accomplishment of the task almost impossible. None of the six imperatives for change can easily be met if the 'people' part of the Clarity equation is not balanced.

Equally, if individuals are not qualified, able or willing to contribute, it is better to discover this at this point rather than have them hold up the development of the team. BAe Hatfield was conscious of this when implementing its Quality Improvement Programme. It chose to make sure that everyone was absolutely clear about and capable of doing what was required. Every shop floor operator received quality training, skills training and cellular team training. The philosophy behind this was to give people the means of achieving results and to secure commitment. 'We're not going to send anyone naked into the world, we're going to give them the tools to do the job and support them.'

The environment needs to be fertile for teams to make optimum contribution. Research among successful teams found that there is often an intrinsic pleasure in belonging to the team which spins off into improved results. Part of this pleasure derives from common goals, common understanding, common agreements on how issues are dealt with and faith in the 'system' of the team. Clarity can provide the 'bump-start' to achieving this pleasure.

Although it is necessary at every stage it is at the Getting Together first phase of development that the team will have the strongest requirement for CLARITY.

AGREEMENTS

Example: A training manager with responsibility for more than 40 instructors made it part of the way things were done that they made team 'contracts'. The instructors spent half their working time in the training situation and the other half in operations. In training they usually formed teams of three. It was rare for them to work with the same tutor team and even rarer to work together in their operational capacity. This meant that each time a tutor team came together they were virtual strangers. They had to work together for a period of up to eight weeks, training an intake of 15 new personnel. The tutor teams had to take on almost total responsibility for the entire preparation, delivery and marking of the pass/fail course, including the welfare of the trainees. Before each programme the team and the manager would talk through the contract and at the end it would be reviewed.

The benefit of taking such a mechanistic approach was that the tutor team had a framework to use to manage itself as there was no team leader as such. It freed up the manager from having to be the team leader day by day. The tutor team developed its ability to take personal accountability, to work effectively in a team and to resolve conflict. Equally, because the team had to design and agree to its own contract members were more committed to its contents than if there was a 'blanket' agreement laid down by the manager that all teams had to adhere to.

The management team in this case had also agreed a 'team statement', which was a point of reference for dealing with any issues that arose. The managment team included on theirs things such as a commitment to a team meeting each week at a certain time; an individual meeting with the senior manager to review progress; not to feed back anything to a third party if unprepared to say it to the subject of the feedback. The item that they committed most readily to was 'having fun is a legitimate indicator of our success'. The team was viewed as highly successful within the organisation; its members took great pleasure in it and there was no lack of candidates for any tutor vacancies.

Below are items tutors included in their contracts:

- Start and finish times.
- Timing and length of breaks.
- Punctuality rules.
- Who does which sessions.
- Allocation of various administrative roles.
- Dress code.
- Smoking/no smoking – where and when.
- Room tidiness – who and when.
- Confidentiality – what it means.
- Honesty and sensitivity.
- Feedback – who, when, how much, style, any specific things you want watched and reported back on.
- Commitment to daily/weekly review.
- Time to let off steam, i.e. 15-minute 'chunter' session at the end of each day where whinges, gripes and entertaining anecdotes can be aired with no judgement or retribution.

- Sitting in on each other's sessions or not.
- Support to each other, i.e. not interrupting in class; not disagreeing with each other's content; showing good listening skills; helping set up and break down training room and equipment; getting tea/coffee for whoever is working up to breaks.

The contracts included really tangible, measurable items and some which were much more 'soft' and intangible. Each of them was relevant to the team and served its purpose in terms of clarifying the way things would be done and who would do what.

We have heard criticism of such formal ways of creating Clarity, perhaps because it can feel uncomfortable and forced. It is our experience, however, that those teams who have tackled this in the early phases of team development suffer much less discomfort and cost at later stages in terms of time, money, energy, emotion and mistake rectification.

BAe Hatfield saw the value of such team agreements/statements when it was implementing its Quality Improvement Programme. Each team was invited to demonstrate its commitment by deciding on a policy statement as a set of common definitions or a framework for all to work with.

COMMITMENT

Commitment is the second part of the balancing act that starts off the team at the Getting On phase. In order to have a 'Top Gun' type team, every member needs to be dedicated to:

- The organisation.
- The team.
- The task.
- Other members.

Only with Commitment can the full benefits of the multiplication of all individuals' energies be realised. Talents and skills will be wasted to the team if any individual lacks Commitment. If some members do not share the team's enthusiasm this can set up difficulties in terms of problem relationships and dynamics. Focus will be diverted away from the main purpose of the team, i.e. the task, towards the way the team is getting along together. Inevitably in later phases of development even more effort will need to be expended on putting things to rights. The committed team will move more quickly through the phases of development to Getting Things Done and will be in a better position actually to get things done when it is in that phase, if attention has been paid to getting full Commitment at the outset. A reminder is useful here that mechanical means need to be applied to get the team working together on Commitment issues. It is not the norm that people will think 'Oh goody! An opportunity to be involved in a change initiative. How can I get involved? I feel so committed to this!' At least it is not the norm in the collective experience of the authors!

Nor in the experience of Lisa Feddon at the BAA.

An effective team will always have a good team spirit, with individual members being prepared to contribute but listen to others also.

Total team commitment happened quite slowly, primarily because this was a new experience. By week three or four the core team could see a clearer picture and enthusiasm was high, by week 12 we could see dramatic improvements.

For the core team, there was clear enthusiasm and commitment to the change and thus improvement to the service. There was at times some degree of dissonance between the core team over the new work procedures laid out and those putting them into practice. The core team's commitment was not always mirrored in the rest of the staff.

If they have a high degree of Clarity of Context and Task, and People issues have had some input, team members are likely to be better placed to become Committed. There is, however, more that can be done.

There are three main themes which will help individuals 'buy in' to membership of a team:

- Ownership.
- Active role.
- Recognition for contribution.

OWNERSHIP

'*They felt they owned it, that was the trick, it was for them to own it rather than us to impose it*'. BAe Hatfield manager about the project to redesign the shop floor layout.

Ownership builds on from Clarity and adds an emotional dimension. This is about bonds that tie members together. It is when the vision or goals become a joint dream. It is when members are protective of their goals, tasks and fellow members – out of pride and a sense of family rather than any 'cover your back' motivation.

Create a Team Identity

- Give it a name.
- Use the word 'we' a lot.
- Design a logo.
- Have a uniform.
- Have team badges.
- Have initiation rites.

> **Example:** *A golfing colleague tells the tale of his experiences in the county golf league. He is a talented amateur player who frequently wins individual tournaments. He had entered a team event with some of his regular golfing partners. They cruised through the early rounds of the tournament. On the day of the final shortly before the start time he was sitting in the lounge reading the newspaper. He knew that one of his team was in the bar having a drink and the third had not yet turned up. This was not unusual so he was unconcerned. He had seen the opposition arrive much earlier.*
>
> *All the visiting players were dressed smartly in matching 'strip'. They had with them a non-playing team member who did all their organising and administration, such as taking care of travel arrange-*

ments. They had gone out to take the opportunity to have a warm up and were now having a last-minute team talk.

Our colleague remained unperturbed because he knew that his team had the combined skills to take the trophy easily.

The third member of the home team arrived just in time to make a punctual start and play commenced.

Unfortunately the visitors won the competition. The losers put their defeat down to the other team's real team spirit and will to win. Their commitment in the form of a team identity had, in some magical way, multiplied their golfing skills.

INVOLVEMENT

- Get everyone working on design of vision/values/goals/tasks/ ground rules/team behaviours.
- Disallow inertia.
- Ensure everyone has a say at every meeting.
- Have each member be 'chairman' in rotation.
- Distribute responsibility.
- Make people accountable for their own results.
- Challenge people to improve on their last effort/output.
- Encourage members to think for themselves.
- Let them ignore official rules.

Example: A Metropolitan Police Chief Superintendent inherited a perennial problem with prostitution in his new area. Many attempts had been made to clear the streets but to date all had failed. A particular difficulty was that the prostitutes knew the shift patterns of the vice officers; they chose to do business between 0300 – 0500 hours on Sundays because the Federation Rules prevented the officers working after 0200 hours on Sundays. It had become an unpopular duty to undertake because the officers knew there was little likelihood of a successful outcome. The new Chief Superintendent told one sergeant that he had six weeks to solve the problem. He handed over responsibility to him totally. He said that he could pick his own team and that they could work any hours they chose. He could manage the resources and rostering as he saw fit. The objective was to arrest and displace the prostitutes.

The chosen team cancelled their days off, by-passed the regulations on duty times and worked totally unsocial hours. This confused the prostitutes, obtained record arrests and the streets were cleared as the offenders moved to other areas!

The officers involved were thrilled with their success. The project was given a break for a month and then another team took it on; and so it went on. Each team became more creative in the solutions it sought.

The posting became a popular one and teams would clamour to have a chance to see if they could improve on previous results.

The Chief Superintendent puts the success of this operation down to the opportunity for freedom and the ability to make their own decisions. The teams felt that they owned the problem and the solution was in their own hands. They enjoyed the autonomy and the challenge.

There was also a very clear, if unofficial, contract between the Chief Superintendent and his team that the team was safe if things did not work out because the ultimate responsibility for the decision to 'go native' lay with the Chief Superintendent.

ACTIVE ROLE

It is crucial that every member has a real part to play. The more real their responsibility the more the chance of them committing to the purpose of the team. Feeling surplus to requirements is the enemy of Commitment and high energy contribution. Even where members clearly understand the need to contribute actively and are highly motivated it can still be difficult to get them all taking responsibility for their own actions. Active role has to mean personal autonomy and accountability.

Example: BAe Hatfield, in implementing its Quality Improvement Programme, encouraged people to take their own initiative, to put forward their own ideas and to play a responsible role in quality inspection. The idea was to develop a climate of creativity, giving responsibility to each employee. This was at times difficult in the workshops where old company culture remained strong and resistant. In the past employees leaned on management to fix the problems. The new culture is about getting those people who are actually doing the job and who really are the experts to solve the problems. By applying teamworking, this enabled the teams to deal with their own problems instead. 'Experts aren't always at the top, often they are at the bottom and identify the problem in the first place'. The philosophy was to empower the teams and give them the expertise to sort out the problem themselves – the long-term aim to reduce the layers of management.

In the early phases of team development when Clarity and Commitment are the key elements, it is self-evident that each member will have a personal need to take on a particular function, both in relation to the task and within the team relationships.

RECOGNITION FOR CONTRIBUTION

In Chapter 4 we talked about how to select team members. If a person has been selected to belong to a team because they bring a special dimension to the team, they will obviously want to feel that they are a valuable part of it. Not only does each person have to have a real part to play in the team's efforts but they need to be recognised for their contribution.

An essential point is that recognition needs to take account of all different types of contribution. To use a football example, if there were to be a 'Man of the Match' award – could it only be presented to the player who scored most goals or to the person who made most contact with the ball? We believe that there must be the possibility for support players to be recognised too. In organisational teams there are often low key players who contribute as much as the high profile members. Without their contribution it would often be that the key players would be unable to operate to such a high level.

Example: A manager in a recently set up, small, autonomous but wholly owned subsidiary that had done phenomenally well in the early stages of operation felt his team were deserving of recognition beyond his personal remit. The recognition system of the parent company was thrust upon him, but the rewards (gifts from a published catalogue) were not welcomed by his team members. There was no match between the style of the reward and reward system to the recipients and their culture. In fact the rewards were worse than being unwelcome, held in contempt by the 'new' team.

TIPS ON HOW TO GAIN COMMITMENT IN A TEAM

To gain Commitment from a team *requires* Commitment. Whatever a leader asks from each member he/she has to be prepared to give. A role model is required, a demonstration of Commitment – to the organisation, the team, the task and each individual. So the leader must: to receive trust, give trust; to receive respect, give it; to obtain information, give information and so on.

Team members have identified the following as some of the things that have helped in the rapid and healthy development of effective teams:

- An initial team building event.
- Initial and ongoing individual meetings with each member.
- Members being invited to give their understanding of goals/ purpose as they see them.
- Leaders who listen to teams' views.
- Leaders who are an integral part of the team.
- Opportunities for personal development.
- Members take on tasks that they prefer, as far as possible.
- Understanding that they may also have to undertake less desirable tasks.
- Leader is available for members.
- Members (and leader) show a genuine interest in each other.
- Concern for personal welfare.
- Encouragement and support of efforts.
- Toughness if necessary, for example, making it clear that team membership depends on commitment.
- Appropriate openness and honesty.
- Information being shared as widely as it can be.
- Team successes (both whole and individual) are promoted

outside the team, for example to peers, bosses and other areas.
- Promotion of the idea of continuous improvement/change as a constant journey rather than the achievement of a single goal.
- The team talks openly about the process of change.
- Enjoyment is an accepted and explicit part of the team culture.

TEAM DEVELOPMENT EVENTS

If a team is a permanent-life team, then considerable time and energy can be devoted to its long-term development over an extended time period. If the team is a temporary team there will be an urgent need for shorter-term, more intensive team development or building. A team development session can rapidly accelerate the processes of establishing relationships and team spirit, while a team left to its own devices will take much longer to develop into a cohesive and productive unit.

There is obviously an optimum balance between the resources (in particular time) available, the proposed duration of the project, the sharpness of the focus of the team, the clarity and complexity of the task and the maturity of the team members. We would recommend that it is always worthwhile investing a planned amount of time and energy in some activity to obtain commitment early in the development of a team.

Options for Running a Team-building Event.

- On home ground with just the team present.
- On home ground facilitated by a third party.
- Off the patch with or without a facilitator.
- Purely focused on the team and its relationships.
- Structured or unstructured format.
- Two dimensional – using a specific task to work on relationship issues also.
- A tailor-made development programme.
- An off-the-shelf team-building programme designed by experts in the field.
- A one-off event as a 'kick start'.

- An initial event with ongoing developments.
- A structured series of events.
- 'Outward bound' type development programme.

More details about team events are in Chapter 7.

COMMUNICATION

Communication is one of the most frequently quoted reasons for blockages and difficulties in organisations. Often teams will express a measure of satisfaction with the way they communicate internally but extreme dissatisfaction about the cross-team communication. Poor communication causes major operational problems as well as emotional and human resource complications. It is the key to delivery on at least three of the change imperatives – awareness, flexibility and co-ordination in the face of complexity.

Communication quite obviously is about keeping people informed. The greatest value is that it:

- Demonstrates to people that they are important.
- Improves self-esteem and motivation.
- Lowers the risk of confusion.
- Makes the early detection of anomalies and errors possible.
- Prevents action based on assumption.
- Helps avoid suspicion and unhelpful competition.
- Generates interest.
- Maintains momentum of change process.
- Improves commitment.
- Facilitates appropriate allocation of resources and scheduling of activities.
- Increases bottom-line results.

Case Study

Nuclear Electric

Workers at Nuclear Electric plc's Oldbury Power Station illustrated that teamwork pays dividends by saving the company £1.5 million. Their fresh approach to dealing with 'outage' created a new record − finishing 3.5 weeks ahead of target.

Complex in-core repairs and overhauls on the gas circulators, turbine and other plant areas took only 12 weeks. In previous years similar jobs had been, at best, completed a day or two either side of schedule.

Communication was the key to the success story according to shut-down manager Chris Baker.

He recognised that the shut-down was a team effort involving nearly everyone on site and kept staff up-to-date with a weekly newsletter and simple bar charts.

'It was important that everyone knew what we were trying to achieve, how we were trying to do it and what their contribution was', says Baker.

The workforce was split into five groups, clear targets were agreed and the teams were given the responsibility to achieve them.

The newsletter gave the job a high profile and kept everyone informed and involved. There was tremendous team spirit from the start.

Comments Baker: 'Everyone seemed to have a new sense of urgency and competitive edge − no one wanted to let the side down. As I walked around the station everyone was asking how we were doing. I haven't experienced anything like that in the past.'

Even the support services not so intimately involved were caught up in the enthusiasm and responded with more urgency.

Computer-based plans were prepared at each stage so each group knew from day to day exactly what its target was and constant re-appraisals of the programme also helped save valuable time.

Case Study

Attendance levels of the workforce were impressive, indicating very high morale. During the 12 weeks only one of the 20 fitters took any time off and that was only a half day. They worked round the clock and productivity levels were up.

'It was an outstanding achievement. The men did more work in 12 weeks in most plant areas than in 22 weeks in past years. Knowing exactly what had to be done and having to make their own decisions made them much more motivated.'

'In the past each person got on with their job but didn't know where they fitted in the overall theme and had no reason to try to do anything more quickly.'

Fuel route craftsman Adrian Beever confirms that more than ever the workers felt more involved and part of a team effort.

'I've worked here for 11 years and it is the first time we have been allowed to get on with the job without interference. We were told much more about the overall job and there did not seem to be so much paperwork slowing things down. We just pulled our socks up and got on with it. It felt good that we got the job done so quickly and probably for the first time it gave me a sense of satisfaction. I was proud to be part of it.'

End Case Study

Communication Matrix

Attention may be paid to the skills of good communication on an interpersonal level. The complex webs and patterns in an organisation make the matter of communication even more tricky. Who must know what? When? Before whom? Who should tell whom? What is the best way to transmit the information?

BAA found out the reality of the communication situation when it set up a team to improve the security in Terminal One at London Heathrow Airport. The stated goal was 'to make security more customer friendly and to achieve a better working environment for security staff'.

An aspect of the Terminal Security Manager's role was to communicate to staff the whys and the hows of the changes taking place, and to communicate in what ways their jobs might be affected – to allay their fears and insecurities about the future repercussions of the change and secure their commitment for the change to be able to happen. All levels of staff were kept informed as much as possible.

On the 'shop floor', supervisors played their role in communicating to staff and keeping them motivated. These secondary teams were there to assist the core team with information gathering, support, help and advice.

Communication to these secondary teams (those doing the job) was seen as vital. It was acknowledged that the rumour machine moves at twice the speed of anything else. The core team and then the team leaders of the operational teams were there to refute the rumours as quickly as they could; talking to staff as often as possible to get the message across in the correct way.

A series of working lunches with managers and team leaders to explain the vision and their part in the change process were organised; achievement of the goal meant looking at planning and manning of areas of operation.

Another issue arising out of this teamworking experience was due to the make-up of the core team itself. The team was made up of a number of employee 'ranks'. While setting up the team it was seen as most important to have members who had differing job roles to provide the team with a greater abundance of expertise and experiential knowledge, irrespective of job level. Conflict arose when team members of a 'lower level' had to instruct or communicate a task requirement to, say, a Duty Officer, who was of a higher rank. The lesson here was to know who should communicate what to whom – using one team member to research and another more 'appropriate' member to teach and communicate, to keep a sense of balance within the organisation and not upset the existing status quo.

It was also necessary to get the appropriate people on board to communicate the change message to others. There was a great need to take care as to how the message was related, the way information was passed on. 'Use key people to spread the message'. 'Communicators' were chosen who would put the correct message across in a truthful manner to the rest of the working teams.

The matrix includes the following combinations:

- Inside the team
  = whole team
  = necessary members
  = individual to individual.
- Leader to team and vice versa.
- To and from the sponsor.
- To and from the customer.
- To and from other teams.
- Throughout the organisation.
- Outside the organisation.

The Body Shop (as illustrated earlier) with the leaderless team in its Oxford Street store found it had to double its concentration on Communication because everyone had to share responsibility for dealing with problems and therefore being informed was even more important than normal. Without this extra attention to Communication there was a greater risk of buck passing, since there were no ranks or clear reporting lines to fall back on. They are considering undertaking further communications training.

Beware! Almost as much damage can be done by over-communicating attempts. Always ask yourself questions along the following lines:

- Is the transfer of this information necessary?
- Why is this being communicated?
- Who exactly *needs* to know?
- Who would it be helpful/useful to?
- How much needs to go?
- What would be the best format?

- What style is appropriate?
- When is the best time for it?
- Can it be put with other information as a package?
- Can someone be responsible as the communications/liaison person in our team?

There are two sides to the need for Communication, a task/ resources side and a people side. Information is also important about how people are feeling; what help and support or encouragement they need. It is the balance of this Communication that will speed the delivery of results.

Communication is one of the highlighted elements at the Getting Things Done stage of development.

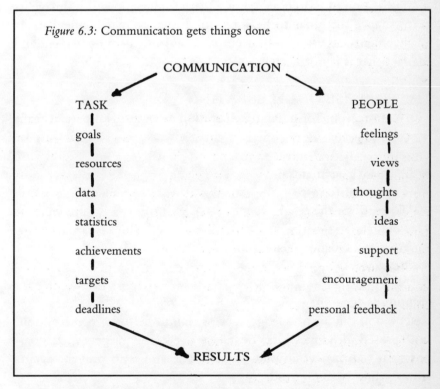

Figure 6.3: Communication gets things done

Teams that have made the investment in good communication have found it pays off. Competition within and between teams has frequently caused ill feeling and failure. Both collaboration and co-operation, in hindsight, are seen to be the foundations of success. Sharing of information widely and freely is essential to the collaboration/co-operation process and helps break down smokestacks and barriers which engender competition.

CELEBRATION

Some people think that Celebration is tantamount to self-congratulation, equatable with smugness, conceit or complacency – each of which would be dangerous in the quest for continuous improvement. Yet consider the danger in *not* being congratulated for endeavours and successes, their risk going unnoticed.

Lack of recognition and reward is known to have adverse effects on motivation of individuals. For a team to develop and improve its performance there has to be some kind of acknowledgement of its achievements, its efforts, its attempts or at least the time it spent and the fact that it is not beaten yet!

THE PURPOSE OF CELEBRATING
The main reasons for having Celebration as an integral part of team development are:

- Acknowledgement.
- Emotional release.
- To reaffirm the team.
- Publicity.
- As a 'punctuation mark'.
- Reward.

Acknowledgement
Celebration can acknowledge success, failure, efforts, contribution, time passed, deadlines met, obstacles overcome, targets met, goalposts moved; in fact anything at all. The aim is to prevent events from sliding by unnoticed.

Public acknowledgement of failure is probably less appropriate. However, if it is accepted that sometimes failure happens then to ignore it totally wastes the opportunity to learn from it. It is healthy to have it acknowledged as having occurred and for members to see that no major harm has befallen the perpetrator(s)!

The idea of celebrating under these circumstances is like having a 'wake' for the failed idea or project that for some reason is destined not to come to fruition.

In most teams, though, it is not realistic to expect constant major successes worth singing and dancing about publicly. However, on long-term projects if there is no element of acknowledgement of endeavour there may be no sense of movement forwards. 'Regular review' is an accepted idea in team development. It misses the element of enjoyment and dynamism that celebration provides. The idea of Celebration can be likened to a ratchet that ensures that things do not slip back.

Emotional release

Celebration serves the purpose of releasing tensions that may have built up during a period of sustained concentration on a task. Rather than individuals taking lone responsibility for dealing with their own stress, Celebration provides a situation for them to talk through their feelings and go through some stress and tension relieving activities. A social Celebration can have healthful benefits.

Reaffirm team

Particularly where individuals have been working on separate tasks the opportunity to get together to Celebrate (whether the focus is on individual or team issues) is important. It is a reminder that they are members of a distinct group and a reaffirmation of team spirit.

Publicity

Clearly if the team has something to shout about and celebrate then there is value in making sure that it is public knowledge. They can take the opportunity to invite others to join in their Celebrations.

Punctuation

A ceremony can mark each stage of development or achievement of a project or a team. Teams coming together can benefit from celebrating their start up. If a team is to be disbanded there are needs of the individual to finish their relationship and membership. Welcome and goodbye ceremonies will help individuals to mark stages in their own development and career. This will enable them to assimilate more rapidly into new teams.

Reward

If the Celebration is sponsored by the leader and/or organisation then it can be seen publicly as a treat or reward for work well done.

On the subject of Celebration, Sir John Egan told us: 'I think looking at next year, we will spend a lot of time telling our staff about the successes that we have had in other parts of the company.'

Examples of teams celebrating

General examples that come most readily to mind are the opening night of a new play at the theatre where everyone gets together to await the results of the critics' reviews. They then have a rousing party if the show is deemed to be a success. Even if the critics have not been kind there is a celebration of sorts – an acknowledgement that they did their best – a commiseration. Imagine if this did not take place and the cast and production team simply went their separate ways. How much more difficult it would be to cope with the criticism and return to work to try again the next day without the support of team mates. Remember how much more exciting it can be to share the joy of success.

Telesales teams practice on-the-job celebration. Each time a member achieves a certain number of calls he/she stands up and shouts it out and their team acknowledges them with a cheer. When a call is converted into an appointment something similar takes place; when a target number of appointments are made individually and collectively then the team stops to celebrate together. In this way they acknowledge the contribution of each member and the collective efforts of the team. Time spent in this way is seen as being as valuable as their task of making sales calls over the phone.

Sports teams also are good Celebrators. Rugby and football teams sing songs in the bath; they adjourn to the bar to drink together and relive the action and share anecdotes. The players in one First Division football team are allowed to 'run amok' when

PHASES OF DEVELOPMENT: ACCELERATING THE PROCESS

they achieve a good result. The key to this celebration is that it is in total contrast to the control and discipline that they must demonstrate while actually playing.

In a training centre where at least one group of 15 new entrant trainees 'passed out' each week it was interesting to observe that although there was an official ceremony organised by the company each group celebrated in its own way by arranging a party, meal or outing of some kind.

Benefits

A quote from the notes from a conference on the Role of Pastoral Councillors in June 1986 at the Diocese Christian Education Centre shows belief in the benefits of Celebration. *'The relationships between members are strengthened through time and attention given to prayerful reflection, socialisation and celebration together.'*

- Increased motivation.
- Refreshed team spirit.
- Alternative method of communication.
- Another shared experience.
- Opportunity to compliment one another/thank one another.

Ways to celebrate

- Publicise your successes.
- Create posters and post them about the workplace.
- Circulate local news sheets advising of progress.
- Have award winners and ceremonies.
- Have wall charts showing levels of performance.
- Declare that celebrating is legitimate.
- Have a team lunch out.
- Create space for celebrations.
- Include celebration in your team agreement.
- Have a weekly celebration spot.
- Hug.
- Get the group together and have them do the 'Ten Ways To . . .' exercise. For example:

- Ten things worth celebrating in this team.
- Ten ways to celebrate in this team.
- Ten reasons to celebrate this week.

'Celebration often means joining with others to share in the delight of a memorable event. We applaud and sing and feast and dance and laugh and cry at rituals that give meaning to our lives.

... A warm embrace is the happiest reward for a special moment and says *I am honoured to be with you and to take part in these festivities. . . Let's celebrate.*'*

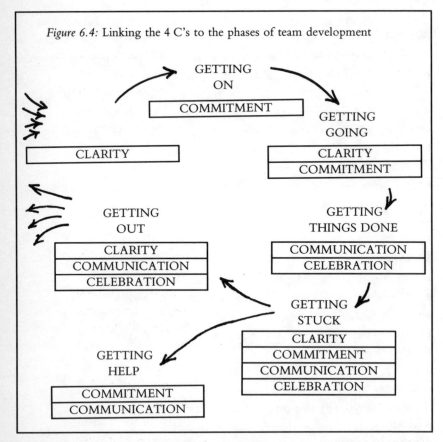

Figure 6.4: Linking the 4 C's to the phases of team development

*From *The Second Little Book of Hugs* (Hug Therapy Z) by Kathleen Keating, drawings by Mimi Noland. Copyright 1987 Kathleen Keating Schloessinger. Published by Collins Angus & Robertson (UK). Excerpted by permission only. *The Little Book of Hugs* is also available from Collins Angus & Robertson.

Linking the Four C's to the Phases of Team Development

Getting Together
Introductions and ice-breakers.
Purpose of the team.
Personal anxieties and insecur-
ities.
Membership issues.
Expectations.
Major need for direction.

Clarity
- context
- task
- people

Getting On
Need for ground rules for
working together.
Development of purpose and
desire to contribute.
Establish standards of performance.
Relationships, roles and
responsibilities.
Identify position and value
to team.

Commitment
- agreements/contracts
- questionnaires
- openness/discussion
- team development
- values & feelings

Getting Going
Challenge and conflict.
Redefintion of rules; acceptable
methods and behaviour.
Needs support and encourage-
ment.

Clarity & Commitment
- facilitation
- support/encourage
- review agreements
- retain task focus

Getting Things Done
Balance people/task focus.
Activity.
Working separately.
Need for recognition.
Achievement/motivation/
achievement spiral.

Communication & Celebration
- share information
- manage relationships
- review/feedback
- publicity

Getting Stuck
External influences.
Lack of achievement.
Organisational blockages.
Resource limitations.
Relationships problems.
Emotional blocks.
Great success.

Clarity, Commitment, Communication & Celebration
– review
– redirection
– get out?
– get help?

Getting Help
Need for third party assistance.

Commitment & Communication
– agreed/understood

Getting Out
Task finished.
Membership change.
Leadership change.
Team redundant.
Project cancelled.
Needs review.

Clarity, Communication, Celebration
– Clarify situation
– Check feelings
– Acknowledge success
– Salvage
– Refocus
– Reallocate responsibilities
– **Celebrate!**

7. Making It Happen: Tips and Techniques

INTRODUCTION

This chapter is designed to offer more detailed practical tips and techniques for those wanting to take responsibility for the development of a team.

Implicit in this chapter is the belief that mechanical means are required to move a team on. The mechanics must be overtly placed so that each member of the team is aware of the process. In relationship building in teams, upon which the achievement of the task frequently depends, trust is the key. Without trust team members will feel that they are being manipulated which will cause resentment and resistance, thus making effective teamworking almost impossible.

In Chapter 5 we mentioned 'talking about the process of change' as a means of gaining commitment within the team. Talking about the process of development is something that supports the change initiative too. This involvement is another part of developing commitment – talking about what is happening among the team and its growth is a fundamental requirement of involvement.

This means that considerable efforts must be made at the front end to drive the process of team development. Clearly there needs to be a sensible balance between the amount of time available to achieve the task and the time spent on the team relationships. It is often tempting to think that people appear to be getting on OK and therefore just leave things be and focus solely on the job in hand.

Equally, because of time pressure it is normal for members to fall into the trap of diving straight into problem solving and 'doing' task oriented things. In our experience, unless the task is so small as to be able to fit into a few moments, or so immediate and urgent that members are prepared to take direct orders, this almost invariably leads to some interpersonal tensions and problems at a later stage. These can either impede task achievement or create such animosity within the team that, although the original task may have been achieved, the ability of the team to operate effectively on any subsequent task is seriously impaired.

It is for this reason that we so strongly advocate doing practical, concrete things right from the outset to accelerate progress through the phases. This means that members of teams can really see that something different is happening and that they feel that they are being actively involved from the beginning. Although it may be extremely difficult to maintain the energy to keep the mechanics going the results will reflect the value of the efforts eventually. A word of caution, however. It is pointless to devote endless hours trying to force the development of a group of people if it is possible to achieve a task merely with a group of able and willing people. The purpose of actively trying to accelerate the growth of a group into a team is to gain the advantage of the potential synergy.

Existing teams can be revitalised by making use of these methods too.

THE EMOTIONS OF CHANGE

Even when there is sufficient skill, talent and creativity, emotions can be the difference between success and failure of a team's efforts. Typically managers have found this area more difficult to deal with.

The following are a selection of emotions people have expressed as their response to corporate change experiences. The list has more negatives than positives. It is our belief that it needn't be that way.

Shock; indifference; apprehension; anticipation; excitement; bewilderment; enthusiasm; frustration; irritation; anger; disappointment; satisfaction; cynicism; pleasure; isolation; pride; fear; elation; sadness; confusion; relief.

It is important to note that individuals will go through different emotional peaks and troughs at varying times. This requires a balancing act, keeping all the emotional plates spinning at once. Because of a natural tendency not to bring feelings to the surface in a work context, it needs to be made safe for members to bring them out in a constructive way. The reason for this is purely pragmatic. If they are an obstacle to achievement then they need to be dealt with. Ignoring them does not mean that they go away, and often if suppressed they will re-emerge at another, perhaps less opportune, time. The skill is to manage the balancing act and be able to challenge and support at the same time.

In the majority of cases people want to make a valid and positive contribution, they want to succeed but they feel blocked. As often as not the source of blockage is not inability nor lack of resources, it is emotional.

The contents of the following pages are designed to bridge the gap between management intention and action mentioned above and also more rapidly move people through an emotional change curve to ensure more effective achievement of the desired results.

Figure 7.1: Challenge and support in balance

HIGH CHALLENGE

Feelings: Fear, anxiety, sometimes anger	**Feelings:** Excitement and enthusiasm
Effects: People avoid involvement Stressful climate Change attempts likely to be damaging and unsuccessful	**Effects:** People want to be involved Co-operation High motivation for change

LOW SUPPORT ——————————————— **HIGH SUPPORT**

Feelings: Boredom, depression	**Feelings:** Complacency, relaxation, warmth
Effects: People will become apathetic	**Effects:** People will seek out and resist any changes to this environment No motivation to change

LOW CHALLENGE

The model above illustrates the need for both challenge and support to develop motivation for change. This shows the need to focus on the development of both the team's task (challenge) and relationships (support).

The purpose of undertaking any development activity is to improve the results or 'output' from individuals and the team. It pays, then, to do some sort of analysis to establish if any training or development needs to take place to bring about this improvement and if so what type, how and by whom.

ESTABLISHING TRAINING AND DEVELOPMENT NEEDS

Before undertaking any training or development programme there are some key points to be considered. Training can be expensive in terms of time, money, credibility and motivation if it is seen or felt to be inappropriate. Conversely, it is of great value if well directed and effective. Particularly in circumstances of change people will be discouraged, (even if they see the personal and organisational benefit of what they have learned) if they believe the training will not make any difference because it will not be valued or supported within the organisation. It may seem simpler and cheaper simply not to plan any training at all. This approach could, however, lead to greater cost later in the development of the team. Even if it does turn out that there is no training requirement it is better to be confident of that at the outset rather than simply take the risk.

It is frequently discovered that the blockages or reasons for poor performance will not be overcome by training but that the fault lies elsewhere in the environment, in reward systems, in management styles, in resourcing, operating systems and equipment problems. This makes it even more essential to do some research, to establish in what ways, other than training and development, output/results can be improved.

Usually training needs analysis concentrates on three areas: knowledge, skill and attitude.

The initial issues are three:

- What does the team need to know?
- What do they need to be able to do (and to what level)?
- What outlook do team members need to have?

This helps establish whether there is a need by identifying any perceived gap between what standard of knowledge, skill and attitude is required and what can currently be delivered. Once the gap is identified then the particular needs can be specified.

Team members will need to be involved in these 'diagnosis' discussions. Members are far more inclined to buy in to the development plans if they have had an input and can see in advance the need and potential benefit. Otherwise they are likely to see it as some sort of punishment or remedial activity.

Questions to ask of team members.

1. What training needs can they identify for themselves, each other and the team as a whole? This is likely to elicit needs in the task related areas of a) technical expertise associated with their immediate task/job and b) needs for skills such as problem solving, change management and so on.

2. What are the main things that go wrong in teamworking in their experience? This will most likely raise relationship issues such as communication problems, interpersonal friction, poor information, between team conflict, lack of trust, unfair and unequal treatment of members, lack of honesty and openness, poor leadership and so on.

In analysing training and development needs for effective change through teamworking there are four areas that will need addressing:

- Technical expertise.
- Project skills, i.e., problem management.
- Team relationship skills.
- Any issues outside the scope of training and development.

The following more general questions will be helpful to establish if there are other issues that need resolving but which fall outside the scope of any training:

- What could be done by others to improve your results?
- What makes it difficult for you to do your job?
- What currently helps you in doing your job?

Another key question is: How important is this in my job? This is to identify if the training really has a value to the project, the team, the individual and organisation now or in the future. People need to feel that there is good reason to undertake learning, otherwise it will be seen as just 'nice to have' or 'flavour of the month'. On the other hand, the team member may be very keen and enthusiastic to undergo some sort of training but may need convincing that the value in relation to cost is insufficient.

There is also one other crucial issue to be considered. Once team members have taken on the new knowledge, skills and attitude how will they be supported back in the workplace? There is evidence of great wastage of development because, despite enthusiasm and commitment among participants, there is no nurturing of it after the event. Again, particularly if teams are intended as agents of change there needs to be support for their 'difference' in the organisation. Recognition, reward, publicity, acknowledgment, support all need to be forthcoming in tangible as well as intangible ways.

Having tackled the trickier questions above, the more practical ones need now to be considered:

- Which members need what training?
- Is anyone else doing something similar – can we share resources? (Consider the risk of dilution versus benefits of cross-fertilisation.)
- Who should do the training? (Comparison: *in-house versus external training*).
  External: expertise in non–company specific areas and chance to meet people from other business for broader outlook.
  Internal: more company focus, especially in culture change; less expensive.

- Can you use people from other parts of the organisation as a resource? Have other teams gone through similar experiences – what can you learn from them?

Training and development need not take a traditional 'classroom' format. Different methods worth considering are: secondment, work experience, coaching, self study, peer assistance, distance learning.

There are various ways of doing the research for your analysis: by questionnaires, in person, in group discussion.

Questionnaires

Written questionnaires are designed with relevant questions for completion and return and can include a list of training topics. They can cover a number of members at once and obtain quantitative data. However, they do risk not obtaining people's heartfelt views.

In Person

This can be a one-to-one interview, either structured with planned questions or not, where an individual gets to talk more freely and his/her contributions are probed. It obtains fresher and possibly more individually meaningful data than a questionnaire; but without a structure some areas and topics may risk being left uncovered.

Group Discussion

This can be a structured or unstructured discussion or brainstorm on what the group needs in terms of development. The value is that each person has a chance to hear what others are saying, though some individuals may feel less free to voice their personal needs.

Information can also be obtained on ongoing training needs from:

- Clarification of job descriptions with job holder.
- Regular performance appraisal.
- Identifying past problems and successes for indications of areas of development need.

Training priorities

It is important to establish the priorities in training needs, especially which areas will provide the greatest opportunity for rapid improvement and success and/or will obviate potential problems or failure. Implementing unnecessary training is counterproductive, so it requires careful focusing. If the whole team is to be involved in the training then the focus will need to be on common, major needs. Any topics that are relevant only to a few need to be targeted and alternative approaches found rather than a whole team event.

Summary

The outcome from your research will probably fall approximately into the following categories:

1. Technical development. For example, specialist knowledge and skills.
2. Project skills development, such as problem solving, creativity.
3. Team relationship development. For example, communication, motivation.
4. Other issues outside the team, such as environment, organisational support and so on.

The main focus of what follows is on points 2 and 3. Obviously point 1 is outside the scope of this book and while the development of team skills may help with point 4, it, too, is outside our remit. We have briefly covered some of the ways in which development can be speeded with the use of external help, but our main concentration is on how the team itself can accelerate its development in-house using techniques that can be built in as everyday activities at minimum cost for maximum effect.

TEAM EVENTS

By a team event we mean a special 'extraordinary' gathering of the team that is specifically for the purpose of development. It will be billed as a 'team event' as part of the process of talking about the team's development. It will therefore take on in people's eyes a special significance. Because change and 'the unknown' are threatening enough to most of us, a team event is likely to be very threatening, especially if it is a new concept and a new team. People may well be fearful of exposure of perceived inadequacies, of emotions being stirred up, of confrontations, of embarrassment. They may be cynical. If they have attended similar events they will bring all sorts of perceptions and memories of their previous experiences. To gain maximum advantage from the initial team-building event members need to arrive with as open an approach as possible. There are a few things that will help to set the scene:

- Ensure people are clear about the purpose of the event.
- Outline what is likely to happen during the event as far as possible without spoiling elements of surprise.
- Describe expectations in terms of people's contribution.
- Explain potential beneficial outcomes.

In order to be clear enough to explain to others, the initiator needs to have thought through the main reasons for the team event. Its purpose can range from initial goal clarification and working methods through developing relationships and solving particular problems.

Apart from making the purpose of the event explicit, below are two further tips for planning for a successful event:

- Ensure all members have clear directions – location, date, time, place.
- Endeavour to make sure they all have time to attend and that other matters are suspended for the duration of the event if possible.

Team events as we have defined them can range from week-long residential outdoor programmes run by external experts to a brief in-house activity designed particularly for a very specific develop-ment need.

Outdoor Events

Team development in the outdoors provides an unusually dynamic experience for teams. Whether for new teams or for pulling an existing team together it can create a deeper and swifter development/change because of the different location, environment, clothing, skill requirements and pressures. It is a great leveller and accesses emotions and issues more rapidly; feedback arrives more immediately and is very much to the point!

Outdoor events can provide either:

- Team **building**, which means that activities are reviewed and processed. Members learn from using existing and new skills and build on their past experiences to enhance for the future.
- Team **bonding**, where the experience alone brings the members closer together and the shared experience can create improved relationships that will be beneficial on return to the workplace.

Below is an example of a typical event.

TEAM BUILDING

A. Known problem and known solutions

Participants form themselves into teams. Each team is assigned a project and then rotates through all the projects (for example crossing a river or an electrified fence). They are briefed exactly on what needs to be achieved and how. Participants have simply to operate as effectively as they can as a team using whatever skill and experience they bring with them. As they undertake each project a new leader for each team will be allocated. These activities begin to break down the initial barriers and identify each individual's skills of planning, organisation, briefing, communication, problem analysis, creativity, time management and listening.

B. Acquisition of new skills

Under an experienced instructor each participant is given the skills of, for example, climbing, caving, abseiling, canoeing, map reading and using a compass. They gain confidence and become familiar with the equipment. These are the skills they will need to use throughout the rest of the programme.

C. Identify the key success criteria of an effective team
Indoor exercise to identify effective qualities and skills to be used in the team. Opportunity to practice and review how they did!

D. Major challenge to use task skills with teamworking
First stage – planning strategy in terms of team briefing, organising, resource planning and control, risk analysis, objective setting, decision making and contingency planning.

The second stage is actually doing the task, which might range from:

a) Having to put together and present a project involving all the outdoor skills plus business skills, presentation skills as well as meeting deadlines.
b) Having to crack a code, locate and obtain vital resources and then spend a night living out of doors. The degree of discomfort depends on the team's ability to acquire the necessary resources. Each person has learned a certain number of the outdoor skills so there is a very real sense of being dependent on one another. Participants feel truly vulnerable and exposed!

The third stage is to review and process the event. A particular strength of the outdoor training event is that participants cannot really hide behind any pretence that the training was not like the real world. Success and failure is much clearer for everyone to see and the results have more of a true meaning, that is the physical and emotional investment is greater.

D. Individual feedback
Each individual receives feedback from every other member of the programme.

Follow-up

A training event some six to eight weeks after the outdoor event provides the opportunity to pick up any outstanding issues and develop original themes. This element enables better transfer of learning and integration to the workplace once the emotional response has calmed down.

TEAM BONDING

Participants are involved in a similar situation but it is not reviewed and processed by facilitators. There are tutors available in case anyone needs support but the main purpose of the exercise is that the team should share an enjoyable and challenging experience, see each other in different circumstances, barriers be dismantled and the team have fun together. One of the benefits of this type of event is that it creates myths and legends that are part of the fabric that bonds the team together. It is as if having an experience that no one else in their organisation has had sets them apart and makes them 'special', creating a unique team spirit. This is part of the sense of being special that successful teams described.

Recent Developments

A recent development in the field of outdoor training is the opportunity to use yacht racing in a similar way. Teams are taught the necessary sailing skills and then embark on a real-life yacht race or voyage. They are supported in this by a skipper and assistant as well as a facilitator.

Indoor Events

Indoor events are designed to access the same issues, feelings and skills as the outdoor event. The activities might include 'set piece' structured exercises to simulate working in and between teams in complex organisations and draw out key learning for individuals and the team as a whole. Other options include setting discussion questions so that the team has to work through some major issues together.

Particularly at the Getting Together and Getting On phases of development the crucial issues of membership, direction, roles and responsibilities, ground rules and relationships need to be worked through comprehensively.

For the more formal style of event or one where there is likely to be conflict or difficulty getting the members to open up and work constructively together it would be sensible to have an external facilitator. If the team is going to manage the process without outside help it is important to be aware of the number of things that require managing to ensure success of the event:

- The physical environment and 'atmosphere'.
- The 'housekeeping'.
- Contribution levels.
- Group relationships.
- Individuals' feelings.
- Time.
- Achievement of results.
- Confirmation and commitment to actions.
- Planning and implementing follow up.

One of the key components of a successful team is being able to value and recognise each member's contribution.

RECOGNISING AND VALUING DIFFERENCES

As discussed in Chapter 4 one of the keys to teamworking is to establish a rich mix in the team make-up. This creates a great opportunity to use the findings from that process as a means of accelerating the team development.

It can be difficult to access all these differences in a positive and constructive way. You don't know what you don't know – until it comes right out and whacks you between the eyes, usually at a time when you do not really want to find out, for example on trying to establish a solution when people's differing standpoints become a block. It is easy to believe that because a team has come together with a particular purpose in mind that everyone shares similar outlooks and interests. There may be several comforting similarities.

However, it is the fundamental differences between individuals that have the most potential for both advantage and chaos.

One useful way of getting to recognise all the variations is to use psychometric instruments. A benefit of using self-completion questionnaires is that each person has to take responsibility for the data fed back because it is based on the way the questions were answered. Although some people express scepticism about psychometric instruments there is no doubt that they provide a thought-provoking vehicle for instigating discussion among team members.

There are a variety of different sorts of instruments available. Some are self-marked, others require administration by a licensed expert. Use of these instruments is best supported by an experienced facilitator.

The three below provide three different insights.

Myers Briggs Type Indicator (MBTI)

MBTI is a personality 'type' indicator requiring licensed administration. It gives information on people's preferred mode of operation, how they take in information and the way in which that information is used to deal with the external world, other people and decision making.

FIRO-B (Fundamental Interpersonal Relationship Orientation – Behaviour)

FIRO-B examines some of the basic ways in which people relate or behave towards each other. It looks at three basic behaviours.

Inclusion – relating in group situations

Control – wanting to influence others

Attention – relating to individuals.

FIRO-B indicates how these forms of behaviour are expressed towards others or wanted from others. It gets to the core of people's feelings pretty quickly. It accesses more meaningful data more rapidly than many instruments looking at behavioural traits.

Strength Deployment Inventory (SDI)

SDI identifies strengths in relating to others, and has the added dimension of a feedback version which provides an individual with a direct comparison with his/her own perception. SDI gives data for two differing circumstances; when things are going well and also under pressure.

Belbin's model of teamworking is another way of getting team members to appreciate the value of each individual. It is covered in greater depth in Chapter 3.

FRAMEWORKS FOR WORKING WELL TOGETHER

Contracts: Creating the Team Ground Rules

Contracts help achieve clarity and commitment within a team. (Some people find the use of the word contract overly formal and will find agreement more acceptable.) Contracts can be agreed as part of a team event or at a meeting specifically set up for the purpose. They have the added function of being a framework for working together, feedback and review.

A simple Getting Started contract would cover similar issues to those mentioned in the example in Chapter 5:

- Timekeeping/punctuality.
- Specific roles and responsibilities.
- Dress code.
- Confidentiality.
- Feedback rules and so on.

The easiest way of doing this is just to show the list of items to the team and ask them to agree a standard on each point. It is also possible for the team to come up with the items to go on the list.

An alternative method is to ask team members to consider and respond to the two following questions.

a) Thinking of good/successful team experiences which I enjoyed, the reasons I thought they were good/successful/enjoyable are:

b) Thinking of bad/unsuccessful team experiences which I found difficult, the reasons I thought they were bad/unsuccessful/difficult are:

The replies will provide the information for the team to establish what are the most important factors to take into account. It is likely that they will cover the usual wide range of issues: unclear direction, lack of resources, lack of organisational support, poor leadership, bad communication, lack of trust etc. The key point to make is to sort out what are the issues that the team can actually control. Although it may not be possible to demand extra resources, the members can make the experience much more satisfactory by positively dealing with those things that are in their gift.

Collate the replies and get the team to group them, prioritise them, eliminate any with potentially limited impact or out of the team's control.

Then, with a list of items which the team believe make up good/successful team criteria the next stage is to ask:

- How will we demonstrate this?
- How will we make sure this happens?
- How will we tell if we are succeeding/failing?
- How will we deal with this if it does not happen?

This forms the framework of ground rules that the team has created for itself and thus is more likely to be committed to.

The next example is a way of generating a team statement that encapsulates the 'style' of the team as well as being a contract. It is more creative and gets the team really working more closely together.

- The team is briefed to think of words which, for the members, sum up how they would describe the team if it is successful. This includes success both in its task/purpose and in its relationships (inside and outside the team).
- Each member of the team chooses three words and writes each on a separate piece of paper.

- The words are mixed up and the team divided into pairs.
- The words are divided amongst the pairs and each pair then has to create a sentence including their six words which would be appropriate as a team statement of intent.
- Once the pairs are happy with their sentence then the whole team discusses each and comes to a final decision about how they will be included in their team statement.
- Finally each member is asked if they can and will commit to operate within the statement/agreement.
- Someone then accepts responsibility for publishing and circulating the statement.

This type of team statement has been most successful where it has been produced in an attractive way and displayed as a sort of team 'charter'.

Questionnaires

Questionnaires are a review mechanism. They check 'climate' and performance and provide the opportunity for team members to spend time alone thinking through their views and feelings before having to go public with them. This can make the process less threatening. A potential disadvantage may be that they might consider the risks of speaking openly and therefore skew their responses. However, if this is the case then the chances are that they would simply remain silent if they had not had the chance to think in advance. Equally they may be able to find a way of expressing themselves which minimises the risks for them.

A team can establish for itself what the items are that it wants to rate and discuss. Below is an example of some points for discussion that are currently in use:

1. Everyone is clear about the purpose, task, roles and responsibilities in the team. The action plan is well defined and we all are committed to it.
2. The atmosphere is one of trust, support, encouragement and fun. We are happy to give suggestions and ideas and are not afraid of making mistakes.

3. The team works cohesively together. Everyone is actively involved. Responsibility is shared. People contribute openly and freely. There are no 'cliques' that cause tensions.
4. Members listen to one another attentively and show respect for each others' views and feelings.
5. We deal with disagreements effectively. We try to see each others' views as much as we try to explain our own.
6. We make our decisions collaboratively rather than by force. We seek positive outcomes rather than defend our own positions.
7. Communication within the team is effective. Everyone has the opportunity to express his/her view. Information is freely available to everyone. Feedback is a normal occurrence.
8. We value the different skills and personalities within the team and we demonstrate this.
9. We regularly review our progress on our task and in our team development. We set time aside for this purpose.
10. We consciously work at managing relationships outside the team. We actively network with the rest of the organisation.

Each of the topics is rated on a scale from 1 – 5.

Always	Often	Sometimes	Rarely	Never
5	4	3	2	1

When each member has honestly completed the questionnaire the data is the foundation of a discussion on how well the team thinks it is doing and provides the opportunity to establish some fresh ground rules.

Teams with Leaders

Team leaders may also want to check the effect that they are having on the team. A questionnaire is equally effective for this purpose. Below is a similar questionnaire but written to check the team leader's practices.

Team Leader's Practice

RATING

DOES NOT   DOES

A. Helps clarify goals, tasks, roles   1   2   3   4   5   6   7
and responsibilities

B. Encourages equal participation from   1   2   3   4   5   6   7
all members

C. Listens and responds non–defensively   1   2   3   4   5   6   7
to views different from their own

D. Provides training, guidance, support   1   2   3   4   5   6   7
and feedback for team members

E. Shares information freely,   1   2   3   4   5   6   7
communicates openly and honestly
with team members

F. Provides training, guidance and   1   2   3   4   5   6   7
support for team members

G. Shares responsibility but is also   1   2   3   4   5   6   7
prepared to take tough decisions to
achieve the task

H. Sets aside time to review progress   1   2   3   4   5   6   7
with the team and with individuals

I. Helps the team by enlisting support   1   2   3   4   5   6   7
from other parts of the organisation
and obtaining necessary resources where
possible

J. Is prepared to help sort out any   1   2   3   4   5   6   7
difficulties the team encounters.
Is impartial while doing this.

Other methods for teams to focus on the way they work together are:

Our Team as an Animal

Members get into small groups and draw a picture depicting the team. They then explain why they have chosen the animal. The animal can be fictitious or an amalgamation of real-life creatures. A variation on this theme could be to use countries instead of animals. Particular benefits of this sort of exercise is that it breaks the ice, gets people 'playing' together on a non-threatening level and also gets their creativity going.

Likes/Dislikes Disclosure

First round: Each person in turn states 'one thing I like about being in a team is . . .' until all likes are exhausted.

Second round: Each person in turn states 'one thing I dislike about being in this team is . . .' until all dislikes are exhausted.

No records are made of these disclosures. It is just a chance to immerse the whole team in information about each other. All the information may not be remembered but certainly there will be a fairly good 'feel' in the group about people's preferences and what sorts of behaviour are acceptable or not.

Storytelling

An innovative way of creating a team identity and common language is to tell stories based on success experiences at work, either as an individual or as a team. As each person tells their tale using imagery as vivid as possible the team (perhaps with the assistance of a facilitator) can identify any themes, imagery or words that are commonly used. These will form the basis of a team identity and language.

In the book *Project Leadership* the authors propose talking with the team through a series of simple graded exercises. The exercises comprise a number of discussion questions – focusing on gaining absolute clarity in the early stages – about the way the team works together, understanding the project in its context and finally roles within the team.

All the above methods and techniques are designed to get the team relationships and working methods off to a good start. This needs balancing by development of task skills.

PROBLEM-SOLVING

Problem solving may include working out how to restructure an organisation, how to design a new product or how to resource all the tasks required to be achieved in a week when half the team members are away from work with 'flu. There is a variety of methods to choose from, and some are broadly described below.

By definition, if there is a problem to be solved there is a challenge. There also may be negative feelings, such as frustration, anxiety, panic. Sometimes the easiest of problems is made difficult because a team is unable to work well in collaboration to solve it. It is far easier to solve problems if a team shares common knowledge on the best methods available.

A logical sequence of steps supported by a selection of techniques will help.

SEVEN-STEP PROBLEM-SOLVING APPROACH

1. Identify and clarify the problem
2. Establish causes
3. Generate options
4. Decide on solution
5. Action plan
6. Implement
7. Follow up

1. Identify and clarify the problem:

- Select which problems need most urgent attention.
- Make sure they are something the team can do something about.
- Ensure they are of value to the organisation and to the team.
- Prioritise problems.

- Include whole team (and other affected parties) in establishing exactly what the problem is.
- Separate the problem into all its component parts and identify where the true breakdown is.
- Define specifically what the desired outcome is and what the current position is to establish the gap to be closed.

2. Establish causes:

- Write down all possible causes.
- Filter until most likely causes remain.
- Research and test likely causes.
- Establish true causes.

3. Generate options:

- Generate as many options as possible.
- Be creative about possible solutions.
- Be prepared to combine solutions.
- Don't eliminate options which at first sound preposterous.

4. Decide on solution:

- Establish which options will be most effective and not affected by any other imminent changes.
- Which is most cost effective and long term?
- Which is most likely to be supported by the majority of interested parties?

5. Action plan:

- Clarify all the steps that need to be taken to implement the chosen solution.
- Spell out what needs to be achieved, by whom, by what date.
- What help and resources do you need?
- What obstacles may impede implementation; how will you overcome these?

- Who do you need to persuade/get on your side and how will you do this without putting people's backs up?
- Plan in checks and reviews.

6. Implementation:

- Communicate your solution to all interested parties.
- Presentation clear and concise, interesting, valid for the needs of the recipient and easy to support.
- Do what needs to be done to agreed standards and deadlines.
- Review progress and amend plan as necessary.
- Keep people informed of progress and amendments.

7. Follow up:

- Keep in touch with interested parties especially to make sure the solution is meeting the need.
- Review and record progress.
- Seek improvements to solution.
- Celebrate and publicise successes.
- Seek help with any ongoing difficulties.

PROBLEM-SOLVING TECHNIQUES

Creative Thinking

There is a saying that 'traditional methods deliver traditional results'. In a change culture traditional results are insufficient. Teams therefore need to use a variety of methods to arouse their creativity.

Historically in organisations, using one's imagination was not rewarded and, in fact, it was frequently considered a drawback to be a 'day-dreamer'.

Not any more. Initiative and innovation are indispensable to the teamworker. A lot of people believe themselves to be lacking in creativity, equating it with artistic ability and not seeing it as an integral part of achieving practical results. They need to be stimulated to break out of the traditional approach to problem solving, which depended almost entirely on logic and technical or specialist expertise.

By combining the logical and creative approaches to problem solving, obstacles are overcome more quickly and the momentum of the change process increases. Because 'non-specialists' can be involved, people can see opportunities for their own development which leads to greater excitement and motivation and therefore more positive contribution.

Barriers to Creative Thinking

Previous experiences cause people to have a negative mindset and they find it difficult to adopt a positive and open minded approach. People may not see the need. They may be fearful of being made to look foolish. Ways of overcoming these obstacles include:

- Explaining the reasons and the method.
- Making it safe/low risk.
- Challenging negative mind sets.
- Making it fun!

If selectors have taken the advantage of the teamworking approach to include a good variety of backgrounds, experiences, qualifications and so on in the mix this can help overcome some of the above problems by involving people who bring different viewpoints to the issues and challenge unhelpful assumptions.

Visualisation

We said earlier in the chapter that day-dreaming used not to be encouraged traditionally. Visualisation, visioning or 'day-dreaming' are, however, excellent methods for creativity in task achievement and team development.

The team gets together and is invited to create a mental image of, say, what successful task achievement would look and feel like to them; or to picture how a successful team looks. They are encouraged to be as imaginative as they can. It helps to spell out that there are no constraints of any kind. Capturing these vision on paper, preferably in picture form using colour and imagery despite any lack of artistic ability, is a way of really freeing up inspiration.

The pictures or collages or diagrams can then be displayed and explained to the rest of the team. There are spin-off benefits from using this approach. Apart from gaining clues to potential solutions to the initial problem, the self-disclosure usually leads to improved understanding, closeness and team spirit.

Brainstorming and mindmapping are two simple and effective techniques to help people break out of their normal linear thinking patterns.

Brainstorming

Brainstorming encourages everyone to be involved. It can reduce judgement and in a sense forces support of colleagues' ideas. It generates energy and hopefully enthusiasm on the back of that energy.

Brainstorming is useful when a quantity of ideas are needed, and especially when attempts have already been made to solve a problem and no solutions seem appropriate. In terms of the seven steps of problem solving, brainstorming is most useful for establishing causes and generating options.

How To Do It

Before

- Create time and space for it. Everyone commits to stay. Ensure no interruptions.
- Flipchart visible to all participants.
- Subject of the brainstorm written up clearly and kept visible.
- Someone ready to write up and remind team of the rules.

Beginning
Either:

- Everyone writes three ideas individually and calls them out one by one in turn.
  or:-
- Everyone in turn is invited to give an idea straight off the top of their head.

- A warm up can be done on any unrelated topic such as Christmas presents for the Prime Minister or the Chief Executive.

During

- Individuals are encouraged to keep up the flow of ideas and shout them out as they arise.
- No criticism, judgement or questions are allowed about any of the ideas.
- Every contribution is written exactly as it is offered.
- All the flipcharts are kept visible.
- Everyone is encouraged to contribute.
- Building on ideas is positively encouraged.

Next

- Take a break when the supply of ideas is absolutely exhausted.
- Invite any further ideas.
- Review the list.
- Organise the contributions where common themes seem to have emerged into categories.

And Then

- Take a more logical look at the suggestions and see if any of them are feasible.
- Ask 'how could we make this one work?' for each of the ideas.

The most essential rules for brainstorming are to ensure that no ideas are put down or criticised, everyone contributes, the exercise is done with fun and energy, wild and crazy ideas are positively encouraged, loads of ideas are expected and something is done with the result of the brainstorm.

Mindmapping

This is a good method for use either in a team or alone. It is helpful if all team members know how to use it so that they will be able to understand other people. This is a technique which many people find really uncomfortable at first because it seems messy and contrary to our normal way of arranging ideas. With perseverance it can become an invaluable tool for situations ranging from writing shopping lists to preparing management presentations.

The benefits of using this method are that the main topic is clearly identified, key ideas are close to the centre, links become easily recognisable and new information can be added easily. It also is often easier to remember what is on the page because the mind remembers the pattern more easily than a list.

A mindmap is a way of 'mapping out' associated ideas. The aim is to jot down ideas so that they branch out from the central issue The keys to successful mindmapping are to:

- Write the main issue in capitals in the centre of a large piece of paper and put a ring round it.
- Write down any words or ideas as they occur and link them to the centre; underline them.
- As new words/ideas occur add them to the mindmap where they seem to fit best.
- Write all ideas and words down, don't stop to worry about commonsense, neatness, spelling or anything else, just free-flow.
- Keep going until no more ideas come.
- Show any links or connections by ringing them or drawing arrows between them. Use different colours to show links.

It does not really matter if the mindmap makes any sense to anyone else. It provides a ready memory jogger. An alternative method to extend understanding of an issue is to list a set of statements and have the team run through them at speed without breaks. Jumping from statement to statement is OK.

- The main point of this problem is . . .
- The problem could also be defined as . . .
- Without constraints we could . . .
- What I'd really like to do is . . .
- A really strange way of looking at it is . . .

When 'endings' are exhausted, return to the original problem and see if any better ideas or solutions have surfaced.

Other common methods for problem solving not covered here because they are amply covered in other books are:

- Ranked pairs.
- Pareto analysis.
- Cause and effect analysis.
- Cost benefit analysis.
- Force field analysis.

These are all ways of finding solutions. Good intentions often do not get implemented because basic principles of goal setting are ignored. Here is a reminder:

Principles of Goal Setting

Clearly defined. Vague goals are rarely met. It is essential to know when you have arrived.

Stretching for top performance. Goals should neither be impossible, because failure discourages and can damage reputations, nor too easy, because then there is no challenge and therefore effort seems pointless.

Sub-goals for manageability. Tackling the whole task at once may be too daunting and may cause paralysis. Help may be required from other sources. Provide a chance to review progress and set fresh plans. Ensure there are opportunities for celebration along the way.

Prioritise. Decide on the best sequence for optimal use of time and resources. Account for other goals when planning in time.

Contingencies. Murphy's law means you need to plan in adequate time for things to go wrong and to be put right.

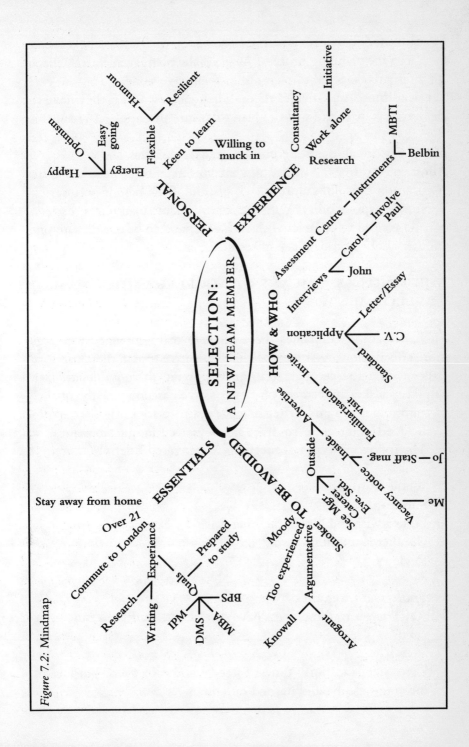

Figure 7.2: Mindmap

Measure, feedback, review. Assess progress and feed achievements back into the planning process. Assess if the plan is still valid. Check for alternatives. Stick to plan rather than have none.

Set deadlines. And stick to them. They create pace. If they have to change, review the rest of the plan to ensure the ripple effect of this change is managed.

Diary. Ensure all plans are put into people's diaries.

Allocate resources. Anticipate what you need to achieve the goal. A common cause of failure is lack of time. Seek help if necessary.

Personal responsibility. Without commitment, planning is useless. Members need to contract with each other and to be tough with one another about non-delivery of results.

MEETINGS AS A MEANS OF ACCELERATING TEAM DEVELOPMENT

There are some guidelines that will help teams manage meetings more effectively so that they become a positive tool in their armoury rather than a source of frustration. Following these guidelines will help keep task achievement on target as well as improve the quality of communication and better manage team relationships. They can be included in the team contract and reviewed in questionnaires.

The following types of meetings are covered briefly:

1. Whole team together.
2. Sub-team.
3. Leader with individual member.
4. Conflict resolution.
5. Reviews.

1. Whole team together

BEFORE: ensure all members have details with sufficient time to be prepared:

- Date, start and finish times, location and directions, purpose of meeting, agenda and desired outcomes.

DURING:

- Declare and clarify aims and desired outcomes.
- Agree finish times.
- Confirm roles.
- Display all agenda items.
- Invite all members to add to agenda.
- Prioritise agenda items and agree which will take preference.
- Offer each member the chance to express a view on each topic.
- Some items may be dealt with by sub-groups or interested individuals. This can generate greater ownership and commitment to the outcomes.
- All groups/individuals present their findings.
- All items discussed – only one at a time.
- All points summarised and conclusions recorded.
- Actions and deadlines agreed.
- Responsibilities allocated.
- Review how the meeting went.

AFTER: Publish action notice and circulate quickly.

NB: Close a topic when:

- More facts are required.
- Views or expertise are required from people not present.
- More time is needed to digest information.
- Agreement is needed.
- Old ground is being covered again.

2. Sub-team Meetings

Follow the above guidelines. The key is to ensure that the results/findings of the meeting are fed back to the rest of the team. In small groups it is often possible to forget about the basic ground rules for working together. While there is room for more informality, there is no reason to let drop the mechanisms for effective meetings.

3. Leader and Individual Member Meetings

The purpose of the initial meeting is to establish rapport and clarify roles and targets. Ongoing meetings are to review individual progress, mutual feedback, goal setting, identify development needs, relationship building, problem solving, coaching and so on. It establishes a sense of value and importance.

Points to Cover
Initial Meeting:

- How member feels about being in the team.
- Leader's expectations of member.
- Member's expectations of leader, peers, organisation.
- Any issues from previous experiences in teams that need resolving.
- Clarification of tasks/roles.
- Member's development needs.

Ongoing Meetings:

- Review and reset goals.
- Review task progress.
- Discuss individual and team development.
- Give and invite feedback.
- Offer help and advice.
- Social/personal issues.

4. Conflict Resolution

Good peacemaking skills are invaluable to teamworking. They are useful both within the team and when faced with opposition from outside:

- Each person in turn makes a clear statement describing how they see the situation, the project, the problem.
- Each person is invited to make a response to the other viewpoints.
- Questions are asked for clarification.

- People listen and try to see the other person's viewpoint.
- No defending, arguing or explaining is allowed.
- Common ground is established and areas of differences are clearly stated.
- People own up to where they might have contributed to the problem.
- Each person lists possible options/solutions.
- Each person lists the consequences of the suggested options.
- Each option is weighed up.
- Either an option is adopted with agreement from all parties OR the differing views are simply accepted. In the latter case it may be that an agreement will have to be made about how the people will work together given the difference.

The important things to remember about dealing with conflict is that although it may only be mischievous war-mongering there is rarely any long-term gain from engaging in war games, tempting though it may be at the time. It is normal to want to convert or obliterate any adversaries but the more we let go and do not pressurise opponents the better chance we have of achieving our aims. Fighting fair usually meets better the requirements of effective teamworking. The aim is to go for a collaborative approach rather than a competitive one – that is win/win/win – where the individuals, the teams and the organisation all benefit from the outcome. If it is not possible to achieve a solution following the above guidelines then it is best to engage the help of an impartial mediator.

5. Review Meetings
Each person in turn:

- States successes in relation to goals.
- Describes their current situation.
- Explains potential obstacles to future success and may receive help from the team on it.
- Is offered the opportunity to express any feelings.
- Gives commitment to actions before next meeting.

The meeting is then reviewed:

- What went well, what could be better next time.
- Any learning gained from the process.

Appreciation of each other and everybody's contribution is expressed. Questionnaires may also be used periodically at review meetings, where they can be invaluable.

Things to Watch for in Team Meetings

The purpose of having specific guidelines is to avoid problems in teams. The guidelines serve to manage both the task and relationship functions of the team. They maintain a focus on getting the job done, by getting everyone involved in tackling the problems, surfacing ideas, facts, opinions, feelings, feedback and alternatives. They keep the meeting on target by preventing topic jumping and digression. Relationships are nurtured when everyone has a chance to contribute and has that contribution treated with respect. Ideas are likely to be expressed with more clarity and listened to. Rejection of ideas is dealt with in a more readily acceptable way so people's emotions are managed more effectively. Support is built in to the process.

All this combines to create a purposeful and workable atmosphere, rather than one in which conflict and disagreement predominate. Teams tend to work more successfully in an atmosphere of directed energy where serious hard work, enjoyment and 'play' go hand in hand.

If any of the following are happening frequently in a team they need to be dealt with within the framework of the team contract or a review meeting.

OVER CONTRIBUTOR – high participation, lots to say, does not allow space for other people to contribute.

UNDER CONTRIBUTOR – does not participate, non-commital.

'MY WAY AT ALL COSTS' – imposes own ideas, intimidates and talks over other members.

BLOCKING – everyone has a responsibility to voice disagreement but not to the exclusion of all else.

LOW ENERGY – the feeling in the room is of apathy and lethargy.

NAVEL CONTEMPLATION – team is self-obsessed to the exclusion of the task.

SOCIALITES – everyone is having a good time but nothing is being achieved.

DEPENDANCY – the team is relying on the leader to take control.

CLIQUES – alliances are forming which are not helpful to the overall team.

RED HERRINGS – constant digression from the point.

INACTIVITY – talking and talking and talking but no action.

FEEDBACK IS THE KEY

The most effective teams have a contract for feedback as a matter of course.

The basic assumptions about feedback are that it:

- Needs mutual trust.
- Is a joint effort.
- Is constructive and supportive.
- Is a skill that needs careful practice.
- Involves good listening.

Effective feedback observes the following conventions:

Balance – good and bad points reflected.

Observed – factual with examples.

Objective – not judgemental.

Specific – avoids generalisation. Focus on actions not the person.

Timely – given at a time when the person can best deal with it.

Each team needs to decide for itself what feedback is valid. A 'circuit' to go round helps if feedback is a new and unfamiliar concept. This gives permission and provides protection of rules in the early stages.

Have Accepted Phrases, such as:

'What I thought was effective about that was . . . because . . .'
'I particularly found . . . helpful because . . .'
'It felt good when you . . . because . . .'
'I would have preferred it if you had . . . because . . .'
'It would have been more helpful for me if . . . because . . .'

This will probably feel stilted and will cause gales of laughter initially. At least, though, it provides a common language, which if introduced well will be a starting point for teams using feedback for the first time.

MAINTAINING THE MOMENTUM

What Chapters 6 and 7 have been all about is accelerating the effective development of the team. The purpose of this is that teamworking will drive change successfully within the organisation. The keys to this are the four C's discussed in Chapter 6 and, in particular, the importance of making the change process and the development process topics for ongoing discussion. They must be talked about. They must be part of the 'air that we breathe'. Teams must keep their eye on the ball of what it is that they are there to achieve. They must recognise that this involves not only whatever the project is, whether it is to displace and arrest prostitutes or design and develop a new control panel, but also the constant development that change culture requires as well as the cultivation of themselves as a team.

A sharp internal focus managing the outside, and the team apart are hallmarks of Superteams. In essence this means developing good relationships outside the team and bringing in any other individuals who can add information or expertise.

A team also needs to continue working effectively when members are apart. Investing energy in the mechanisms described in this chapter means that this is more likely to happen naturally. Keeping in touch needs to become the norm in addition to raising early warning signals. Someone, if not the leader, needs to take the role of overall co-ordination.

We finish this chapter with a variety of other ideas that will also make a significant contribution to the speedy development of a team. There is the risk that once a team has undergone some initial 'events' and established its contract and rules about how team members will work together, things will be allowed to slip and slide back to the way they were done before. Particularly if events are run by an 'outsider' and especially away from the workplace, the learning or development may not be so readily seen as an integral part of the development and change process. If a meeting is once run without sticking to the agreements, or someone breaks a part of the contract, or an individual feels unsupported by the rest of the team – *and nothing is done about it* – confidence and trust will begin to diminish and that is the beginning of Getting Stuck or even prematurely Getting Out. The team needs to stick to the principles it applied at the beginning for them to become 'the way things are done around here'. In time they will not seem like meticulously applied techniques but natural and will evolve into new ways of growing and developing.

Successful Teams:

1. Create trust between each other. Deliver on promises – do what they say they will; meet deadlines; are on time for meetings; don't talk about each other behind one another's backs.
2. Plan in time for the team. Start or end the day with a 15-minute informal 'catch up' to keep each other informed of progress.
3. Establish traditions of having coffee, lunch or tea breaks at the same place at a certain time each day so that members know where they can relax together briefly.
4. Have regular 'honesty' sessions. A bit like an amnesty, where people have the opportunity to get things off their chest and really say what they think without risk of damage to relationships. It will be important that people are able to take responsibility for their own feelings rather than make personal attacks on other team members. Each member will need to be prepared to act as an impartial referee.

5. Review potential learning from each new experience, either as a group or perhaps have an individual present his/her own findings. Simple review questions such as 'What did we learn from that?', 'What went well and why?', 'What could have gone better and why?, What would or could we do differently and better next time?' would be an adequate framework to begin with.

6. Write their own 'ten ways to . . .' book. Every time something needs considering have a 'ten ways to . . .' brainstorm. For example, ten ways to brighten up our environment.

7. Socialise together. Take the opportunity to see each other in a different light. Have fun together. Capitalise on good feelings back in the workplace.

8. Network with other teams. Develop good relationships within the organisation. Do good PR by publicising plans and achievements.

9. Record developments, improvements and changes so that the team can look back and enjoy its success.

10. Have initiation rites for integration of new members and give departing members a great send-off.

Let the last word go to Sir John Egan of BAA. 'There is a lot to keeping this thing going, it is not enough just getting it going.'

Section 4

Troubleshooting

8. The Team's Internal Problems

INTRODUCTION

The reasons why some teams are more successful than others are complex and varied. Successful teams bring together a rich mix of competencies, personalities, experiences and values. The literature on effective teamworking and our own experience indicates that some of the following qualities contribute towards increasing a team's effectiveness:

SECRETS OF EFFECTIVE TEAMS

- **PURPOSE AND GOALS**
  They are persistent and obsessive in the pursuit of their goals, but creatively flexible in how they get there. They constantly ask themselves the question, 'What are we trying to achieve?'
- **REMOVE BARRIERS**
  They try to remove barriers and obstacles and are willing and able to confront people or situations that are not helpful.
- **PERFORMANCE EXPECTATIONS**
  They are committed to quality in their own performance and their expectations of each other are very high.
- **UNDERSTAND THEIR ENVIRONMENT**
  They appear to have a good understanding of the philosophy, strategy and values of their organisation.

- **CLEAR VISION**
  They have a clear vision of what they are trying to achieve. They use this vision to provide them with direction. They also have very clear strategies of moving beyond their vision into the action stage.

- **BUILD NETWORKS**
  They are good at building networks both inside and outside the organisation by identifying individuals who can help them achieve their goal or support them in other ways.

- **OPEN AND AVAILABLE**
  They are visible and available to others. Although they have strong values and communicate to others what they stand for, they are also willing to receive feedback and advice from other people.

- **DRIVEN BY SUCCESS**
  They are driven by success and thrive on energy, excitement and commitment, which come with feelings of success. They enjoy the recognition and rewards that success brings.

- **TAKE INITIATIVE**
  They are action–orientated. They do not wait for things to happen to them. They initiate a lot of activities and make things happen. They respond quickly and positively to any problems or opportunities that they see.

- **ASSUME RESPONSIBILITY**
  They appear to be in touch with their parent organisation's goals and are committed to their organisation's success. They thrive in a supportive and open culture where they can assume responsibility and produce results.

- **INFLUENCE EFFECTIVELY**
  They influence their organisation and other teams within it. They tend to use their credibility rather then their authority to get things done.

- **REMAIN FLEXIBLE**
  They work best with broad guidelines and principles rather than with rigid rules. In this way, they are able to remain flexible.

- **URGENT AND CRITICAL**
  They are able to distinguish between the important activities and

the urgent activities. They welcome change and are able to integrate it in their plans smoothly.

- **SHARED LEADERSHIP**
  They like leaders who can provide them with direction and help to maintain the team's energy and commitment. They expect the leader to negotiate with others in the organisation for support and resources. Leadership shifts from time to time depending on the circumstances, the needs of the group and the skills of team members. Team members are prepared to assume leadership when necessary.

- **COMMUNICATION**
  They maintain a high level of communication even when they are working apart. Team members feel free to express their feelings about the task and the team's operations.

- **INNOVATE**
  They tend to be innovative and creative and prepared to take risks in order to enhance the team's performance.

- **CONTINUOUS IMPROVEMENT**
  They are interested in continuously improving their own performance. They look for ways to do things differently and to do things better.

- **CO-OPERATION VERSUS COMPETITION**
  They are able to work with others easily and focus on co-operation rather than working against others.

It is, however, inevitable that things go wrong or teams get into trouble. There are many different things that can have an influence on the smooth running of a team. Some of these elements will be the result of the internal working of the team and others will be a result of external factors or issues to do with boundaries and relationships. Here we give a wide variety of examples to illustrate how teams can get into trouble and some techniques to help them get back on track. The Troubleshooting Techniques could be interventions made by the team leader or someone external to the team. They can also be used by teams themselves to try to get unstuck and back on track. During our research we were very fortunate in that individual team members and whole teams were prepared to relate their experiences very openly and honestly to us. In previous chapters we have generally identified specific teams when illustrating a point. However, in this chapter, for obvious reasons, we have chosen to protect the confidentiality of the teams so that the relevant points can be illustrated fully without causing any embarrassment. The examples provided in this chapter are not a complete and exhaustive list of reasons why teams can get into trouble, but they are some of the most common ones.

TELL-TALE SIGNS OF AN INEFFECTIVE TEAM

Teams that are not functioning effectively are not necessarily doing things that are opposite to what effective teams may be doing. A particular team may rank highly on some of the elements mentioned earlier but it might still not be addressing some critical areas. The needs of each team will differ depending on its phase of development. In turn, these needs have to be met for the team to be successful. For example, in the very early phases a team needs clarity, direction and agreement on goals. This team may enjoy good relationships and a relaxed atmosphere but it will not be effective unless it is clear about its purpose and its goals (see example on 'clarity of purpose' later in this chapter). However, in a later phase of a team's life, conflict may well arise, which will need careful handling. A team that does not have good process skills may not be able to resolve differences between team members effectively. They may have clarity of purpose and goals but may get stuck because they cannot resolve conflict.

There are a number of tell-tale signs that may indicate that a team is in trouble. Once again, this list is not exhaustive but it highlights some signs to look out for.

- Team members are unable to describe the team's mission. This is especially important in the early phases of a team's life but the problem may also occur when a team has been together for a long time and has lost its focus. Alternatively, you may find that every team member is unable to agree with a mission statement.

- If the team meetings are conducted in an uneasy and tense atmosphere, that is a clear sign that all is not well with the team. If no one is prepared to make the effort to ease the tension, the team is likely to be heading for more trouble.
- Some teams enjoy the social side of being part of a team so much that no task gets accomplished. The level of involvement and participation may be very high and team members may enjoy the team interaction. However, if no one is able to be 'task-urgent', this is likely to lead to missed deadlines.
- Listening is key to effective teamworking. If the level of listening is much lower than the level of talking, this is likely to indicate problems. Lack of listening will inevitably lead to misunderstandings, possible conflict and confusion. Communication among team members is likely to be poor.
- If disagreements and differences are not discussed and debated openly, this is likely to signal some internal problems. A tell-tale sign is when you hear about disagreements and differences in private, one-to-one conversations rather than during team meetings.
- When a team has been together for some time and the trust levels are still low, the glue that binds the team together is missing.
- Confusion over who is doing what, duplication of work and no early warning signals of late delivery of work or non-attendance at team meetings can indicate problems.
- All teams require help and support of various kinds from outside. If significant people outside the team are not co-operating, this may indicate that the team is not 'managing the invisible team appropriately'.
- If a team is reluctant to give entry to anyone who is different from other team members, it will lead to a team full of very similar people. This may lead to the team getting stuck because members have allowed themselves to get too narrow and blinkered.
- If a team is reluctant to stop and assess how it is doing this may indicate that members of the team are out of touch with each other.

FRAGMENTATION AND SPEED

One of the key consequences of rapid change, especially once in the middle of it, is fragmentation. Not just a feeling of fragmentation but the actual number of demands fighting for attention.

Henry Mintzberg's work is well documented, showing how fragmented even 'regular' managerial work can be. During change, this process gets magnified many times over. Rosabeth Moss Kanter in the *Change Masters* puts it well, by saying that change mastery is not the job of a 'one-minute manager'. It requires the ability to stay with the fragmentation, not necessarily being able to make sense of all the different pieces, certainly not being able to put all the pieces together at once. The key skill for a team is to be able to see some of these fragments as if in a kaleidoscope, to look for emerging patterns.

During the early stages of a team's work, fragmentation is often a part of life. A team dealing with a major change that involved merging two organisations commented:

'The norm was working on about 50 to 70 problems simultaneously. The interruption was constant, either by telephone or by the hundreds of people who came in and out with queries, suggestions, looking for support or just to make sure that we were still there. Our office was also a corridor leading to the administrative office. While interviewing potential candidates for jobs or discussing the possibility of additional resources with someone, people passing through the corridor/office was a normal occurrence.'

Fragmentation demands flexibility and the ability to be able to move from one subject to another, quickly but intelligently. It is about being able to go from financial to legal to emotional problems, all in the space of a few minutes.

'One particular day comes to mind when there were about seven people looking for attention, for a few minutes of our time. They were all urgent issues. We recall taking each person at a time, listening very carefully to what they had to say, entering into a discussion, giving them a decision, advice or guidance. When we asked the last person how we could help – he had been waiting for 30 minutes for his turn to get time

with us – his question was 'have you seen the coffee tray?'

During times of change especially, the trivial and the major problems seem to get thrown in together unceremoniously. The skill is being able to distinguish which one is which and deal with them appropriately.

'Fragmentation also occurred in terms of our style and behaviour. There was constant tension because tough behaviour needed to be counter-balanced with compassion and concern. We had to recognise that our natural style of working was not necessarily appropriate or effective. This meant a lot more emotional energy was needed to adjust to a style which was appropriate for the situation but not necessarily our favourite'.

The absent and shifting workforce meant that there was a need for constant briefing and debriefing, often having to go over the same issues or concerns many times over.

'Written communication alone was not enough. We had to be there to let people know what was happening. That is what provided some of the psychological comfort for the staff'.

'Fragmentation was a way of life. Fighting it did not get us anywhere. Trying to bring some structure to the various fragments often left people neglected or opportunities missed. The art was in trying to generate energy to deal with all the different pieces as quickly as possible.'

During times of change the actual number of demands fighting for a team's attention can lead to fragmentation. This can be a frustrating time for the team, when progress is slow and can easily get bogged down in trivial detail.

Troubleshooting Techniques

- It is important to stay with the fragmentation, not necessarily being able to make sense of all the different pieces.
- Be alert to the fact that during this phase, it may not be possible to get everything done perfectly.
- Letting go of some things is vital.
- Allocate one or two team members to deal with the immediate problems so that fragmentation does not continue for long periods of time.

- The ability to move from one subject to another quickly and smoothly is helpful.
- Discriminate between trivial and major issues and address them appropriately.
- Match appropriate styles to circumstances. (Leaders and team members). Be alert to the importance of using an 'appropriate' rather than the most familiar style.
- Teams are most likely to experience this problem during the Getting Things Done phase.

LEARNING ON THE RUN

The team leader sometimes feels that he/she has to be an expert in all areas of work. This can lead to the leader taking time to master every aspect of the work and in the process possibly not using team members' expertise. The members do not feel trusted and can feel depowered.

The team leader of a new product development team comments:

'There did not seem to be enough time to take a particular subject and master it, to fully understand it. The learning that had to take place had to be on the run. For example, there was a time when there was need for a decision on the legal aspect of a particular area. Because of various circumstances, there was not time enough to consult properly with the lawyer. So it came down to: "Brief me on the legal aspects of this issue. You have about ten minutes and then I must take a decision or at least be able to talk about it intelligently." The job of the team member briefing me was to ensure that she gave me all the relevant information succinctly. My job was to learn fast, to make sure I understood the key ingredients and ask the right questions to be able to glean this information.

The learning was not confined to one area. This project required me to learn about information technology, software, financial controls, media relationships and many other areas. Learning was always on the run. Getting expert advice was important. The skill was in being able to ask the right questions and having enough detail to make a decision. The biggest block that had to be overcome was not trying to be an expert in every area but using every available resource in the team to get things done. The time of change required me to dive into the unknown constantly and to give up illusions of mastery or expertise. The psychological shift was having to manage something new without being able to master it first, without having all the answers or being an authority on the subject. Trust and trusting others judgement became a key issue.'

Troubleshooting Techniques

- There isn't always enough time to take a particular subject and master it fully. Don't try to be an expert in every area.
- Use every resource available, both within and outside the immediate team.
- Integrate learning on the run as part of everyday life.
- Trusting other team members is vital.
- Enjoy the acquisition of new knowledge. The Getting Going phase is where learning on the run is most necessary.

BROADENING HORIZONS

A customer service team in an ailing car manufacturing company was set up to help reverse the trend and make the company profitable. The threat of closure was ever increasing. This team found that the rest of the organisation was becoming dependent on them and not embracing the change themselves.

The team members gave us their account of how they broadened their horizons:

'The immediate and urgent problems facing our organisation forced us into a survival mode. Because of the speed of response needed there did not seem to be any time to develop people or coach them. Not only was it easier to do it ourselves but to some extent it was the only way, to be directive. The anxiety levels were so high that even competent people had chosen dependency as a way of operating. Our rationale was that we had to work with what we had, just to keep our heads above water'.

'As we understood the length and breadth of this project, we also

understood the urgent need to develop people. Having got ourselves into survival mode and responding to dependency, we now had to learn to start developing people. This meant that our behaviour had to change and our own level of tolerance had to go up. If we were going to progress this change then we would initially have to tolerate mistakes and learn to live with efficiency that was perhaps 90 per cent of what we felt it should be. We also had to change our own behaviour by replacing our responsibility for doing a particular job with being responsible for seeing that systems and procedures were in place so that work was done by others. Control over what was done lay not in doing it ourselves but in the ability to decide what was important. Often in the early days of this change effort it felt like we were the only ones to tackle a job and that ranged from deciding the best way of counselling staff to ensuring that up-to-date information was available.

'Confidence and consistency appeared to be very important. We were aware of the danger of sending out messages saying, "you've got to take more charge" and then rescuing someone the minute they hit the first stumbling block. In doing this we would be reinforcing the dependency by not changing our own behaviour. It was an easy trap to fall into.

'In broadening our horizons, we also had to move from day-to-day survival to setting goals and then driving ourselves and everyone else towards them. Broadening horizons brought more confidence, excitement and some sense of direction for the new customer service approach but it did not mean leaving people alone completely. We were expected to lead, to push and to be out in front showing real teeth.

'This phase meant that everyone working on this project had to start combining toughness and self-confidence with humility and compassion. It could not be one or the other. Both were needed, sometimes simultaneously.

'Broadening horizons may be seen as normal, regular managerial activity. In times of change the focus is often on the change, it has to be, but unless the team is able to broaden that focus and leap forward to the next change, the chances are that the project may get stuck at the vision stage or not be integrated into the organisation. It may appear to stand alone.'

Troubleshooting Techniques

- Move from doing it all alone to bringing in other people by coaching and developing them.
- Broaden horizons by moving from the survival mode to setting longer-term goals for the team and the rest of the organisation.
- Start thinking about what needs to be done beyond just the immediate change.
- This example illustrates moving from Getting Going to Getting Things Done.

ARTICULATING AMBIGUITY

A multi-disciplinary team was appointed to examine the current education system in Spain and recommend an appropriate system for the next decade. Resources had already been cut drastically and there was much anxiety among educators about the possible direction that this team may take.

The team found itself immobilised because it was trying to take account of all the assumptions and uncertainties before it could really start on its research. In addition, team members were faced with a lot of questions that they could not answer.

Their account states that:

'This project required a lot of different people to be articulate on topics that had barely existed before. More importantly, there was often an assumption by people external to the education system that there were answers or points of view on various subjects. The fact that the situation was ambiguous and uncertain, full of assumptions, was often disregarded.

'Creating a scenario of what might be, with all the assumptions and uncertainties thrown in, helped to provide a starting point. By creating this kind of scenario for the education system, we were able to start reducing ambiguity and therefore the anxiety that often goes with it. On the other hand, creating just one scenario was often not enough. In order to increase the chances of success, we had to create a number of different

scenarios, dreaming up options and working on problems from many different angles.

'When we talked about articulating ambiguity, what we found was that even though we were not experts on a certain subject or had not yet fully mastered all the details of a particular problem, it seemed important to start constructing a point of view. This often helped to make the situation or the subject less ambiguous. The next stage was having the courage to present it to different people – that again helped to reduce anxiety for everyone. Although it may not have been the answer or the point of view we finally ended up with, it did help to start the debate, to get people interested and clarify their thoughts by someone having articulated what, for most people, might have been a vague feeling.

'Articulating ambiguity clearly provided not only an intellectual challenge but it was often coupled with the obvious test of reactions from others testing its reality.'

Troubleshooting Techniques

- Create a scenario of what might be.
- Include all the uncertainties and assumptions.
- Start the debate by articulating that which might only be a vague feeling for other people.
- Start the communication process early. Don't try to get all questions answered before you start talking to interested parties.
- Move from Getting Going to Getting Things Done.

THE 'EEK' FACTOR

Change can often immobilise people; either because of the task that faces them or indeed the unknown elements of change. It is often not recognised that a team appointed to bring about change may itself be confronted by this 'eek' factor.

The leader of a medical team sent to Romania to work with sick children comments:

'There is something about change that even when intellectually a person is excited by it and looking forward to it, it can still immobilise.

'Over and over again during our time in Romania I came across this factor in myself and in other people. There were times when competent people were immobilised, were unable to respond or to take a decision. There were child care specialists who had worked in the area for many years who were clearly very experienced, yet attempting to tap into this experience was difficult at times. Somehow the magnitude of change and the speed with which it was moving seemed to have reduced some people to filling the space with words but no decisions, no recommendation and certainly no action. Good, competent medics had become afraid of the very thing they were there to do.

'Although we had experienced medical staff and experienced child care specialists, the magnitude, depth and gravity of the problems often left some of them unable to respond quickly . . .

'The "eek" factor struck our team many times during this assignment. At times this lasted only momentarily and then we were able to plunge in and get on with what we had to do. At other times, the "eek" factor remained with a particular team member for longer, sometimes days, immobilising not only that individual but other people around them and slowing down or bringing to a halt progress in a particular direction. What we had to find was a way of acknowledging the "eek" factor also, but more importantly, spinning ourselves out of it and into the next stage. Sometimes, not always, change was fun but it always demanded courage and risk taking.'

Troubleshooting Techniques

- Acknowledge the immobilisation that can occur as a result of the 'eek' factor.
- Get beyond it by focusing on the overall goal of the team.
- The only way to find out how something will turn out is by doing it.
- Have the courage to try to do things differently.
- Provide support and encouragement for individual team members to help them spin out of this stage.

- The 'eek' factor is clearly an example of teams visiting the Getting Stuck phase of their development.

CONFLICT

It would be naive to pretend that teams are always cohesive and so committed to the task and each other that conflict never occurs. Just the opposite. There is probably more conflict in high performing teams than in ordinary teams. Conflict is a necessary and useful part of team life. Some teams can smooth it over, others allow it to become destructive, others look at it directly and do all they can to resolve it. Conflict, properly managed and constructively employed can lead to a greater understanding among team members.

Conflict can occur for many different reasons, and if not properly managed it can hinder a team's progress for long periods of time. One of the most common causes is limited resources. Team members often find themselves competing for a share of what is available. While a certain amount of competition is healthy, too much has consequences that are not only bad for the team but can have undesirable results for the whole organisation.

In one photographic team, there were a number of different lines; each team member cutting and packaging different types of film and photographic paper. Three team members each had a number of different lines. The maintenance department served all the team members. Inevitably, there was a particular day when all the machines broke down simultaneously. Each team member insisted that his/her breakdown was the most urgent. There were heated arguments and a lot of time was lost as each team member pushed for priority. The situation was difficult to resolve and this conflict seemed to trigger a series of other conflicts among team members that had been bubbling under the surface for a few weeks. This resulted in the team missing its deadlines, members spending time arguing and blaming each other and for that period of time totally losing sight of the team's objective. In this particular example, it took an intervention from the team's sponsor to help get the team back on track.

If conflict in teams is not handled properly, it has a habit of reappearing under different guises. Managing the team's internal conflict is perhaps the most difficult and most time-consuming aspect because team members have to find a way of talking about the conflict, resolving it and getting on with what they are there to do in the first place.

Troubleshooting Techniques

- Live through it, it will eventually be over. In other words, sweat it out.
- Wear down the conflict by pushing until there is no more energy to continue the conflict.
- Rise above individual conflict and focus on what is best for the team.
- It's important to keep the team together; don't isolate people.
- Before the next team meeting, send in a diplomat to smooth the way.
- Separate out the tasks of the people involved in the conflict. Make them less interdependent.
- Consult a third party who can act as an honest broker between the members in conflict.
- Use the authority of the leader to decide how to proceed if all else fails.

Conflict can happen at any phase of development – this example illustrates it as an everyday part of the process.

BEYOND VISION

Teams sometimes get so excited by the vision they have created that they get stuck at this stage. They are unable to formulate strategies for moving beyond vision. Alternatively, the planning phase takes so long that they miss opportunities.

The importance for teams to alternate planning and implementing in short 'plan-do' cycles was noted in *Superteams*. Essentially this means getting away from the linear and traditionally used process of planning an event, intervention or product from beginning to end before the implementation process can start. This can cause difficulties for teams in a number of ways, especially in a rapidly changing business environment. By the time the team's planning process has been completed, the product may already be obsolete. Competitors will have brought something new to the market.

One of the biggest barriers to implementing change and moving beyond creating a vision is the attitude that teams have towards planning. Too much time and energy may be devoted to trying to predict the unpredictable in an effort to reduce risk, uncertainty and ambiguity. This often results in highly complex and sophisticated plans, which in fact induce rigidity and inhibit creativity and innovation. The traditional way in which planning is done has the effect of extending lead times and reducing quality and productivity. It also often makes it difficult to experience those successes that are so important in maintaining commitment, high energy levels and the willingness to pursue further activities and overcome problems.

Increasingly, teams are having to find different ways of working in their attempts to move beyond vision and in dealing with uncertain situations and a constantly changing marketplace. We often use a simple exercise on training programmes where a team is given a project and asked to devise the most efficient way of doing it. A number of key things invariably happen:

- Almost always a separate sub-team of planners is set up and those responsible for implementation are largely excluded from the planning process.
- The planning team delivers the results of the planning process to the implementing team, telling it what has to be done, dictating timescales and setting out a plan of how it is to be done. This is only done after the detailed plan is completed.
- The 'doing' phase of the project is always a separate activity that follows after the detailed planning phase, as in a relay race.
- Before the implementing team can do anything, it often has communication problems because the key elements of the plan are expressed in the planning team's jargon.

- A lot of time is spent arguing on exactly how long each of the activities is going to take and in what order they should be done.
- The activities in the implementation phase are ordered in a linear fashion, one activity only starting after the previous one has been competed (another relay race).

The common thread running though all these situations is that 'things haven't gone according to plan'. Planning, which is a very persuasive form of thinking, cannot by definition deal with ambiguous, uncertain and complex problems that teams face today, especially during times of rapid change.

Troubleshooting Techniques

- Plan for implementation early.
- Get away from the traditional, linear planning process. Use short plan–do cycles. Each cycle can provide feedback and data which can be used to predict future activities.
- Planning and doing may need to start in parallel. Plan the broad activities and set milestones instead of planing for every detail.
- Planners and doers need to work together from an early stage. Plan both what has to be done and how it will be done.
- Implementing vision is an untidy and messy process. Create strategies for moving beyond creating a vision without trying to plan out every last detail.
- Teams moving from Getting Going to Getting Things Done.

CLARITY OF PURPOSE

Support teams were created during a week-long corporate culture change programme. Managers from all levels, functions and disciplines attended the programme, which formed part of a larger culture change effort. During the week, people worked on various projects in teams of seven or eight. Each team had a tutor attached to it. After the programme, the support team were encouraged to meet, creating their own time and finding their own resources. They were to meet to support each other in carrying forward the messages of the corporate programme.

One of the first problems was the fact that the support team members were often at different corners of the globe. Some of the more enterprising members found a way round that by combining a business trip with a support team meeting. Others were less successful. After the initial high of the programme and promises of 'we must meet within the next month', when the team did meet for the first time, they still had things to talk about from the programme and feedback from questionnaires received after the programme had to be shared. Thereafter, the teams fizzled out rapidly. They did not seem to be serving a purpose any more. Perhaps if some of the principles of effective teamworking could have been applied – for example, dealing with a specific issue and being action oriented – these teams could have contributed more fully to the change process in this company. Unstructured, with no objective or purpose, the teams were of limited value. What they did was to go some way towards breaking down organisational barriers and give a little more insight to people about what other functions did. In our opinion, this was a missed opportunity; the teams were fired up and ready to contribute but they needed a focus.

TROUBLESHOOTING TECHNIQUES

- Be clear about why a team is being set up and what it is there to do.
- Define the purpose of the team, the objectives and the expected outcomes.
- Provide a clear focus for the teams.
- Ensure that team members can define and accept the vision, mission, goal or task of the team.
- The Getting Together phase is crucial if teams are to achieve anything.

WHEN NOTHING SEEMS TO WORK

It is rare to come across a team where 'nothing seems to have worked'. Usually, there are some elements of teamworking or some aspects of the task itself that can be the saving grace. The following case–study is depressing but it is also very illustrative of a number of key factors that need to be in place for effective teamworking. We have chosen to report this case very fully, while, for obvious reasons, protecting the identity of the team. The team had existed for 12 months but had not delivered in either their own terms or in terms of what the 'sponsor' hoped for. The team consisted of six people who were charged with responsibility for a quality issue which was leading this firm to lose market share. The comments are from team members:

> 'There were no set roles for us and no leader to orchestrate the team efforts. We did not know what the ground-rules were. It was the personality of certain members that dictated how the team worked and how meetings were organised; because of this, some team members were pitching in more than others. Laying down some ground rules and allocating team roles might have alleviated this problem and avoided any friction and resentment felt by some members about others over the uneven work load.
>
> 'There also appeared to be lack of commitment and involvement from some team members, even though they knew that it was an important task. Team members often did not attend the meetings that had been set, for a number of reasons. In particular because they had "other things, more important to do" and in one case, a senior manager pulled one team member from the team without explanation to the rest of the team. Having team members pulled out by their bosses without any explanation was not very encouraging. Bad feelings also occurred when non-attendance of team members was "punished" by assigning them tasks in their absence.
>
> 'Probably one of the greatest difficulties that we experienced was the lack of supervision and direction of the team's activities and its members. There was no one person who was championing the cause or pulling it all together, no focal point for the team. With the lack of ground rules,

there was no way of monitoring the team's activities. This often resulted in team members feeling disorientated and there were often unspoken and unaimed feelings of resentment towards other members. This was either because they were not pulling their weight or because they were not attending the scheduled meetings. When things went a bit flat in the group, due to non-attendance, someone getting pulled out from the team or because there was a bad atmosphere around, there was a tendency for people to feel demotivated and to pull themselves away from the team experience rather than to try to pull together and "make it work".

'We experienced other difficulties, when team meetings had to fit in with many other teams and work commitments. It became a real juggling act, just to fix up a time when everyone could be there. As the team involved three senior managers, they often had to pull out of meetings at the last minute or turn up late or leave early (without even the courtesy of communicating to the rest of the team, who had managed to get there despite other commitments) due to other priorities.*

'We were given one year to deal with this problem. This was really too long and it had a demotivating effect on the team members. It was so much harder to maintain momentum, because the time frame imposed on us was just too long.*

'In retrospect, we felt that it should have been made clear to all team members what the ground rules were, what the expectations were and that the team was here to stay and that everyone would attend. We should also have found a way of showing courtesy and communicating more effectively with each other. I am sure we would have benefited from having a team leader, to help us to focus and to monitor our team's efforts and to be clear about the roles and responsibilities expected from each team member. The leader could have helped us to clarify each others' perceptions of what we felt we could contribute to the team and what we felt we owed to the team effort. We needed to look at the whole issue of participation – what jobs should be taken by whom? – to ensure that everyone was contributing evenly in the teamworking process. If you are assigned to a team, then you should be made to participate. Obviously, the team members' expertise is invaluable, which is why they are there in the first place. We needed to be much more aware of the processes involved in working as a team rather than only concentrating on the results. In this way, it may be possible to break* *down the problems into smaller issues, its constituent parts, otherwise tackling the problem appears to be "big, unwieldy and takes too long".'*

Troubleshooting Techniques

Leadership

- Determine what kind of leadership role may be necessary for the particular team.
- Provide clear direction and create a climate that stimulates high performance.
- Manage team members' performance by defining, monitoring and rewarding performance.
- Constantly analyse how the team is working and how it can be improved.
- Be clear about which roles need to be fixed and which ones can be flexible.

Membership

- Clarify each team member's responsibilities and roles.
- Specify the level of involvement and commitment that will be necessary.
- Identify and utilise each team member's expertise.

Planning

- Plan 'What' needs to be done and 'How' it will be done.
- Develop internal success criteria. Articulate standards, expectations and objectives.
- Establish who will do what and to what standards, what are the time limits and how the team will conduct itself.
- Set hard criteria by articulating time, cost, resources and technical standards.
- Set soft criteria by articulating attitudes, skills and behaviour.
- Agree a set of ground-rules which indicate 'the way we do things around here'.

- Involve the whole team in the planning process. Use the plan to provide a way for the team to monitor its performance against expectations.
- Set realistic milestones within the overall project plan.

All excellent examples of what happens if the first three phases of development do not take place – it becomes almost impossible to succeed in the Getting Things Done phase.

MOVING ON

There must come a point in any team's life when it is time to move on, either for individual team members or for the team as a whole because its particular work has been completed. The hardest part of letting go is a feeling of there being a lot more that needs to be done and the work not yet being complete. However, it may now be the work of a different kind of team member to take the work further. In our consulting practice, we have often come across teams whose work is done, team members who need to move on for organisational reasons or personal ones, yet who may get stuck, unable to let go or not being allowed to let go. This can often kill the change that has been started. Tradition, history and bureaucracy can set in.

The art is in being able to decide when to hang on and when it is time to let go. A team that does not persist, push or shove will not be able to get the change rolling forward, yet if it does not let go at the appropriate time, the same team can get in the way of future change and innovation.

Troubleshooting Techniques

- Keep the momentum going until the end but recognise when it is time to move on.

- The team leader needs to look after the interests of the team members and of the organisation.
- Have a structured approach to hand over the product or the service and to help the team to move on.
- Shows the need to recognise and manage the Getting Out phase.

9. Managing External Boundaries and Relationships

INTRODUCTION

Teams do not exist in isolation. They are usually part of a larger organisation. At times, teams can get so inward looking that they lose touch with the reality of the rest of the company. At other times, it is the rest of the company that can be the cause of problems for the team. Often the issues centre around managing boundaries and relationships. The following pages illustrate some of the more common reasons why teams may find themselves unable to proceed smoothly. The 'invisible team' can help or hinder teamworking.

MANAGING EXPECTATIONS

Teams in organisational settings are established with the purpose of delivering a product or service to another group or individual, often referred to as the 'sponsor'. In some of the more radical illustrations we have quoted earlier in this book, where a whole organisation structure has been based on teamworking, the sponsor can be regarded as the board of directors. Where they are also integrated in a teamworking culture the sponsors are the customers/clients and, where appropriate, the shareholders.

If a gap emerges between what the sponsor expects and what the team expects, then problems can arise. The gap can appear for a variety of different reasons such as the desire of the team to go its own way (see DIFFERENT AGENDAS below). It may emerge, however, as an accidental by-product of a different set of intentions. In the case of one of our clients, the head office had asked a Project Team to deliver results on an innovative and high profile project, in a very short space of time. In briefing the Project Team, they had also managed to convey to them that they could do pretty much what they liked, as long as they produced the results. The Project Team, perhaps alarmed at the seriousness of the directive but also hearing correctly the underlying message about the importance of the project, acted accordingly. It started to borrow resources and spend unauthorised budgets in order to get the job done. Both parties ended up bewildered and frustrated. The head office sponsors reacted badly because they claimed that they had never given their express permission for some of the spending and what they saw as the commandeering of resources. With equal indignation, the Project Team claimed that it had responded very responsibly by making every effort to ensure that it delivered the end product.

Having witnessed the earlier days of a small manufacturing company making a big shift in culture towards organisation wide teamworking it is clear how initial over-enthusiasm can lead to a later mismatch in expectations. In order to get the process started, the sponsors, who were mainly the directors of the firm, gave everyone a lot of messages to the effect that they were competent, capable people with hidden potential and they should seize the opportunity that teamworking presented. The change in culture was a messy process and not without cynicism and resistance from some sections of the company. In the face of this opposition, the directors re-doubled their efforts and strongly reinforced their earlier messages.

The company had chosen to use self-managing teams with very little formal structure and a reporting link to the directors, who themselves formed a team. Once the teams had been formed, some problems began to emerge. The less mature individuals had taken on board the message which said 'anyone can do anything, if they only try' very literally. A team had been formed to take on the responsibility for the internal marketing of the next phase of teamworking. The membership consisted of some people experienced in marketing and some complete novices who were swept away by the spirit of doing something new and who were willing to give it a try. Their first attempt at an internal marketing poster was extraordinarily naive and had very little motivational impact. One of the more experienced marketing managers knew it was inadequate, voiced a faint protest but didn't press the point because she felt it was against the spirit of teamworking. The end result was that the posters were released and received a lukewarm response from most of the company but an icy reception from the team of directors.

In the ensuing arguments it became clear that expectations were out of line. A number of people had taken the message to seize opportunities at face value and were prepared to do so, whether or not they were skilled. Some of the more experienced managers who were formerly in senior positions and who had now been integrated into one of the teams were reluctant to define standards in case it was seen as a covert attempt to reintroduce hierarchy. The directors' team had expected that standards would be maintained throughout the culture change and had underestimated the impact of their calls for people to take the initiative for tackling new challenges.

Troubleshooting Techniques

- Spend time with the sponsors testing what their expectations are. If they are not very clear or forthcoming try some examples such as 'if we were to go and recruit a new team member without consulting you – how would you feel about that?'
- Express the team's expectations as fully as possible, especially in critical areas such as the limits of the team's authority.
- Be prepared for the expectations of both sides to change over time and be open to negotiation.
- In the event of a clash of expectations put more time into the processes described above.

The first phase of a team's life depends on absolute clarity.

Different agendas

It is the very success of a team-based way of working that can sometimes cause problems within an organisation. We noted in Chapter 1 that the oxygen of involvement in a team can produce a deep level of commitment and a sense of group identity on the part of the individual members. A major benefit from the individual's point of view is a greater sense of satisfaction and fulfilment; from the organisation's standpoint, the benefit is the pay-off of greater output and a more responsible workforce. Problems emerge when a team takes on a set of values or ways of working which essentially depart from the culture of the organisation.

We saw the effects of a divergence between team and corporate cultures in a major company in the leisure sector. The senior management had correctly identified the power of instilling a customer care culture in the company and had chosen a number of initiatives, including a call for employees to join voluntary teams to examine ways of improving customer care. These customer care teams were launched amid a fanfare of internal publicity involving the circulation of a special newsletter, the offer of substantial prizes for the most innovative ideas and time off from work for the customer care team leaders. The teams ran reasonably well for a year and although some of the initial enthusiasm had tailed off, the teams had been consistently supported by senior management.

At the end of the first year we were called in to analyse progress to date and provide suggestions for revitalising teams for the coming year. During our research we were struck by three things. All the surviving teams were remarkably cohesive, they were very resistant to change and they had all evolved a pattern of working which celebrated brainstorming but very little else. Many of the teams had come to define the process of serving the customer in the very narrow terms of their own area of responsibility. They were not particularly interested in how their operation impacted on other areas of the company and how they could combine resources and ideas to provide a better total service. In fact, most teams were resistant to our suggestions that their membership would benefit from people joining them from other teams.

From the beginning, the teams had learned the skills of brainstorming and clearly still found it an enjoyable process. It was noticeable, however, that over the course of a year, the number of ideas capable of successful implementation had tailed off very rapidly. Although there was no visible depletion of innovative energy there was a dwindling concern for the organisational relevance and the commercial practicality of the ideas. A growing amount of the output of the teams either focused on high cost options for enhancing customer satisfaction or placed a strong emphasis on enhancing employee satisfaction with only a tenuous link with customer care. It was as if the process of being in the team and the fun of brainstorming had taken over from the original purpose of the team's formation.

Senior managers were very disappointed to hear the direction that the customer care teams had taken, but because of their voluntary nature felt reluctant to intervene. They allowed them to decline naturally and chose to accept the occasional morsel of a useful idea from the huge brainstormed output. This was a classic case of a team evolving such a different agenda from the original blueprint that the end product was barely recognisable.

More disturbingly, the teams experienced themselves as distanced from senior management, whom they saw as having lost interest in the initiative and unwilling to commit money to potentially useful ideas.

Troubleshooting Techniques

- Teams need to be provided with a reason to keep their agenda in line with the rest of the organisation so that some of their goals clearly serve a 'super-ordinate' goal.
- Training and coaching of team members should stress cohesiveness and co-operation as a global concept, extending beyond the boundaries of the team itself with tangible rewards for people who are seen to practise the concept.
- The agendas of both team and organisation should be made as explicit as possible.

- Both the team and the organisation need to feed back regularly and in depth on their progress towards their respective goals.
- Illustrates the need to be able to assess whether the team is still in the Getting Things Done phase or whether it should be working through the Getting Out phase.

INTEGRATING WITH THE HIERARCHY

The comparative lack of hierarchy within many teams is one of the dimensions that lends flexibility and speed to teamworking, as we have seen in Chapter 1. This can create problems when the team needs to integrate with an organisational structure that is more hierarchical than itself.

Case Study

Dead on Arrival

A manufacturer of visual display units for a range of computer applications was struggling with a particularly intractable quality problem. The company had grown at a phenomenal rate on the back of the information technology boom of the early 1980s, with much care and attention from the senior management and an enthusiastic workforce. When we first met the directors, they were proud of their quality achievement and could boast a complete absence of 'dead on arrival' (DOAs) deliveries (their term for a set of kit that was found by the customer not to be working, from the moment it was unpacked). The directors acknowledged that as they passed the 400 employees mark they could not guarantee to know their staff individually, that the business would lose some of its 'family' feel and that the risk of DOAs would greatly increase.

When the first DOA was announced, the directors acted swiftly and set up a quality guarantee task force. This task force was drawn

Case Study

almost exclusively from the shop floor operatives who were closest to the daily problems. The directors were so concerned about the significance of the DOAs that they gave the task force time away from daily duties and the resources that they needed on the condition that they solved the problem quickly and effectively. At the same time, they let it be known that they expected full co-operation with the task force from the rest of the company.

The task force swiftly located what they thought was a critical problem with dust contamination at one of the assembly stages. On the day they made the discovery, the Production Manager and his assistant were out on site visits so they reported their findings immediately to one of the directors, who was delighted and urged them to pursue their line of investigation further.

Although the company was quite small and reasonably informal, everyone was used to a fairly traditional reporting structure. On their return, both the Production Manager and assistant complained that they had not been consulted and argued that the task force should have reported their findings through them. In the ensuing confrontation, the director intervened on behalf of the task force, arguing that the nature and urgency of the problem took precedence over the normal reporting protocol. At the same time, the directors had to work hard to manage the wounded pride and hurt feelings of the Production Manager and assistant.

A further conflict emerged when the task force was asked to interview one of the technical specialists. The specialist felt threatened by the interview because he was accustomed to being able to guide and direct the activities of the operatives from a position of superior knowledge. In this particular instance the task force operatives knew more about some of the technical details than the specialist, simply because they had been conducting such detailed research into a quality problem. As a result of feeling threatened, he was not as forthcoming as he might have been and the operatives felt he was withholding information deliberately and accused him of doing so. Again, the directors had to intervene to mediate in a difficult interpersonal conflict.

Although hierarchies create barriers and slow down a number of processes, they sometimes lend people – and satisfy needs for – status and security. If these props are being removed it requires careful handling and an explanation of the reasons. Where this has not happened the stakeholders in the hierarchy are reluctant to focus their attention on the benefits less structured ways of working can bring.

Troubleshooting Techniques

- Spend time explaining to all concerned the benefits of working with and without hierarchies, when two systems are expected to co-exist.
- To those expected to continue to work in a hierarchical fashion point out the advantages of recognising people for their contribution as well as their position. Make it clear that they are likely to witness unusual ways of working on the part of teams using flat structures.
- For those operating in a hierarchy who feel undermined or threatened by having to witness a very different way of working, find ways of recognising their contribution, reward signs of co-operation and discourage competitive or inflexible behaviour.
- Spend time with teams coaching them in the skills of influencing others who are working in a different way and encourage ways of influencing others that will attempt to 'pull' people on side rather than 'pushing' them to a desired conclusion.

- Teams who have really made it to the Getting Things Done phase need to work hard at managing the outside in order not to get stuck by external forces.

POLARISATION

Some teams lose heart because they find that they are not very popular. The issue that is central to their work may lead outsiders to take very different stances. The team can feel pulled from one direction to another, sometimes losing friends and making enemies.

The Spanish team exploring an alternative education system described their experience:

'Any change tends to produce a polarity of views. Our project was not different. It produced polarisation at all sorts of levels. There were those people who thought it was a great idea and wished we had done something like this earlier. There were other people who said the whole concept of an alternative education system was wrong. We had to acknowledge both points of view.

'Whatever else happened, this particular change did not leave anyone who came into contact with it untouched or unconcerned. Somehow it seemed to drive people towards taking vastly exaggerated stances, one way or the other. One example was of someone who helped us with some training, a very mild mannered professor. He was drawn into a debate where he almost felt forced to take a side and portray his views in a letter that was so strongly worded and which was so out of character that it totally baffled everyone.

'Polarisation was a difficult issue to deal with. It was difficult not to try to smooth things over, but instead to try to explain the reality as it was, to give answers where answers existed and to try to win people over who were clearly opposed to the whole idea. The only way to cope with this situation was in a Zen-like fashion, to go with the flow, to keep the debate alive and the issue in focus. The reasons for this were numerous. We needed funds to continue the project, and we needed to continuously remind ourselves that we were also in the business of political, social and legal change and that required not only heightened awareness but in depth debate of the issue from all the different angles.

While instinctively, we wanted everyone to support the idea and promote it, it was useless trying to turn a highly complex issue into a simple one. Polarisation during the early part of any change effort is almost inevitable. We needed to work with our supporters and with our critics despite the fact that it was time consuming. The fact that the critics had a point of view was better than indifference.'

Troubleshooting Techniques

- Acknowledge the full range of views, especially at the exploration stage of the project.
- Try not to smooth over that which is a complex issue.
- Work with supporters and critics, as both are important in the long run.
- Keep an open mind and listen to the different ideas. Try not to close the debate too soon.
- Remember the need to bring 'invisible team' members through the first three phases so that they join in the Getting Things Done phase rather than cause blockages.

THE SIEGE MENTALITY

Teams have often reported a feeling of 'the whole world being against us and the project' and yet being prepared to persist with the project and what they believe in. If a team is undertaking some new, different or innovative work, then it needs to stand up and take all the criticisms, and passionately continue to believe in what it is trying to do.

Start-up teams or early phases of change projects cannot always deliver on those things that mature organisations can. Yet the pressure, mostly external but at times internal as well, is intense to deliver on things like products, figures, decisions, solutions. The pressure and criticism mount as attempts are made to hold them off. Other people do not believe that the team may not have the data and are often accused of withholding information, of being difficult and secretive. The team has to be brave and say 'we are not ready to talk about . . .' whatever the subject under discussion might have been.

The team can end up feeling as if it is under siege.

Such attacks on the team seem to heighten the siege mentality. One of the teams who took part in our research commented:

'At times it felt like we were paranoid, but it could just have been the situation we found ourselves in. The enemy was not only outside but also within. Keeping an eye open for that was equally important. For example, one or two significant people in the organisation gave out messages that were totally different from what we were actually trying to do, thereby almost dragging the team in a completely different direction. We had leaks of information to the press. We were dealing with highly confidential and sensitive information. We were aware that information was being leaked which was not helping us. The culprit had to be someone internal, someone closely related to our project. This category was perhaps the most frightening, the most difficult to assess and the most harmful.

'The main skill (apart from courage and optimism) in dealing with these situations was the ability to say "No, we are not ready, we don't have the answer". That often left us feeling isolated, criticised and locked in but that also helped us to survive, to pull up the drawbridge until we could respond or felt safe to do so. The siege mentality seemed to be part of the change process, sometimes driven by external forces and sometimes by internal influences. Knowing that we were in a state of siege, not panicking, being able to say "no" or "not yet" helped us through those times.

'Of course, such an attitude can be interpreted as protective, defensive and unhelpful. We were open to the criticism that if we didn't have something to hide, why were we being secretive and if we believed in the change that we were introducing, why weren't we letting people in to examine it. The reality was that we didn't have all the answers, not everything was sorted out and effort put into answering accusations deflected us from our true purpose. In this way, the siege mentality afforded us some protection and helped us to move forward at times.'

Troubleshooting Techniques

- Pull up the drawbridge if it feels necessary to do so.
- It is legitimate to say 'No we don't have all the answers just yet'.
- Don't panic. Conserve energy for the project.
- Keep interested parties informed of the team's progress, but avoid being pressurised into giving details before you are ready to do so.

Getting Things Done means holding off sometimes. The need for this needs to be communicated.

IS THIS FOR REAL?

A number of cross-functional task forces were set up in a small but highly successful architectural design company. The teams had a specific focus and were asked to do certain things within given time frames. It seemed as if setting up the teams had released a lot of extra energy within the company. The task forces achieved more in a few weeks than the whole organisation had achieved over a number of years. The problems arose when the company tried to start the implementation process. The sponsors of these teams were senior managers, who were also the founding fathers of the company. While they were keen to get the process of change started and were happy to set up the teams, they weren't ready to manage the consequences of what it meant for them. Fear and insecurity gripped them as the younger executives were seen to be taking over and pushing the organisation in a direction perhaps not anticipated by the founding fathers.

The blocks appeared in strange ways – for example, not being able to get an appointment with the sponsor for a presentation on the outcome of the project; the paper was not written in the style that the sponsors were used to and so on. In this case, the teams were working extremely efficiently but faltering commitment from the sponsors, driven by fear, insecurity and perhaps not enough involvement by the team leader led to problems at the time when the sponsor was most needed, that is, at the implementation stage.

Troubleshooting Techniques

- Clarify the sponsor's roles and responsibilities early. Ensure that you have his/her commitment.
- Test the organisation's commitment by negotiating success criteria with the relevant people. Be clear about what they expect from the team and articulate the team's expectations of them.
- Keep the sponsor involved throughout the project.
- Agree a broad plan with the sponsor and schedule regular times for progress meetings and reports back.
- The first three phases of development require continued reinforcement of clarity and commitment from outside as well as within the team.

MANAGING THE INVISIBLE TEAM

Teams do not operate in a vacuum and they cannot be successful if they use only their own resources. Teams that become purely inward-looking eventually fail because they lose contact with what is going on around them. External contacts are vital. Key people outside the team, such as customers, clients, users and sponsors have expectations of the team and also make demands of it. Each of these external roles, if managed well, can contribute significantly to the team's success. If the 'invisible team' is not well managed it can get in the way of the team's progress. The client and the customer can often be an invaluable source of guidance, information and ideas, yet many teams neglect them.

Teams usually need a sponsor who can serve as godfather, mentor and promoter. A good sponsor can increase the life of a team and provide access to resources like budget, staff and publicity. Multi-disciplinary teams need the co-operation of the functional departments from which team members are drawn. The managers of the functional departments can support the team by encouraging their staff to give priority to the team's requests. Service departments can provide information, staff, expertise, facilities and equipment that can be vital to the success of the team. Managing boundaries is an important aspect of teamwork, and selecting the best person to do the job is a key decision. Lack of information about the team can lead to a lack of credibility. Ultimately, a poor image can hamper team success. It is important for the team, (especially in the early days), to inform others, understand and overcome objectives, understand the different points of view and motives of all the parties involved, and influence and persuade key people on how the idea can benefit the organisation.

Troubleshooting Techniques

- Select the best person for the team to manage boundaries and the 'invisible team'.
- Share the recognition and credit for team successes with the 'invisible team'.
- Keep the 'invisible team' informed of actions that may have an impact on them.
- Encourage contact, communication and feedback from client, customers and sponsors.

Teams need to record and publicise phases of development right from the point of Getting Together.

THE PRESSURE ON FAST DELIVERY

The need to produce results in a much shorter space of time, identified as a Change Imperative in the Introduction, can create extraordinary pressures on the people involved. While teamworking can be a vehicle for speeding up processes and sharing the burdens of pressure, there are limits to what it can achieve. Opponents of teamworking will often point to the time taken by a team in consultation and in discussion. At the same time they may highlight the effectiveness of the single manager making quick-fire decisions without the need for consultation. Yet complex decisions can rarely be taken by a lone individual. More commonly, such a decision has to struggle up through several layers of management only to struggle down again once it has achieved the official seal of approval.

Even if ponderous hierarchies could be replaced by a set of Clint

Eastwood, 'men–with–no–name' managers who fired off decisions rather like the great cowboy actor shoots villains, the critics of the speed of team decision making are often missing the point. Some decisions are unsuitable to be taken by a single individual. This is particularly true if the successful implementation of the decision demands wholehearted commitment on the part of those required to execute it. Groups of highly paid and highly marketable specialists are renowned for choosing to exercise their career choices if they feel that their employers are ignoring their views or feelings. In many service sector jobs in which organisations are expecting their staff to treat their customers with understanding and empathy, a style of management that imposes autocratic decisions on the people who deal with the customers is unlikely to produce the desired result simply because it is so incongruous. The mixed message implicit here is 'treat your customers in a caring and adult fashion but don't expect us to do the same to you'.

Decisions that have many different variables will involve opinion as well as fact; those which lead to a range of possible outcomes with no single 'correct solution' are almost always beyond the reach of a single individual. These decisions demand input from a number of sources and the power of analysis by several different people.

A way to determine which decisions require a team approach and which can be taken by managers working alone is provided by two US authorities on participative management, Vroom and Jago. They outline a good set of rule of thumb guides to help managers to determine which mode they should be operating in. Their guidelines extend beyond a simple solo decision/group decision choice and explore consultation processes with individuals as well as groups. This neatly mirrors the point raised in *Superteams* that people can operate in a teamworking fashion ('the team apart') even when they are not all gathered together in one place. One of the many important messages behind the Vroom and Jago model is that a collective decision making process takes time and that time is an important ingredient in allowing the benefits of team decision making to take place. Commitment to a decision, especially if it is an unpopular one with some team members, only comes with the proper expenditure of time (even if it is only to allow the process of voicing concerns or disagreement).

Having worked with the Vroom and Jago model ourselves, in helping managers to learn about participative management, we have often witnessed a phenomenon that we have come to describe as 'the veneer of consultation'. A manager will opt for a highly participative decision making style in a given situation, often giving the impression of having handed over to his/her team altogether. If the team does not look like making rapid progress, the manager's growing impatience will often cause him/her to interfere and demand an instant decision with the threat of an imposed decision if it is not forthcoming. The end result is often a poor-quality decision because it has been forced, or one to which there is little commitment because the manager has imposed it.

We worked with a manager who intellectually believed in the value of participative management, but emotionally could not come to terms with the fact that it does not always progress smoothly. When he managed to gain agreement from the organisation that his department should be given room to expand on to a new floor of the building, he decided that he would hand over the process of planning office allocation to the members of his department. They were unused to sole responsibility and very quickly became bogged down in a series of counter-productive squabbles. Instead of intervening to help, he became frustrated with them and set in place a 'guillotine motion' whereby failure to reach a decision within 15 minutes meant that they handed the prerogative of decision making back to him. The 15 minutes was taken up with further debate about the manager's behaviour at the end of which he took the decision. This had the unfortunate effect of producing a plan that everyone felt free to gripe about – and did so – over the ensuing months. Not only that, there grew to be a healthy mistrust of his attempts at participative management and people would stop trying to become a self-managing group and wait instead for the inevitable imposed decision.

The frustration and impatience of managers who will not wait for consensus reaching processes to take their natural course can strangle the development of teamworking. This is particularly true in the early stages of a complex teamworking programme that is scheduled to last a long time or even permanently. If teams are not allowed or helped to sort out their own problems early on they may not develop the maturity they need for tough decision making. One of the ways that they may be prevented from developing is if the pressure to move quickly is so severe they either do not get time to sort out their internal workings or managers intervene to wrestle back control of a project.

Troubleshooting Techniques

- Be fair when assessing the time it is taking a team to make decisions.
- If a team's processes still seem to be slow, share the problem with the team but give it some latitude, especially in the early phases of development.
- If intervention does prove necessary, the motivation should be to find permanent ways of speeding up the team's processes for future success rather than just a quick fix of today's problem.
- Intervention described above may take the form of training and an attempt to get the team to take on board faster ways of working for its own good and that of the company.
- Teams need time to work through the first three phases of development.

Conclusion

The choice to adopt teamworking involves risk. It is possible to map out traditional, hierarchical control and command structures which give the appearance at least of being ordered, rational and logical. In pyramid fashion, direction flows from the top to the bottom and the results of tasks carried out flow dutifully back from the bottom to the top. Throwing out or even amending what to some feels like the only way to run an organisation is risky.

The two problems with the pyramid model are that it doesn't actually work as smoothly as the organisation chart might suggest and it is woefully inadequate to deal with the current scope and pace of change.

Joseph Heller lifts the lid off organisational life in *Something Happened* when he illustrates the immensely complex web of jealousy, competition and back-stabbing that can accompany the sharply defined pecking order that a pyramid of people often implies. Even if a command and control structure worked on a purely rational basis it does not have anything like the speed, responsiveness and flexibility to deal with a world rendered highly unpredictable by huge swings in economic fortunes, the phenomenal rate of invention, ecological disasters, and political upheaval in all shapes and forms.

Teamworking is, quite simply, a risk that has to be taken because the pay-offs are immense. These pay-offs are not guaranteed, however, and require effort. The purpose of this book is to provide a guide to focusing that effort to get the best from bringing teams together, from developing them and from troubleshooting. Success in these three areas greatly reduces the risk element.

Some risks are deeply unattractive, involving the choice between two unpleasant courses of action. In contrast, the strategic choice to use teams has the potential to provide outcomes which are engaging, energising and fun, as many of the cases illustrate. Many teamworking converts find it hard to imagine ever having done anything else.

Teamworking is not an optional extra – it is vital for success. In the words of Sir Graham Day, Chairman of British Aerospace, 'survival is not compulsory'.

Bibliography

Akin G. and Schultheiss E. (1990) *Jazz bands and Missionaries: Organisation Development through stories and metaphor*, Journal of Managerial Psychology, Volume 5, November 1990.

Belbin M. (1991) *Management Teams: Why they succeed or fail*, London: Heineman Professional Publishing.

Boydell T.H. (1971) A guide to the identification of Training Needs, British Association for Commercial and Industrial Education.

Briggs K. and Briggs Myers I. (1976) *MYERS-BRIGGS TYPE INDICATOR*, Palo Alto: Consulting Psychologists Press Inc.

Briner W., Geddes M. and Hastings C. (1990) *Project Leadership*, Aldershot: Gower Publishing.

Chaudhry-Lawton R. and Lawton R. (1992) *Ignition! Sparking Organizational Change,* London: Century Business.

De Bono E. (1990) *Six Thinking Hats*, London: Penguin Books.

Evans R. and Russell P. (1989) *The Creative Manager*, London: Unwin Hyman 1989.

Fairbairns J. (1991) *Plugging the gap in Training Needs Analysis*, Personnel Management, February 1991.

Fowler A. (1991) *How to identify Training Needs*, Personnel Management Plus, November 1991.

Hampton D. (1988) *Inside Management: A Selection of readings from Business Week*, Maidenhead: McGraw-Hill International.

Hastings C., Bixby P. and Chaudhry-Lawton R. (1986) *Superteams: A Blueprint for Organisational success*, London: Gower Publishing.

Heller J. (1976) *Something Happened*, London: Corgi Books.

Hersey P. and Blanchard K. (1977) *Management of Organisational Behaviour: Utilising Human Resources,* New Jersey: Prentice Hall.

Hunt J. (1986) *Managing People at Work: A Manager's Guide to Behaviour in Organisations*, Maidenhead: McGraw-Hill.

Keating K. (1987) *The Second Little Book of Hugs*, London: Collins Angus and Robertson.

Kilmann R. and Covin T. (1985) *Corporate Transformation: Revitalising organisations for a competitive world*, San Francisco: Jossey-Bass.

Kirton M. (1989) *Adaptors and Innovators: Styles of Creativity and Problem-Solving*, London: Routledge

Lombardo M. (1985) *Five Challenging Assignments* Issues and Obervations, Volume 5, No. 2. May 1985. Centre for Creative Leadership.

Mintzberg H. (1973) *The Nature of Managerial Work,* New York: Harper and Row.

Moss Kanter R. (1985) *The Change Masters: Corporate entrepreneurs at work*, London: Unwin Hyman Paperbacks.

Moss Kanter R. (1989) *When Giants learn to Dance: Mastering the challenges of Strategy, Management and Careers in the 1990s*, New York and London: Simon and Schuster.

Naisbitt J. and Aburdene P. (1990) *Mega-Trends 2000*, London: Sidgwick & Jackson.

Parker G. (1990) *Team Players and Teamwork*, San Francisco: Jossey-Bass Management Series

Pegg M. (1992) *Positive Leadership*, London: Mercury Business Books

Peters T. and Austin N. (1985) *A Passion for Excellence: The Leadership Difference*, London: Collins

Peters T. (1987) *Thriving on Chaos: Handbook for a Management Revolution*, New York: Alfred A. Knopf

Pettigrew A. and Whipp R. (1991) *Managing Change for Competitive Success*, Oxford: Blackwell Publishers.

Porter E. and Maloney S. (1973) *STRENGTH DEPLOYMENT INVENTORY*, Pacific Palisades; Personal Strengths Publishing Inc.

Sadler P (1991) *Designing Organisations: The foundation for excellence*, London: Mercury Business Books.

Schutz W. (1967) *FIRO–B*, Palo Alto: Consulting Psychologists Press.

Thorn P. (1991) *Training Needs Analysis in theory and practice*, Banking and Financial Training, Volume 7, No. 5. November–December 1991.

Vroom V. and Jago A. (1988) *The New Leadership: Managing Participation in Organisations*, New Jersey: Prentice-Hall

Waterman R. (1987) *The Renewal Factor: How the best get and keep the competitive edge*, New York: Bantam Books.

Taking Chances: How Four Companies Spawn New Products by Encouraging Risks, The Wall Street Journal, September 18, 1980.

Index